GOING THE DISTANCE

HOW TO STAY FIT FOR A LIFETIME OF MINISTRY

PETER BRAIN

FOREWORD BY DAVID JACKMAN

Going the Distance
© Peter Brain and Matthias Media 2004
2nd edition 2006

Matthias Media
(St Matthias Press Ltd. ACN 067 558 365)
PO Box 225
Kingsford NSW 2032
Australia
Telephone: (02) 9663 1478; international: +61-2-9663-1478
Facsimile: (02) 9663 3265; international: +61-2-9663-3265
Email: info@matthiasmedia.com.au
Internet: www.matthiasmedia.com.au

Matthias Media (USA)
Telephone: 724 964 8152; international: +1-724-964-8152
Facsimile: 724 964 8166; international: +1-724-964-8166
Email: sales@matthiasmedia.com
Internet: www.matthiasmedia.com

Scripture quotations are from The Holy Bible, English Standard Version, copyright © 2001 by Crossway Bibles, a publishing ministry of Good News Publishers. Used by permission. All rights reserved.

ISBN 978 1 921068 42 3

Work of Dr Archibald Hart reproduced with permission.
Work of Dr Pat Cleary in *Southern Cross*, February 1997, reproduced with permission.
Work of Dr Kath Donovan reproduced with permission.
'Appendix I: Bible study and discussion guide' written by Denis Kirkaldy.

All rights reserved. Except as may be permitted by the Copyright Act, no part of this publication may be reproduced in any form or by any means without prior permission from the publisher.

Cover design and typesetting by Lankshear Design Pty Ltd.

Contents

Foreword 5
Acknowledgements 7
1 The importance of self-care 9
2 Burnout—friend or foe? 25
3 Stress and the demands of ministry 39
4 Stress and adrenalin 51
5 Depression doesn't have to be depressing 67
6 Anger: using it constructively 83
7 The pastor's family 99
8 Sexual temptation in the ministry 123
9 Friendship 143
10 Principles and strategies of self-care 159
11 Where the rubber hits the road—a maintenance plan 171
12 A word for local church members 185
13 A word for local church leaders 201
14 A word for denominational leaders 215
15 Finishing the race 229
16 Justification by faith—a truth that works! 243
17 Summing up 255
   Appendix I: Bible study and discussion guide 259
   Appendix II: Our life and doctrine 277
   Appendix III: Staying happy in ministry 281
   Bibliography 283

Foreword

IT WAS OVER COFFEE, after lunch, that the young pastor, at whose morning service I had preached that day, eventually shared with me his great anxiety. He didn't know whether he should talk about it really, but it was so pressing that he needed to off-load to somebody. He had been in the ministry for five years, but already one-third of his year group from college, who had entered the ministry at the same time as him, had left. His fear was that he would soon join them.

As we explored the causes and possible remedies, it became clear that his experience at college had generated a totally unrealistic set of expectations of what he and his friends might be going to achieve. They had not been at all prepared for the hard realities of ministry, so that when they hit the unmoveable object of church members' traditions and prejudice, and the sheer intransigence of elders in whose vocabulary 'change' was equivalent to 'heresy', the force of their naïve enthusiasm was found to be less than irresistible. Friction resulted and, more often than not, the minister had left.

Sadly, this was no unhappy exception. Nor is it an exaggeration to say that many associations of churches are currently facing a crisis in terms of recruiting young candidates for local church ministry. And even where the recruitment is active, the wastage is alarming. I have spoken to many able young men who have seen the burnt out, turned-out casualties of local congregational ministry and who have come to the conclusion that there must be better ways to use their energy and gifts in God's service.

That is why I am so delighted that this book has been written. There is not the slightest doubt that it is needed, at a time when demand was never higher in the ministry and the pressures were never greater to 'succeed'. This is a book of unusual insight and pertinent, practical wisdom for both the minister and the congregation, to enable them to live together in mutual respect and love, so as to model in their relationships the liberating grace of God, to whom they all belong.

This book is full of uncommon sense, because it is written from the inside, out of years of experience in pastoral leadership, during which both sides of the coin have been examined on many occasions. There are many areas of the pastor-teacher's own life which need careful examination, but which are so often glossed over, or ignored, in coping with the constant demands of 'the work'. The opening chapter stresses the importance of *self*-care and that is a recurring note throughout the book. The pastor is the person who can do most, with God's help, to change his own situation and experience.

The author is overflowing with good, practical advice about one's relationship with God, with spouse and family, with church leaders and church members, with the world at large and with oneself. Analysis is accompanied by strategic action plans, which can really facilitate necessary change and development. Undergirding it all is the liberating doctrine of justification by faith, which the author uses to great practical effect in evaluating one's role and 'performance'.

Rooted in the realities of what local church life is actually like, the book is the product of mature reflection on how Biblical principles of ministry impact the practicalities of a day-by-day ministry which glorifies God and is a blessing to people. Chapters distinguishing burnout from stress, recognizing and dealing with both, are of immense value, as are the practical sections on using anger constructively, on the pastor's family, on sexual temptation and on the necessity of friendship. Every church leader and every church member would benefit from reading this book, not least for the chapters devoted to them, explaining what things look like from the pastor's point of view and encouraging their love, support and prayer.

This is a gem of a book, full of good things, and I am delighted to be able to recommend it very warmly. My only regret is that it was not available thirty years ago!

David Jackman
London
December 2003

Acknowledgements

THEY SAY IT TAKES a whole village to raise a child. It certainly takes a wide range of brothers and sisters to nurture and encourage a Christian. My experience has been that God, in His mercy, has brought many people, lay and ordained, across my path, who have nurtured me and modelled Christian love.

The opportunity to attend Dr. Arch Hart's Fuller Theological Seminary course 'The minister's personal life: coping with the emotional hazards of ministry' was given by Dr. Peter Carnley, Archbishop of Perth, and the Perth Diocesan Trustees, and for this I am very grateful. Bishop Tony Nichols (Diocese of North West Australia) and Dr Allan Chapple (Trinity Theological College) gave me the opportunity to further develop the material with fellow pastors and their spouses. Thank you for your fellowship and encouragement. Thanks are also due to the Trustees of the Australian Research Theology Foundation and my good friend and pastor, Rev. Gordon Thomas, for enabling me to put my material into book form. I appreciated very much the Perth clergy and lay leaders who completed my questionnaire in 1992. This was invaluable to me in earthing my reading and helping me organize my thoughts. My hope is that in sharing this with others I can pass on the benefits I have derived from other pastors and fellow Christians.

I am deeply in debt to Dr. Arch Hart, whose lectures came at a vital time in our ministry, and to the men and women of St. Luke's Anglican Church, Maddington and St. Peter's Anglican Church, Wanneroo, whose fellowship and friendship were so important to our entire family.

I am very thankful for Denis Kirkaldy's encouragement and time in the preparation of the study guide.

My wife, Christine, and our family have been wonderful to me and without their understanding, love and constant encouragement my life and ministry would be very much the poorer. I thank God for you. The help and work of Jean Bowra and Mary Straiton along with the Matthias Media team in the production of this book has been much appreciated, with special thanks to Kirsten Birkett for her patient editorial work.

Peter Brain
2003

I
The importance of self-care

*My life was given to me to spend for God.
I have no intention of hoarding it or wasting it,
but I intend to spend this one life wisely.*
JAMES A. BERKELEY

Self-care—the key to a faithful ministry

All pastors want to be faithful. Our attitude to self-care will keep us from premature burnout, joyless survival and the unsatisfying experience of living on the edge.

A positive attitude, coupled with an intentional pattern of self-care, is all about helping us function well in our relationships with others. It will help us value and develop good support systems that fellow Christians will want to offer us, and will enable us to keep our focus for ministry clear and sharp. In the words of a German proverb, we will be able "to keep the main thing the main thing".

Christmas Evans, a British evangelist, once made the comment, "I'd rather burn out than rust out in the service of the Lord". Many pastors operate on a similar principle. James Berkeley's comment outlines an alternative:

> I admire the bravado. It sounds dedicated, bold, and stirring. However, when I view the burnt-outs and the almost burnt-outs who lie by the ecclesiastical road, the glory fails to reach me. I see pain and waste and unfinished service. Is there not a third alternative to either burning out or rusting out? In Acts 20:24, Paul stated, "I consider my life worth nothing to me, if only I may finish the race and complete the task the Lord Jesus has given me". Herein lies the model I choose to follow. I want neither to burn out nor rust out. I want to finish out the race (Berkeley, in Robbins (ed.), p. 154).

An intentional self-care on the part of pastors is not a matter of selfish pampering, it is essential to maintaining an effective ministry over the long term.

Why is self-care important?

The nature of pastoral ministry makes self-care important. My own experience convinces me of the greatness of pastoral ministry. Pastors taught me the Christian faith by their credible example and clear teaching. Nothing could be greater than to be at the forefront of God's purposes in building up his people.

This is confirmed by Scripture in many places. The apostle Paul's farewell to the Ephesian elders, recorded in Acts 20:17-38, demonstrates the greatness of all ministry. He says in verse 28:

> Pay careful attention to yourselves and to all the flock, in which the Holy Spirit has made you overseer, to care for the church of God, which he obtained with his own blood.

These words remind us of how important every congregation is. It is a task of great importance to pastor people who are a part of God's church.

The gravity of the work of a pastor is reflected in the ordination charges of different churches. It is certainly seen in the Anglican ordinal:

> You have heard, my brothers, in your private examination, in the sermon, and in the readings from Holy Scripture, how great is the dignity and importance of this office to which you are called. And now again I exhort you, in the name of our Lord Jesus Christ, that you remember the dignity of the high office and charge to which you are called: that is to say, to be messengers, watchmen, and stewards of the Lord's family; to seek for Christ's sheep who are scattered abroad, and for his children who are surrounded by temptation in this world, that they may be saved through Christ for ever.
>
> Have always therefore printed in your mind how great a treasure is committed to your care. For they are the sheep of Christ, whom he bought with his death, and for whom he shed his blood. The church and congregation whom you must serve is his bride and his body. And if it should come about that the church, or any of its members, is hurt or hindered as a result of your negligence, you know the greatness of the fault and the judgement that will follow. Accordingly, consider within yourselves the purpose of your ministry to the children of God; and see that you never cease your labour, your care, and diligence, until you have done all that lies in you, according to your bounden duty, to bring all such as are or will be committed to your care, to that understanding in the faith and knowledge of God, and to that maturity in Christ which leaves no place among you for error in religion or viciousness in life (AAPB, pp. 609-610).

The work of a pastor is unique. Christian psychologist Dr Arch Hart has commented that "ministry is a unique vocation and if undertaken seriously the most dangerous occupation around ... in choosing ministry one chooses to command an outpost of unequalled danger which threatens from without and within".

The uniqueness of the pastor's work is its essential Godward focus. It is a ministry of prayer and the word. Whilst its daily functions share much in common with other 'people professions', its uniqueness derives from the relationship the pastor has with God as his under-shepherd, someone who is responsible to prayerfully minister God's word to people. Hart, himself a psychologist, remarked of pastors that "no one else can pray the pastoral prayer". This does not mean that many Christians do not pray for their work and their friends, but that when pastors minister, they are expected to and ought to pray for those with whom they work.

The greatness and uniqueness of the pastor's work leads us to recognize the *seriousness* of the work. This is felt in the tone of Acts 20 and the ordinal quoted above. False teaching is just one of the reasons the pastor needs always to be alert and sharp. Self-care enables that alertness.

Two hobbies from which I gain great satisfaction are woodwork and scone making. I tell my friends (who are often surprised at my scone making) that I enjoy these activities "because I can see the finished project". This is especially so with scones, which are made inside of half an hour. By contrast, pastoring, like parenting, is always a work in progress, an unfinished task.

The core activities of pastoring—prayer, preparation, pastoral visiting, discipling and counselling—are never ending. Every pastor would like to spend more time in each of these activities, and so the unfinished nature of our work is always on our minds. Each of these aspects of ministry combine to cause us pastors to push ourselves hard. We believe in the work. We want to honour God and to serve people, so we tend to work hard. Of itself, hard work is not a problem; but it can become one if we neglect our families, ignore the physical and emotional strains upon our bodies and minds, and become frantically busy.

Intentional self-care can be likened to the safety valve on the old pressure cookers, designed to stop us from blowing up (and indeed, as often happens, blowing off at others!). This is not self-indulgence; it is a wise mechanism that makes for a healthy pastor.

The nature of church

The fact that ministry takes place within the church furnishes us with further reasons for thoughtful care patterns to be established by pastors. The voluntary nature of church membership is always on the pastor's mind. People sometimes vote with their feet in order to taste others, sermons, or because their children find a more relevant kids' or teens' program at another church. Every pastor knows the heartache of surveying Sunday's congregation and observing where the empty seats are. Irregular attendance patterns are often signs of deeper problems. Of course, the pressures of modern life can account for their irregular patterns of attendance, yet the pastor and the regular congregational members all feel keenly the absence, and possible defection, of their brothers and sisters. When members leave to go to other churches, or drop out of church completely, this becomes a real pressure that pastors need plenty of healthy reserves to cope with.

Very often lay people are happy for their pastors to 'do it all'. Sometimes this is due to a genuine lack of confidence and maturity, but often can be traced to an unwillingness to get too involved. It could be argued that, from time to time, this is the fault of pastors who try to do everything, or who fail to teach about gifts and 'every member' ministry. Whatever the reason, such expectations often leave the pastor drained from the feeling that it is all up to him or her.

On the other hand, some pastors feel pressured by the *high* expectations of lay people. This can especially be so when gifted lay people want to perform functions that belong primarily to the ordained pastor and to his office and responsibility. This may especially be the case with preaching. Lay people need to understand that they very often have another focus and significant area of life from which they derive much sense of worth and joy—for example, their work. For the pastor, work and church are the same.

This is not to suggest that pastors should not share significant areas of ministry, but to highlight the need for pastors to have a balanced view of themselves. Sympathetic congregational members will contribute to the pastor's health. Healthy and balanced pastors, who are able to handle both the low and high expectations of lay people, will be those who have had time to reflect upon the great truths of justification by faith and the priesthood and ministry of all believers. Such reflection will in turn enable a balanced ministry that will be able to encourage lay ministry, and will give the pastor the assertiveness necessary to handle constructively both these low and high expectations.

The problems of human society

The trend away from denominational allegiance has been noted in Australia and other Western countries. This is evident amongst 'baby boomers', and commonplace in the 'baby busters' generation. When people move to a new suburb it can no longer be assumed that people will transfer to a church of the same denomination. When we add to this the highly mobile society where people move regularly, the stress of losing members is very real.

It is estimated that in Perth, Western Austalia, where I ministered for some years, people move every five years on average. When loved and valued members move, a grieving process takes place. Add to this the fellowship lost, and the financial loss of those who take stewardship seriously, we can see that we have a recurring pressure on congregations and their pastors alike.

In North West mining towns, pastors typically find, on arriving back in February after vacation, that half their congregation has moved back to the city. Even with a strong sense of 'kingdom ministry', this fact of modern life means that pastors are wise to build into their lives support structures that will equip them to handle such loss. This too is an important aspect of self-care.

Our society has a low view of church and Christianity in general, and of pastors in particular, and this also must be taken into account. Television advertising and movies portray pastors as wimpish or foolish. Many in our community see us as 'dinosaurian' relics of a past era, or as a genuine drain on society. This is often reflected in questions that are asked of us, for example—"How do you fill your day?" To be fair to those who ask these questions, my own experience is that, when I outline my schedule and work pattern, they usually express a general appreciation of the work. Yet the misguided view of a minister's life is still there; and what is not understood is usually undervalued and sometimes ridiculed. This question of image is not helpful when a pastor's or evangelist's failures come to light and fall under the scrutiny of publicity. Certain kinds of sin (such as sexual sin, or greed that leads to misappropriation of funds) bring sadness, pain, embarrassment and grief to the whole church—not least to pastors. This, too, is a real pressure on the pastor's sense of worth. Self-care can help a pastor maintain a healthy sense of worth.

Competition exists between churches in the same locality. This is a fact of life that every pastor is conscious of. It not only makes even gracious church discipline difficult, but also makes it easy for Christians to move from church to church even when they don't move homes. When we add to this the ability of large churches to offer specialist ministries, especially to teens and children, pastors of smaller churches have an additional source of pressure to deal with.

The pressures of church growth

There is a *worldly and self-centred mindset*, that we Christians easily imbibe, that asks "What can we get from this church?" rather than the more Christlike "What can we put into our church?". Pastors can feel this by succumbing to the unhealthy 'numbers game'. Closely related to this pressure are the expectations conveyed to pastors by some church growth literature, concepts and speakers. The helpful insights of speakers, especially those from North America, are often lost, and can even do damage to the morale of pastors in the very different Australian context. In my own experience, there have been times when rather than encouraging me to listen and then distil insights, church growth speakers have driven me to a sense of despair and unhelpful self-deprecation.

This has not always been the fault of the speakers. It has often arisen from my own tiredness, lack of vision, loneliness and the disappointments associated with leadership. Sometimes, however, it has been the result of triumphalist and unthoughtful presentations that fail to note and take seriously the cultural differences in church attendance patterns. The practice of inviting pastors of major US churches to speak in Australia or elsewhere, when the reality is that the overwhelming majority of churches in the USA have less than 75 members, is one that needs to be questioned.

These observations are not meant to encourage smallness, or to imply that we ought to languish in despair or fail to learn from the thoughtful insights of others whom God is using. However, the often selective reporting of church growth literature can contribute to a fragile sense of worth among pastors.

Other clergy

Even the proper exhortations of church leaders can discourage as well as build up pastors. Archbishop of Canterbury, George Carey, once issued the challenge:

> Churches die when leaders die. Churches die from the top downward. Show me a growing church and you will show me a visionary leadership. It is leaders who make growth. When you have spiritual leaders, men of prayer, women of prayer—imaginative, alert, intelligent—there we have growth.

On hearing this, the potential for despair amongst hard-working and faithful pastors is very real. I'm not suggesting that he was wrong in issuing the challenge, nor that he should have qualified it (thus making it die the death of a thousand qualifications). What I am suggesting is that pastors should have in place such a pattern of self-care that enables them to *assess* and *receive* exhortations, challenges and criticisms honestly, but without being destroyed by them.

Leaders always need to take into account church membership (some churches don't want to grow) and community context (some are prouder and harder than others) when issuing challenges. They must remember that it is not always wise to measure growth numerically and that churches are always in process. In other words, growth usually takes time and is mostly built upon the diligent work of others.

It is in this context that 'clergy talk' can be sometimes unhelpful. Pastors can fall into the 'numbers game'—we talk of the numbers of people attending, the size of the pastoral team and the church budget. But how honest are we as we do so? Some pastors 'count feet', I'm told! Do we include children? We are easily tempted to give the maximum number, or the best day, rather than a realistic average. By doing so (and it is quite natural for pastors to do this) we miss the real opportunities of caring for and encouraging each other. The squandered opportunity may cause discouraged fellow pastors to measure themselves against us, and conclude that their ministry is ineffective. Had we been more considerate, we may have had the chance to strengthen our fellow. The exhortation of Hebrews 10:24—"let us *consider* how to stir up one another to love and good deeds"—reminds us of the responsibility and opportunity that thoughtful and considerate words can play in the pastoral care of one another.

Personal expectations

There are further reasons why pastors need to pay attention to self-care. Very often it is our *own* expectations that set us up for our greatest problems. Four observations, all from my own experience, serve to illustrate my concerns.

In 1992 I surveyed Perth Anglican Clergy concerning various ministry matters. The results would, I'm sure, be applicable to any number of other church regions around the Western world. I asked them to answer the question "on average I work___ days,___hours each week". I then compared their answers to the answers given to the question addressed to congregational leaders "how many days or hours do you expect your Rector/minister to work?" The results were:

	PASTOR'S ACTUALS		LEADERS' EXPECTATIONS	
	Average	Range	Average	Range
Hours	60	50–85	45	37.5–54
Days	6.0	6–6.5	5.25	5-6

One pastor who noted the large discrepancy between his actual work pattern and his leaders' expectations was greatly helped to overcome the pressure that he (mistakenly) felt from his lay leaders. Such realizations may help pastors to be free to give time to the congregation, rather than to be driven by false or imagined expectations. We are very often driven people, and our own worst enemy.

Along with this drivenness is the *Messiah complex* that is alive amongst us pastors. This desire, which manifests itself in the need to be seen and approved of by people, makes it very hard for us to even say 'no', and drives us to attempt everything. The great irony of this is that our Messiah, who was both God and perfect man, did not attempt everything, and did not need to be always seen by people.

Dr Broughton Knox, a trainer of pastors for over 40 years, regularly made two observations concerning this complex to his students. Speaking of his Anglican denomination he would say, "our problem is one hundred percentism". We think we have to be seen attempting everything. To do so is to court disaster. The more realistic and responsible approach is for us to do the things we are called to do, and then the things we can responsibly undertake. The outcome of this more balanced and realistic approach is less tiredness, and a more faithful and joyful ministry.

Broughton Knox also noted that there is a continual temptation to skimp on the core pastoral responsibilities of prayer and preparation for preaching (Knox, pp. 239-242). Why? Because people don't see the pastor doing them. Dr Knox was quick to point out that the discerning congregational member will soon know when sermon preparation hasn't taken place! Prayerlessness may not be noticed by others, but it robs the pastor, since God has clearly told us that he delights to strengthen, guide and comfort his servants. Only driveness, with the resultant desire to be seen by people rather than by our gracious God, can account for this mistake, with its resultant guilt and energy-sapping lifestyle.

My own experience has confirmed time and time again that attention to these two core activities, of prayer and preparation for preaching, are fundamental to my self-care. This should not surprise me, since they are fundamental to every Christian's relationship with God. Prayer and Bible reading form the staple diet and are, together with church, a means of grace appointed by God for our growth. As a pastor, attendance to these core activities—which I have been set aside to do—will actually be God's means of sustaining me. Commitment to intentional self-care will mean that I will allow myself, indeed discipline myself, to set time aside for these unseen activities.

For some pastors, the call to ministry is equated with always being *on call*. This can easily be the result of an inner drivenness (to be seen or to prove ourselves), rather than a well thought out commitment to pastoral ministry. Of course, pastors want to be always available to people. Being available, however, is different to always being 'on call'. Never resting, or always dropping everything in response to the latest crisis or telephone call, is not healthy. Crisis-based ministry will rarely achieve much, and will be difficult to sustain with any sense of satisfaction or joy. A pastor who is available and refreshed will be able to fulfil his or her duty more effectively than one who is worn out by crisis care, or dependant upon the crisis to set the agenda. Most crises can wait for a few hours, or even a day or two. They have often been weeks, even years, in the making! The confident and caring appointment made for tomorrow or the next evening is a loving indication of the pastor's desire to care and fulfil the pastoral responsibility. When we are so busy that we drop everything for every crisis, we find that many people from our congregation won't call us, because we appear to be so rushed and busy all the time.

The cost for family and friends

Most pastors have families to care for. All pastors do well to take the time to nurture friendships. Yet we easily take for granted the loyalty of family and friends to ourselves and to (our) ministry. This means we easily presume upon this loyalty and squeeze them out, in time and in emotional energy and attention. Since this rarely happens overnight, and is a process that gradually becomes more and more habitual, we pastors must pay special attention to nurturing our families and friendships. We may not notice this process, but we can be certain that our spouses and families do. We do well to attend to their signals.

This became very clear to me when my wife, who is very committed to ministry, remarked to friends, "Life is often easier when Peter is not home". That cry from her heart pierced mine, not only because I love her and our children dearly, but also because I consider that I owe them a commitment and care that takes priority over the church.

Richard Foth comments wisely,

> the idea of ministry versus marriage is a false dichotomy. We must not pit one against the other ... marriage gives rise to ministry. It is ministry's foundation. Out of our service to our wives we build a superstructure of ministry to the rest of the congregation (Merrill, p. 56).

Self-care will ensure that a proper balance is in place. It prevents bad habits becoming ingrained that cause resentment, indifference or anger in the pastor's family.

Our son's athletic coach drummed into him the saying, "practice makes permanent". Bad habits become ingrained. By contrast, self-care allows good habits to emerge and grow. Part of our humanity is to enjoy the relationships that God gives to us. Healthy self-care will make sure that time and patterns of living enable our relationships to grow.

Positive reasons for self-care

Self-care is therefore a way of recognizing our ministry as a good, God-given gift. According to Dr Hart, "Most ministers don't burn out because they forget they are ministers, they burn out because they forget they are people". Surely this is why God gave us the command to rest from our labour one day in seven. It is his gracious provision, because he knows our bodies and minds need regular rest. Just as he has kindly built into every 24 hours time to sleep, so he has given a weekly day of rest. By keeping God's Sabbath command, we are agreeing with God our heavenly Father that our bodies "being fearfully and wonderfully made" require the refreshment of rest.

Clearly God wants us to work creatively. It is part of what it means to be made in his image, but to do so we need to rest regularly. Failure to rest regularly means our work becomes drudgery and an end in itself. Inefficiency sets in, as the law of diminishing returns takes over. On the other hand, a proper balance of work and refreshment, of work, family and friends, can ensure that our work is seen as a way of serving others.

As pastors we feel sometimes that since we are involved in God's work, we can ignore this creation ordinance of rest, and the physical aspects of life like sleep, exercise and balanced diet. This is a form of Gnosticism, which, in devaluing the body, fails to benefit from the resources of creation that our gracious creator and sustainer delights to give to men and women. We do well, as pastors, to remember that we were created before we were recreated, we were born before we were born again. We have bodies that enable us to minister. Robert Murray McCheyne remarked towards the end of his short life, "God gave me the gospel and a horse. I've killed the horse, so I can no longer preach the gospel". (He was speaking of his body.) Self-care is a way of enabling us to remain as fresh and enthusiastic for the work of pastoring for as long as possible.

Far from being a reason for self-indulgent laziness or an incentive for pastoral hypochondriacs, self-care is really a way of ensuring that we will remain effective in the great work God has given us to do. The phrases I hate hearing the most from parishioners are "I didn't want to bother you, you are always so busy" or "you always look so tired". I'm a pastor because I want to minister to people.

Self-care helps me engage in the art of being an "unhurried pastor". This phrase, used by Eugene Peterson (Peterson, p. 141), has nothing to do with laziness, but everything to do with availability and freshness for the task. Self-care will help us practice this art. Peterson says "pastors are busy because they are lazy!" They are too lazy to work out priorities and then to put them into practice. The unhurried pastor will establish self-care patterns that will enable him or herself time to set priorities (itself essential to self-care) which will allow freshness and vitality to thrive.

In building self-care principles and patterns into our lifestyle we are offering other people, especially fellow Christians, a healthy pattern for Christian discipleship. Certainly this will be so for the pastor's family. If the pastor can never stop still long enough to enjoy friendships and relationships, it will come as no surprise if his or her family cannot or will not do the same, especially toward the pastor. On the other hand, a balanced pastoral life will model the importance of service and hard work, while affirming the place for rest and the nurture of family and friendships.

Many church members have high-pressure jobs. This is the case with self-employed people, and those who work for large corporations. There is often pressure to work longer and longer hours, either 'at the office' or with work brought home. The pastor can model balance by thoughtful self-care. Often the danger for driven pastors is to reason, "if my lay people work that long then so should I"—but not if they are failing to rest, or failing to give time to their prior relationships of family and church. Working hard is a challenge to the lazy self-centred hedonism of our age, but resting and relating well is a challenge to the workaholic. This might be called the accountability of self-care, which serves to help us keep the balance, at the same time providing a model to others. Self-care means that we cooperate with the God who made us and who will equip us for a faithful ministry.

Self-care means that we will build into our lives patterns that demonstrate our reliance upon God. Passages from 2 Corinthians demonstrate a resolute commitment to the hard work of ministry *and* an equal resolve to rely upon God (11:28-31, 4:7-18). Reliance upon God will be especially important to pastors who are feeling lonely. The practised pattern of daily dependence will always deliver to us the comfort and strength that we require. Where this practised pattern has been neglected, the going will surely be tougher. This is not to say that God will not come through for us, but it is to affirm that we will have cheated ourselves of the care we could otherwise have experienced.

Self-care maintains a close relationship with God, and provides a pattern by which that primary relationship is nurtured.

An important distinction

Is self-care at odds with our Lord's clear gospel call for self-denial? Our Lord's words "if anyone would come after me, let him deny himself and take up his cross daily and follow me" (Luke 9:23) are clear and uncompromising.

Dr Hart makes an important distinction when he notes that this call to self-denial refers to our "motivational self", whereas self-care deals with our "structural self". Hard work and consistent sacrifice is required by virtue of us being Christians—it cannot be otherwise if we are to follow in Jesus' footsteps. Yet being human, we need rest, refreshment and encouragement. No one can prescribe for another in this area, yet some observations can be made that may help pastors live creatively with this tension. As with other issues of discipleship, the ability to talk about the tension, and to find that others are seeking to work through it, can be as profitable as it is reassuring

Three popular statements encapsulate the issue for us. Each of these have been very powerful summary statements in my own desire to follow Christ generally and specifically as a pastor.

- 'Only one life that will soon be past, only what's done for Christ will last'
- 'We are saved to serve'
- 'Jesus is to be Lord of all or not at all'

My own feeling is that each of these pithy statements are an accurate expression of Scripture. They stir our hearts and minds to self-examination, challenging our level of commitment, and under God can evoke a new obedience and stimulate perseverance. Yet with this, my own conviction remains that devoted service and obedience not only will flow out of a base of thoughtful self-care, but will be fuelled by it. For example, the saying "Lord of all or not at all", will involve the pastor (indeed every Christian) in subjecting to Christ not only their work in ministry, but also their bodies, minds and spirit, that make the work possible.

Pastors will need to be vigilant and intentional in carving out time and establishing strategies of care, since a dozen good things will conspire to keep them as intentions only. Denominational and local church leaders can help local church pastors greatly, by giving them permission and encouragement to pursue healthy patterns of care. There is little doubt that everyone benefits when this happens.

Intentional self-care that takes up the opportunities and disciplines offered by the very nature of pastoral ministry, will enable the pastor to keep fresh and thus remain at his or her work. Built into the task are means for self-care. Prayer, preparation from God's word and time spent with those people whom God calls into his church, can all contribute to the pastor's health. God's grace in calling us, using us to bring others to himself, providing us with a day of rest, and going before us to work in others, all help pastors face their task with confidence. Self-denial does not mean denying our humanity expressed in a need for rest, friendship, strength, wisdom and support. Rather, it involves a willingness to deny self-interest. Expressed positively, this will mean accepting the means and provision for care that God so graciously puts in our way as pastors.

The reason for self-care is not so that pastors can become indulgent hypochondriacs, always concerned about their own welfare, or even to avoid the twin ravages of growing older and the fatigue of hard work and pastoral concern. A recent cartoon of a parishioner dressed in sports gear, armed with an ice hockey stick, sitting opposite her pastor at his desk has the telling caption: "No Miss. The reason this church believes in the grace of God is not so that it leaves us more time for our hobbies!" All Christians are meant to be workers. We are saved to serve and work. Pastors have work to do, work that is vital.

The assassinated former Archbishop of Uganda said "He who is forever watching the wind will never sow". Self-care must never be a cover for selfishness, or a cowardly holding back in the interests of self-protection. However, like the mother of the fourth-century apologist Origen, who acted wisely to hide her son's trousers in order to keep him from a premature and unnecessary martyrdom, pastors will understand the wisdom of self-care. Its wisdom is to ensure, as far as humanly possible, a wise and orderly work that conserves and lengthens a pastor's ministry.

2
Burnout—friend or foe?

*Most ministers don't burn out because
they forget they are ministers. They burn out
because they forget they are people.*
A. D. Hart

*Every day I die a little. The big question is:
"Am I dying too fast?"*
A. D. Hart

*God gave me the gospel and a horse.
Now I have worn out the horse and can no
longer preach the gospel.*
Robert Murray McCheyne

Alarming statistics

"Most clergy close to burnout" was the headline of an article in the *Sydney Morning Herald* of October 5, 1995. The survey, conducted by Dr Ian Hay of Brisbane's Griffith University, of 142 Anglican clergy in Southern Queensland, found that:

> five percent were so burnt out that immediate remedial action was thought necessary to restore their physical and mental health. Another 20 percent said burnout was a factor in their lives, and 45 percent were bordering on burnout.

My own survey of Perth clergy conducted in 1992 showed that 27 percent of all pastors had "burnt out, suffered a break down or serious illness whilst in full-time ministry". The figure went up to 44 percent for those who had been ordained for more than 15 years. The statistics are alarming because they represent real people: pastors, their families and the congregations of which they are a part. All suffer as a consequence of burnout.

The Brisbane survey confirms the interpersonal damage that accrues from a burning out pastor. "Feelings of loneliness, isolation and tiredness were common ... one in seven clergy felt lonely, tired and irritated much of the time."

Burnout can be largely attributed to lack of self-care. Established strategies that are built carefully into our daily lifestyle and ministry can make an enormous difference in minimizing the harmful effects of burnout. Clearly, to know the importance of self-care, and even to have established strategies in place, is vital, but these need to be planned, practised, pursued and persevered in. Self-care strategies are like All-Bran—you eat it when you don't need it, so you won't need it!

However, even practised strategies are not enough. A belief system that enables us to understand ourselves, handle success and failure and cope with a variety of often competing expectations, is essential in combating the ravaging effects of burnout.

Friend or foe?

Because its consequences are so devastating, it is important that we recognize the symptoms of burnout quickly, and be encouraged in the knowledge that it is a "reversible spiral". The feeling of being out of control, so common in burnout, is likened by the authors of *How to Beat Burnout* to being in a plane plummeting to the earth in a nosedive. They affirm, however, that when responsibility is taken to overcome its dive, a potentially devastating result is avoided. This is good news indeed for pastors and others whose work is with people. Burnout is commonplace with those who work in the caring professions, and especially amongst highly committed and responsible people. The ability to take responsibility in firstly recognizing, and then reversing, the spiral will be maximized by those who already have thoughtful self-care strategies in place. Not only will these strategies go a long way in preventing burnout from becoming serious; they will make us more likely to respond to those around us who would alert us to, and then help us out of, the burnout spiral.

Since every pastor is an individual, it is important for each to take personal responsibility in combating the effect of burnout. In reality, it can become a friend, not a foe, if recognized early, and appropriate action taken.

> Decide to take the initiative yourself, realizing that taking care of self is a responsibility given us by God. Without meeting that responsibility we will never be able to succeed in the life-long purposes he has for us (Minirth et al., 1986, p. 103).

Though the initiative is in the hands of the pastor, members of the congregation and denominational leaders can provide the encouragement for recovery by their active support when burnout occurs. This will mean that the pastor will not be made to feel a failure, or a 'slacker', should extra time off need to be taken. The preventative strategies a pastor has in place should be known and supported by the church leadership. Whether it be a golf game, or the real sense of belonging and positive refocus given by a fellow pastor who may meet for weeks with the despairing pastor, it does not matter. The important aspect is that 'permission' is given.

This 'permission' is given when those in authority expect and encourage the pastor to take good time off, and to pursue activities that will promote health. This need was highlighted in my 1992 survey by a number of pastors who did not pursue strategies of self-care because of lack of money, time and the "expectations of others". Hopefully the expectations of church leaders regarding hours to be spent working will be such that they encourage pastors to take more evenings off, and work fewer hours.

Certainly if pastors are encouraged by their leaders to pursue meaningful strategies, problems of unrealistic and unhealthy expectations could be overcome. My survey revealed that there is a strong commitment on the part of many local church leaders to look after their pastors. A strong desire to support in the practical tasks of church work and the pastoral role were noted.

Symptoms

Researchers have identified three symptoms of burnout:

- a sense of being drained emotionally
- a reduced sense of personal accomplishment
- a sense of depersonalization, of distance and disconnection in relationships

My own ministry would confirm this research, as I have experienced each of these to one degree or another. It is, needless to say, somewhat disturbing, since a large part of my work, together with my understanding of ministry, is about being involved closely with people.

Certainly it is true that a spiral effect can easily come into play. One discouragement can fuel another, and soon even genuine gestures of fellowship, encouragement and support are misread and either rejected or not able to be received. This in turn adds to the emotional drain, minimizes accomplishment and tends to depersonalize the pastor's relationships with church members.

Dr Hay's survey of clergy described the effects of burnout in different but similar categories:

frustrated in accomplishing tasks	(17%)
alone and isolated	(14%)
carrying feelings of guilt	(14%)
cynical about parishioners	(10%)
withdrawn from parishioners	(7%)
unenthusiastic about their job	(5%)

When we become burnt out there is a great temptation to work harder and harder, either to make up for time lost in inefficient work patterns, or to try to re-establish the sense of job satisfaction we had previously experienced. Whilst our work and accomplishments do not form the basis of our acceptance with God, they can provide us with a strong sense of confidence and wellbeing. When this is reduced, it inevitably leads to frustration, as we work harder to overcome a sense of guilt that our motives and achievements are not good; it also leads to a crippling loss of perspective that sees everything as waste and failure. The downward spiral can seem out of control.

Before we look at ways out of this spiral (and remember it is reversible when responsibility is taken), we would do well to think about the three major symptoms of burnout.

1. The sense of being drained emotionally

This feeling causes us not to care for the work any more. There is no emotional energy left in the tank. The reserves have been drained, and we either no longer care about replenishing them, or if we do care we don't really know how to go about it. Change seems impossible. The circumstances that brought us to this point seem insurmountable. We really don't know how to change things even if we wanted to.

2. A reduced sense of personal accomplishment

I like the story of the pastor who, at 2 pm each day of the week, would drive from his office through town across the railway bridge and then wait patiently for the 2.15 pm train to go past. This happened for months. People were curious. One elder was commissioned to go and find out why this daily ritual had become so important to the pastor. After the 2.15 had gone past, the elder who was sitting in his car beside the pastor asked him why he came to watch the train. "That's easy", explained the pastor, "it's the only thing in my day that I don't have to push!"

Sometimes it is easy for pastors to feel like this. Even if it is not the fault of parishioners, but a result of our own unrealistic expectations of ourselves, a reduced sense of personal accomplishment begins to dominate our thinking. This can be magnified when we work in an area where other churches seem to be doing better than ours. How careful and truthful we need to be when we talk about our 'successes' with fellow pastors. An innocent remark from a church member about the new initiatives at a nearby church can send a discouraged pastor further down the burnout spiral. These can hardly be avoided, but certainly comparisons that are designed to be putdowns must be avoided at all costs if colleagues or parishioners are to be encouragers.

Midlife can often be a vulnerable time for pastors. Accomplishments may have been modest, dreams and hopes may not have been realized, and positions of influence look less and less likely to be achieved. Current patterns where churches seek pastors under 45 years of age make this problem even more serious for midlife and older clergy.

When the sense of accomplishment is down, the spiral easily comes into effect. Only the negatives are seen, the glass is always half empty and rarely seen to be half full. Good friends, a caring spouse, and encouraging local and denominational leaders are especially important in beating this one.

A sense of depersonalization, distance and disconnection in relationships

"I love the ministry, it's people I can't stand." This quip, borrowed (I believe) from school teachers, is a natural reaction to spending much time with many people. We all have our days when we need space. "A little peace and quiet is what I need", is what my mother used to say when life was especially demanding. We all understand this. Indeed, time alone is essential to our emotional health. However, when the quip is no longer said in jest, and when the desire to keep away from people becomes ingrained and supported by a studied avoidance of parishioners, we know we are in trouble.

This first happened to me many years ago. I remember the evening well. I went to visit a couple who had not been to church for some time. The telltale signs of a lessening involvement were there. After being very keen for a couple of years, their church attendance became erratic. I had called on them a number of times, and we still got on well together. However, this visit would be the last, and it would not be by appointment because I suspected that if I had phoned they would have politely said no. I drove to their home. I stopped. I couldn't get out. I drove around the block and the same thing happened. And a third time. Perhaps it was because this was a difficult visit, I reasoned. However, neither could I make the other two friendly back-up visits I had planned, to people who had recently visited our church. I drove home, reported the incident to my wife, who knew exactly what had happened. As one who normally loved visiting and believes that home visiting is an important aspect of local church ministry, this was unfamiliar and disconcerting territory to be in. I can't remember if either of us used the term 'burnout', but that is exactly what was happening.

Most of us become pastors because we love people, so when we find ourselves not wanting to engage with parishioners at a real, personal level we not only know that there is a problem but we really feel it. Keeping people at arm's length is not a satisfactory solution. We want our relationships to count. We want to be warm and accepting. We want to have impact on people for good. Sometimes when pastors are in burnout, they feel that resignation from pastoral ministry, or a move to another congregation, is the solution. If the latter occurs the problem is only transferred, and the final devastating consequences postponed to another time and place.

A better way

There is a better way. Burnout is an invitation for us to take stock. The pastor who reaches the point of fantasizing about a new church—worse still, a new wife—who will appreciate him better, needs a major readjustment. Given some goodwill on the part of his wife, children and congregation, his whole life and ministry can be radically reshaped, renewed and rejuvenated through counselling.

In my own case, I took every evening off for the next two weeks. The local leadership was more than happy for me to do this, since they saw no value in a tired, disengaged pastor. Extra rest, 'time out' and time with family gave me refreshment. Thankfully the spiral was broken by early intervention.

Burnout symptoms, when seen as a *warning light*, can be a real friend. They become an opportunity to step back, to take remedial action and then either to implement or redouble one's efforts in establishing patterns of self-care.

When the symptoms appear, attention *sooner rather than later* is best. It's like the fuel or oil warning light in the car. If the oil is not attended to, big damage can be expected. Since most of the factors that lead to burnout are in our power to modify, we do well to respond to the warning symptoms as soon as they begin to manifest themselves. Good friends, thoughtful parishioners, sensitive leaders and caring spouses will be ideal 'warning lights' for us. They should be heeded, since they can often see us better than we can see ourselves. At least, they will not be rationalizing or avoiding the issue, as we pastors are so prone to do.

We will consider the question of sexual temptation in ministry in a later chapter, but in order to illustrate the 'sooner rather than later' principle, we do well to note how burnout can be a contributing factor in sexual infidelity or inappropriate thought and behaviour patterns. Burnout leaves us fatigued and discouraged through disappointments with ministry. This can easily cause us to look for something or someone to give us a lift, or at least to sympathize with us. In fact, we can feel that we deserve some attention. We may even reason that since we have been working so hard for God, he actually owes us some favours. How much more vulnerable we are to sin's deceits and Satan's deceptions when we are fatigued, frustrated and discouraged. When this is coupled with possible isolation from spouse, family and friends, we become easy targets for inappropriate relationships. We look for compliments, we respond to interest shown. With vulnerability high, and emotional and spiritual strength lowered, we can seek comfort from the wrong people. H. B. London observes that people who take notice of and look for compliments from people in power (such as pastors), also notice our vulnerability.

Burnout symptoms attended to sooner rather than later can keep us from serious trouble. A garment can be salvaged and repaired if the tear is quickly attended to. When the telltale symptoms of burnout emerge, quick attention will bring rewards. The counsel of thoughtful friends and a preparedness to take advice will prove to be invaluable.

Careful thought and quick action can reverse the burnout symptoms

Repairs can sometimes be done on the job, by rescheduling one's program. More time can be taken for prayer, personal Bible reading and reflection; times can be marked into the diary to be sure that good time is actually spent with one's spouse and supportive friends and colleagues. Such measures will go a long way towards recovery.

For myself, I find a need to be at home more often in the evenings when the burnout warning lights are on. Yes, there is a price to pay in congregational life when I cannot visit as often as I would like, but it is nowhere near as high a price as if I burned out totally. The horse would be then well and truly ridden into the ground, and I couldn't preach the gospel.

Sometimes 'time out' is required. It may be a few days or several weeks that is needed. Many pastors feel that they just couldn't request time off when they are fatigued. Certainly there are some churches and members who would misunderstand such a request, and who expect their pastor to soldier on regardless. I am convinced, however, that the vast majority of church members and local church leaders have enormous love, respect and good will toward their pastors. This is especially so where pastors work hard and in consultation with their leaders. When a pastor is known to be consistently faithful, church leaders would much prefer their pastor to have some time off in order to rest or seek counselling instead of watching him or her struggle on, clearly hurting. In other words, out of love and respect they would want appropriate action to be taken. Church leaders also know about diminishing returns. They know that burning-out pastors achieve less in six days than healthy pastors in five, that their despair will rub off onto the congregation, and that the ultimate price—breakdown and resignation—benefits no one.

Denominational leaders can also encourage 'time out'. They are able to create a culture within congregations and amongst pastors which sees burnout as illness not as failure, and where preventative and remedial strategies are regarded as sensible stewardship of our bodies, and not laziness. When this teaching is backed by the modelling of healthy and balanced work patterns, pastors will be more likely to adopt preventative and remedial measures that enable burnout symptoms to be friends, rather than destructive foes.

However, experience shows me that at the end of the day I must take responsibility to have good patterns of self-care in place. Others can encourage me and provide the culture that will see me supported in these strategies, but I must be prepared to keep at it. Strategies need to be constantly worked at and affirmed. Although sickness is catching, health is not! For this reason, strategies for pastoral health need to be constantly reworked and shaped, endorsed, and above all, persevered with. Denominational and local church leaders offer pastors a great gift when they enquire as to whether they have strategies for self-care, and how they are keeping them going!

Several years ago, my wife and I drove from San Francisco to Los Angeles along the coast road. This was an unnerving experience for me. The rugged cliffs, winding road and unfamiliar driving position gave rise to feelings of panic and fear. Thankfully, at regular intervals along this road were 'turnout bays'. What a welcome relief these proved to be. We could stop the car, let drivers pass, relax, enjoy the breathtaking view and then start again.

As I reflected upon this experience, I saw illustrations for a number of valuable lessons about burnout and self-care. Those 'turnout bays' provided me with the opportunity to refocus and get the situation in perspective. Yes, it was a new situation, and the cliff was steep; but the car was working well, the road was safe and wide enough, other drivers courteous, and I had driven safely enough over similar terrain in Australia. 'Time out' was afforded by the 'turnouts'. The situation that was causing fear, concern and even panic could be surveyed and a new perspective gained. This is really what self-care in the ministry is about. It is about recognizing that some situations will take their toll, but that God has graciously provided other resources to enable us to cope. Such 'time out' of the mainstream of pressure and constant activity can be as short as an hour.

The following equations may help demonstrate the role of 'time out' in self-care.

- Burnout + Turnout = Appropriate and controlled life
- Burnout − Turnout = Disaster

Self-care is designed to deal with burnout in such a way so as to ensure a controlled life appropriate to our aging. Hart's question is salutary: "Every day I die a little. The big question is "Am I dying too fast?"

Turnouts that will refresh can include:
- time away from the phone reading the Psalms
- a walk around the local park
- coffee with a trusted friend
- smelling the roses
- swimming some laps
- a weekend or few days away
- more time given to prayer or preparation
- pursuing a hobby

By regaining perspective, ministry is enabled to continue. It is a mistake for pastors to delay taking 'time out' because they feel they cannot afford the time or money. There is no virtue or joy in allowing the law of diminishing returns to have its way in our lives. Caring church members will appreciate and encourage 'time out' of the normal routine. They will certainly do so when they see the benefits.

It might be objected that self-care is an attempt to forestall the normal dying process, and to forget that our lives are in God's hands. Certainly self-care cannot ensure a long life that finds its end in retirement and beyond. Many faithful pastors, who have worked hard and have sought to rest properly, die before their three score years and ten. Without a doubt, there is great potential for health in the humble recognition that our lives are in God's hands. Remembering this means we will not wait to do worthwhile things 'next year', but will make the most of today. It is precisely because life is a gift to us that we ought to be good stewards of it. Yes, we will work hard, but at the same time we will use the means God has given to us to be effective in our work. Sensible living is surely to be preferred to burnout as a much wiser use of the resource of our bodies.

Common symptoms of burnout

If burnout is reversible, if the symptoms can be like the friendly warning light urging us to top up the oil (remember the chorus "give me oil in my lamp keep me burning?"), then how can we recognize them in advance so that we can respond as quickly as possible?

An inability to say no

In burnout, we often feel unappreciated and underachieving, which means we are prone to say yes to everything that comes our way. Why? Because it gives us a boost. Someone appreciates us. Coupled with this, we often feel duty bound to please everyone, so we say yes. But, like a boomerang, our decision returns to hurt us; we become overwhelmed by the extra commitment, or feel bitter and resentful because of the pressure of others' expectations. How often, when faced with deadlines, do we think "it seemed like a good idea at the time"! Hart's one liner "your no's give value to your yes's" is worthy of our reflection.

2. A need to succeed

All pastors want to do well. This is especially so in one's first pastoral charge. The pressure to succeed can come from within the pastor, and from outside. Church and denominational leaders must exercise great care in communicating expectations to pastors. This is doubly so when other churches in the locality are doing well. Unrealistic expectations can be crippling and contribute to burnout, especially among sincere and faithful pastors. But what is success? Success is found in the meeting of standards. But in ministry, whose standard do we measure up to? Since pastors are at the service of many people, there will be differing expectations about success.

J. I. Packer has an excellent epilogue on success in his study of Nehemiah (Packer, pp. 205-6). It is well worth reading for its balanced wisdom and encouragement to faithfulness in ministry, seeking God's verdict, not man's, on our work. He writes:

> Wisdom says: leave success ratings to God, and live your Christianity as a religion of faithfulness rather than an idolatry of achievement.

Gene Habecker's suggestions that "excellence in leadership differs from success" and that "excellence is a quality" and that as such "everyone has the possibility of performing in an excellent way, whereas not everyone will be seen to be successful" are helpful in reminding us to live and work for God's applause and not that of people. When God is no longer the one in our grandstand, we are going to find it difficult not only to say no, but to be realistic in the way we view ourselves and our ministry. Our sense of purpose and accomplishment will decrease. When this happens, we need to refocus upon God, not any unrealistic goals we and others may have set before us.

3. The expectations and demands of churches

We cannot escape these. They are part and parcel of ministry. Furthermore, they are multiple and often competing. If we think we can meet everyone's expectations and demands we will burnout quickly, and if we are hard working, spectacularly.

What is required here is not an absence of goals, but rather clearly worked out, agreed and articulated goals. Such goals are best worked out in consultation with, or at least with the endorsement of, local church leadership, and will serve as an essential guide and framework for the pastor's work. Not every worthwhile thing can be done by a church or by pastors. Not all demands or expectations can be met. A well-thought-through set of priorities, agreed to by the pastor and church leadership, will establish a grid that can be appealed to when other demands are made.

If endorsed by leadership, the pastor will find that his choices will be supported, and the debilitating effects of competing and unrealistic demands and criticism will be minimized.

4 Long working hours

As we saw in the first chapter, long work hours are more often on account of pastors' drivenness than church members' expectations. Church members do not expect us to work excessive hours, and they will not thank us when we run ourselves into the ground. Experience shows me that burnout is upon me when all I can do is try to work longer. It is a sure sign that I'm too tired to think clearly or imaginatively. Instead of increasing my sense of accomplishment, it actually works the other way, and has the detrimental effect of distancing me from my greatest supporters and encouragers, my wife and family. If my working hours increase because I want to avoid my family, then I'm really in trouble. The warning light is on. The engine is about to seize. Remedial action must be swift.

5 Lack of exercise and healthy habits

It is easy for us to allow work to consume us, and for exercise and healthy eating patterns to slip. In turn, this becomes an unhealthy way of life that causes us further discouragement born of guilt, and an inability to break out of the cycle. This is all the more so if we had previously kept to a healthy exercise and eating regime.

An old advertising poster ran the line 'what you eat today walks and talks tomorrow'. There is much truth in that. When unhealthy eating habits are combined with lack of exercise, and with sedentary leisure times in front of the TV, sleep often becomes a problem. The short 'dream sleep' phase of each sleeping cycle, so important to our psychological refreshment, no longer delivers to us its full benefit if our sleep hours become shallow or disturbed. When exercise, eating and sleeping are no longer healthy and helpful to us, we know that we need to change our behaviour patterns. Each is meant to sustain us. Each is a gift of God and a reminder to us that our complex body engines need regular replenishment if they are to remain functional.

Friend or foe?

Burnout can be devastating, a relentless foe that will keep on capturing pastors, and robbing us of joy in ministry and life in general. Though probably inevitable, its symptoms, if spotted early, can be reversed. They become an invitation to recover our perspective. Its symptoms can be likened to a caring friend who says, "It's time to slow down, to regroup, to turn out for a while". Far from being an invitation to be self-indulgent, the preventative strategies we put in place, like the regular servicing of our motor car, will work to keep us on track and running well for as long as possible.

3

Stress and the demands of ministry: learning to say no

The ministry can, from an emotional point of view, be regarded as the most hazardous occupation around. It takes great effort to be happy in ministry and the key to happiness is self-care.
A. D. Hart

Your no's give value to your yes's.
A. D. Hart

And, apart from other things, there is the daily pressure on me of my anxiety for all the churches.
2 Corinthians 11:28

Accept it: there will be stress in life and ministry. As psychologist Dr Pat Cleary says:

> Stress is personal wear and tear associated with earning our living, caring for our families, Christian ministry, studying for exams, grieving for a loved one and so on. Stress presents itself as tense muscles, increased blood pressure, disturbed digestion, increased metabolic rate and body temperature, disrupted sleep, restlessness, anxiety, guilt, feelings of helplessness and hopelessness, apathy, self pity, inefficiency, disorganization, indecisiveness, wishful thinking. The list goes on.
>
> But we don't just experience the stress of life; we also create it! So stress management needs to deal with these all too familiar reactions as well as ways to avoid creating unnecessary stress (Cleary, 1997).

Understanding what stress involves alerts us to the need to minimize and manage stress constructively. Demands which cause stress will come to all pastors. Within ourselves we have a mixed bag of emotions. The people we work with, like ourselves, are sinners. We all have different agendas, expectations and backgrounds. The potential for stress is enormous.

A pastor friend told me that one Sunday evening he came home late, and was complaining to his wife about all the problems of his parish. After patiently listening, she remarked, "Well, mate, that's why you've got the job, isn't it!"

We cannot run from demands in the church. We will actually make them worse when we deny their existence, try to avoid them or view them as obstacles to be removed. Part of the pastor's work is to work with church members in working through and meeting these demands. The key is to face them realistically with God's help and wisdom.

Sources of stress

Figure 1: **STRESS IN THE MINISTRY** Dr A. D. Hart April 1989

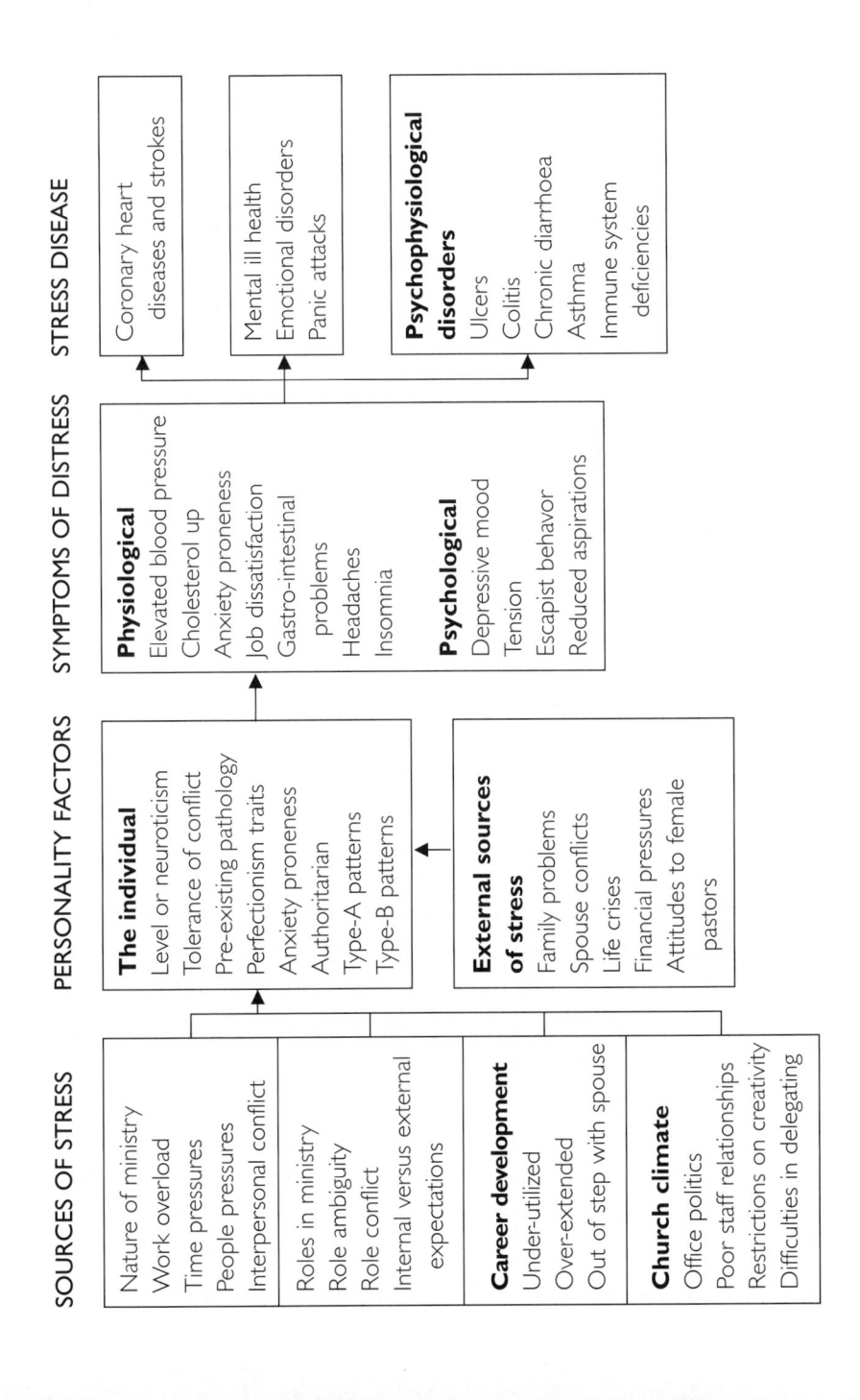

SOURCES OF STRESS

Nature of ministry
Work overload
Time pressures
People pressures
Interpersonal conflict

Roles in ministry
Role ambiguity
Role conflict
Internal versus external expectations

Career development
Under-utilized
Over-extended
Out of step with spouse

Church climate
Office politics
Poor staff relationships
Restrictions on creativity
Difficulties in delegating

PERSONALITY FACTORS

The individual
Level or neuroticism
Tolerance of conflict
Pre-existing pathology
Perfectionism traits
Anxiety proneness
Authoritarian
Type-A patterns
Type-B patterns

External sources of stress
Family problems
Spouse conflicts
Life crises
Financial pressures
Attitudes to female pastors

SYMPTOMS OF DISTRESS

Physiological
Elevated blood pressure
Cholesterol up
Anxiety proneness
Job dissatisfaction
Gastro-intestinal problems
Headaches
Insomnia

Psychological
Depressive mood
Tension
Escapist behavor
Reduced aspirations

STRESS DISEASE

Coronary heart diseases and strokes

Mental ill health
Emotional disorders
Panic attacks

Psychophysiological disorders
Ulcers
Colitis
Chronic diarrhoea
Asthma
Immune system deficiencies

Notice the mix of factors that lead to demands and stress upon pastors. Hardly any of the sources of stress can be avoided, or should even be regarded as bad. What should be noted is that they need to be recognized, understood and then dealt with. An understanding of these demands will not only help pastors to be realistic about their task, but will also make it more acceptable to seek help from God and others, and encourage the development of meaningful personal strategies in response. This will in turn help pastors to be more effective in ministry.

The connection between effective, happy and healthy pastors, and healthy churches, is a matter of observation and common sense. The need for a real strategy of self-care to be in place is heightened by the preventative power of such strategies. Most of us do not fall into damaging and sinful behaviour patterns overnight. Attitudes develop, and thought patterns are nurtured, which may lead into harmful patterns of responding to demands. As it has been said:

> If you sow a thought you reap an act,
> If you sow an act you reap a habit,
> If you sow a habit you reap a character,
> If you sow a character you reap a destiny.

This progression works for good as well as bad. A strategy of self-care that includes the input of others can be particularly beneficial in encouraging this progression in a positive direction. Thoughtful strategies will help eliminate the negative and accentuate the positive. The caring yet firm corrective input from a trusted person, be they church member, spouse, fellow pastor or denominational leader, may be just the word we need to help us break the deadly spiral of sinful, self-defeating thought patterns and ministry practices. On the other hand, words of affirmation or encouragement that strengthen us, give us understanding or lift our confidence, will also be of immense help in enabling us to embark on a road of growth. I sometimes need help in transforming a thought into an appropriate action that would assist me in dealing with conflicting or competing demands of church leaders. Such words will have had the effect of delivering life to my ministry, rather than confirming patterns of death.

Conflicting and competing demands upon the pastor may be caused by people who are wilful, innocent, confused or impatient. There is no doubt that demands are made upon pastors by members, leaders or denominational leaders, because they want to use us for their own purposes. On other occasions, demands are innocently heaped upon us, especially if we are known to be a willing horse who gets things done.

Stress can also come from the pastor's own actions. Sometimes pastors confuse people by saying that the ministry is to be shared by all Christians, and then fail to delegate, share or train members in ministry. There are times when we fail to take any kind of lead on anything, and church members begin to make demands upon us because they want something to happen.

All self-care has a cost. There is a price to pay. A stand needs to be taken. For some pastors it is emotionally far easier, though never satisfying, not to make any moves at all. Some will seek to fulfil every demand from whomever it comes, whilst others will be content to allow a state of confusion or even anger to prevail. Neither of these methods is helpful, and both exact a toll. The former exacts a toll on the health and vitality of the pastor and his or her family, because not all demands can or should be met. The latter puts a burden on the congregation, who may become complacent, angry or both. In both cases, neither pastor nor people can be happy, nor can the church grow to its potential. Rather than pay the toll of neglect, it is in the long run much wiser to pay the price of a firm, thought out and articulated strategy. There are at least *three* strands to a strategy that will adequately deal with the demands of ministry:

- Articulating priorities
- Being assertive
- No's give value to yes's.

Articulating priorities

A willingness to take every opportunity to articulate priorities will deliver immediate and long-term benefits to pastor and people. This of course presupposes that the pastor has some well thought out priorities for ministry. The pastor will be in a position of greater strength and understanding if these priorities have been worked through with the congregational leadership.

The time for articulation and affirmation of priorities is at the time when demands are made upon the pastor. This should take place in every situation, whether it be a request in the vestry, or elders meeting, or a request from a church organization. Whilst this may take more time and some courage in the short term, the effort will be repaid in the long term. It will face up to the realities that not every request can be met, or even if they are, that not every person or group will be happy anyway. At the end of the day, everyone will at least know that their pastor is seeking to lead in an open and purposeful way.

When we are clear about our priorities, demands will not be viewed as possible threats to the pastor's image if we say no, but as opportunities to explain our ministry aims and strategies. We also affirm to ourselves that our value is not tied to meeting everyone's demands. At the same time, we will be gaining credibility in our style of ministry, since the aims and purpose of our ministry will be clear for all to see. This in turn will enable work to be accomplished, and will serve to strengthen our own sense of value. The cost of saying "no" to some requests, and the time and effort of articulating both the strategy and its reasons, will be richly repaid in the long term.

Being assertive

The ability to be assertive is closely related to the articulation of priorities. The whole concept of assertiveness for Christians is difficult ground indeed. The voluntary nature of congregations, together with the power many congregational and denominational leadership structures have over pastors, make it very easy for pastors to lose their assertiveness. A pastor's mindset can develop into a pattern of "it would be wrong for me as a Christian and a pastor to be assertive in either refusing demands or even articulating priorities". When a pastor becomes non- or under-assertive, it simply fuels the anger within. At this point, it is important to note that good assertiveness is never expressed in anger. In other words, aggressiveness is not assertiveness. The under-assertive person only has the ability to express themselves with the courage of anger, and this is where so much damage can occur. The situation is inflamed, the pastor is full of regret and anxiety, and the people are hurt, offended or confused.

If the pastor is unable to be assertive in saying "no" to demands that cannot be fulfilled, many harmful consequences follow:

- workloads reach intolerable heights
- depression can easily follow

- conflict situations and people are avoided
- stronger or influential people can easily manipulate us
- we are always always apologizing, thus assuming responsibility for everything that happens, leading to anxiety and guilt
- we are always fantasizing after the event as to how we should have responded, thus wasting energy in winning the game of the mind
- we can easily develop pathological ways of expressing our anger; these include sabotage, scapegoating and hostility towards kids or spouse
- it will lead too physical damage brought about by, and contributing to, lack of satisfaction in work (Hart, Fuller lectures, 1st May 1991).

Assertiveness can be developed once we recognize that it is a legitimate way of behaviour for the Christian pastor. It is best learnt and practised in the non-important areas of life, such as expecting quality for what we have paid for in a store or for a service rendered. When practised in these areas, we will know how to be assertive in the important issues of life, especially in responding to demands. There is a very practical issue at stake here. Nobody would want to suggest that pastors should not be free to 'go the extra mile'. A pastor may well respond to a demand that is out of the ordinary but is singularly appropriate at the time, even if it falls outside the generally accepted and previously articulated guidelines. Indeed, to have learnt to be assertive increases the opportunity to be flexible. It is when I am angry or feel cornered by a request that it is easy to act in a rigid and protective way.

Assertiveness will first help me to claim my right to say "no", and then willingly give up that right and respond to the request. No longer will I view the request as a demand that I cannot possibly escape, but a request that I am free to respond to if I so choose. To offer a person a sacrifice of time or energy, it must first be mine to offer.

When I feel that a demand must be met because of the asker's expectations, then I can only say "yes" begrudgingly. In this case a certain amount of bitterness and anger will be present. Guilt may well be mingled with bitterness if I actually enjoyed what I did, or the recipient was particularly grateful and full of praise. When I realize that I can say "no" to demands and expectations, I can then willingly give my "yes" without feeling pressured. Freedom follows sacrifice that is freely given.

The example of our Lord and Saviour is important at this point. It is because he did not *have* to become incarnate, or even go to the cross, that his birth and atoning death are so full of wonder, grace and example. His voluntary self-giving thus serves as the most compelling motivation to service and ministry. This appears to be Paul's way of encouraging servant ministry in Philippians 2:1-12.

No's give value to yes's

The third strategy is the affirmation that our no's give value to our yes's. There will always be demands and opportunities for pastors to do many good things. It is not a matter of simply choosing between right and wrong, or helpful and unhelpful activities, but choosing the action that best furthers our goals. To say "yes" to everything will mean we have not given any real value or priority to anything. The importance of saying "no" is that it is our mechanism against overload, and a key to being able to fulfil God's will in our lives.

Both Jesus and the apostles needed to make choices so that they could fulfil God's purposes. Being confident enough to be able to say "no" is surely an important mechanism that busy pastors need to employ if they are going to be purposeful in ministry. To do so will require confidence that our value depends more upon our faithfulness to God than upon our response to other people.

How to say "no"

Dr Hart helpfully outlines three simple principles in being able to say "no". These principles work on the assumption that how we say "no" to people is in the end more important than the fact that we say "no".

In the first place it is important that we clarify the request. In seeking to understand the nature of the request, we are putting ourselves in a position to clarify the kind of commitment required from us, at the same time respecting the person making the request.

Then it is important *to assess the reasonableness of the request.* Many pastors find that it is helpful to ask for some time to do this. Consultation with one's diary, family and church leadership can help clarify the request. If at that particular moment we are not feeling appreciated or valued by our church, or we are going through a trough of depression, it is tempting to respond immediately with an affirmative answer. A request to speak somewhere else becomes a way of escape and a well needed tonic: "at least someone around here values me and what I have to offer". Asking for time to consider can enable these motives to be worked through. The time of reflection will help us enjoy the tonic of having been asked, without going through the pain of adding yet another demand to a schedule that may well be a contributing factor to the church's lack of appreciation or our own depression. Time requested will of course be given by any thoughtful person, and will be seen as a legitimate way of assessing whether the request can be dealt with in a conscientious fashion.

When the time comes for an answer to be given and the request is turned down, it can prove helpful to share the process with the person who asked. For example, if the church leadership have in consultation with the pastor decided that, as a matter of stewardship, mission and fellowship, it is right for their pastor to be away four weekends a year, and to fulfil this request would make number five or mean two successive weekends away, then this should be shared. This is honest, and of course makes it easier for people to accept a "no" answer.

The third principle may at first glance run counter to the one just outlined. Having decided to say "no", *there is no good purpose served in giving an extensive explanation* for saying "no". Sharing the process is sufficient, and by giving up the inclination to engage in a long apology with many reasons, we will find that our proneness to guilt will not be fed.

Each of these principles reminds us that it is as much our right to say "no" as it is to say "yes" to requests. As we have seen previously, this is not a recipe for complacency or laziness, but a strategy that will enhance our ministries. It will do this because we will then be free to pursue ministry goals with confidence and a good conscience, whether they be in the mainstream of our pastoral duties, or in fulfilling the requests that come to us from time to time.

Confidence is required to say no

We need to be realistic about ourselves and about God, if we are going to be able to say "no" and persevere with strategies that will keep stress to a minimum.

In the final chapter, I outline how the doctrine of justification by faith helps us gain confidence in combating many of the stresses and demands of ministry. In order to say "no", I need to be sure and comfortable that my status before God is settled, not by the amount of work I do or the size of the church I'm ministering in, but by my acceptance by God the Father. This acceptance is based upon the life and death of Jesus Christ, and secured by my wholehearted acceptance of what he accomplished for me.

When this wonderful teaching of Scripture is central to my own thinking and living, not only can I say "no", but I can say "yes" for the right reasons. Furthermore, I will be much more likely to be able to accept warranted, and even unwarranted, personal criticism. It is a doctrine that works in the rough and tumble of ministry.

Ten preventative measures

Psychologist Pat Cleary offers a number of ways we can prepare ourselves to be less stressed. The ten listed below flow out of the healthy basis of justification by faith.

- Live less in the future, not focusing and brooding on what *might* go wrong, what people *might* say, and things that we can't control.
- Realize that failure is not a terminal illness, so we don't have to wait till we think we've got everything perfect and under control before we move forward.
- Reject the ideas:
    You shall at all costs avoid getting into trouble.
    You shall always protect your reputation, even if it means being dishonest.
    You shall at all costs avoid saying anything that people may not like.
    You shall always feel responsible if anyone is upset in your presence.
- Let go of the compulsion to prove ourselves (to ourselves and others) by our efforts and achievements. Our value comes from who we are; a friend, partner, parent, child of God; from our relationships not our products.
- Admit our limitations and aim to honour God rather than our own ego. Perfectionists aren't perfect, they just feel they have to be (or pretend to be)!

- Accept that naughtiness, carelessness, foolishness, laziness and selfishness are all part of the human condition. We will be less surprised and less condemning when we and others fail. Being judgemental can be a stress problem!
- Come to terms with being one of the 'all' that Paul wrote about ... *for all have sinned and fall short of the glory of God* ... (Romans 3:23).
- Accept that we can't be in more than one place at a time and remember that there are only 168 hours in the week to be divided among all that we have to do. We can only spend more time on one thing at the expense of another. We are created within time and time is not elastic, so it is not ungodly nor a failure to say politely, "No, I'm sorry, I can't help you tomorrow".
- Challenge the unhelpful idea that work, study, ministry, and so on, are the normal state of the human organism and that rest is ungodly: "there's always something good we could be doing".
- Come to understand God's grace. We will see that we live in relationship with him and that within that relationship we plan, we strive, we serve. We will not be rejected from that relationship whether we succeed or fail. When we fail, we repent while remaining within that relationship (Cleary, p. 15).

4

Stress and adrenalin: understanding your body clock

No one can live without experiencing some degrees of stress. It is not even necessarily bad for you; it is also the spice of life, for any emotion, any activity, causes stress.
H. SELYE

Stress has a real tendency to suppress our immune system.
WILLIAM HULME

If you stop playing the Messiah, you will have considerably less stress.
A. D. HART

IT TOOK ME YEARS to understand why after Sunday morning services my hands were cold. People would remark on it as I greeted them at the door, especially after the second of the morning services.

I love church, and I especially love preaching God's word and fellowshipping with my brothers and sisters. But it all takes energy. Energy is expended in leading, speaking and being concerned that all is going well. "I wonder why Tom wasn't there today?", "I do hope someone talks to that new couple …", and so the concerns go on, all while I'm trying to be available for people.

Why the cold hands? The well-intentioned remark "cold hands warm heart" was comforting, but not convincing. No, the key had to do with how my body responds to stressful events.

The following chart, reproduced from Dr Kath Donovan's book *Growing Through Stress*, helps us understand why we feel the way we do when stressed (Donovan, p. 46).

Figure 2: **Symptoms of the stress response**

Part of Body	What Happens	Why	What we Feel
Heart	Beats faster	To get blood, glucose and oxygen quickly to brain and muscles	Thumping
Lungs	Air passages enlarge, breathing faster	To get oxygen into blood quickly	Breathless
Brain	Increased supply of blood with glucose and oxygen	Ready for action	Mind alert
Muscles	Increase in blood carrying glucose and oxygen	Ready for action	Tense
Skin	Less blood because it has gone to brain and muscle; more perspiration	Blood needed elsewhere to cool body	Cold clammy and looking pale
Stomach	Less blood	Blood needed elsewhere	In knot

Dr Donovan describes these "biochemical and physiological changes" as

> directed towards preparing the body to protect itself against whatever threatens, by fight or flight. It does this by directing blood, oxygen and glucose to the organs which would be most involved in protective action—brain and large muscles. This results in extra clarity of thought, and increased strength. This happens at the expense of temporarily less vital organs such as the skin and stomach (Donovan, p. 46).

This is the "gearing up for action" side of the stress response.

Stress cannot be avoided in life and ministry. There will always be emergencies to attend to, difficult circumstances and people that need attention, regular deadlines to meet, plus our own expectations driving us.

What is important is our *response* to stress, and the way we manage our lives so as to avoid unnecessary stress. My cold hands alert me to the fact that I am "fearfully and wonderfully made". God has designed my body with the ability to work hard, respond to tough and difficult situations, and to carry out a number of responsibilities diligently.

An attitude of wonder and amazement at the way God has designed our body should lead us to a fresh appreciation of why we need to rest regularly. The same God who has given us the command to rest has also enabled medical research to discover the way our body works. In regard to stress, Dr Hart's insights as to the way adrenalin works in the 'gearing up' process, and the even more important let-down response (Dr Donovan calls this the "calming down" side of the stress response), go a long way towards keeping us from abusing what God has given us.

Those cold hands are a reminder to me that considerable energy has been expended in getting me to the line on Sunday morning. Adrenalin has been released from my adrenal glands to give me the energy needed for what I consider my most important public pastoral responsibility. It is also my most enjoyable.

Good stress

Sometimes we feel that only bad stress (that is, stress caused by difficult people, circumstances or confrontations), is potentially damaging. Good stress, caused by things we enjoy, can be even more damaging. This is because we don't see the need to avoid or alleviate the stress; rather, we thrive on these "good stress" situations. To put it another way: it is not stress as such that will kill us, it is how much stress we allow in our lives.

A stressed person is like an engine that can only function in high gear. The engine keeps racing, everything is done at a frantic pace, rest is impossible even if the need is acknowledged, and eventually the whole engine blows up.

That is, our body cannot continue to function with high levels of stress. Something will give way, and illness will follow.

Our adrenalin alarm system

The 'fight or flight' response is the way God has designed our bodies to cope with life's pressures. Hart explains how adrenalin is the hidden link in triggering our bodies' responses.

> When the state of alarm or emergency is triggered, our various physiological systems are bathed in adrenalin, which disrupts normal functioning and produces a heightened state of arousal. In the immediate 'emergency' reaction, the heart beats faster, digestion is speeded up, and a host of hormones is released into the bloodstream to prepare us for dealing with the emergency.
>
> We will go into these changes in a little more detail later. For now, we just need to understand that God has created us to be creatures of extreme complexity. Whenever we are threatened physically or psychologically, a complex chain of responses is set in motion to prepare us for what has been described as the 'fight or flight' response. It's as simple as that. When we are under stress, our bodies are prepared either to attack what is threatening us or to run away from it.
>
> This is the *alarm* system that is triggered by stress. Its purpose is to alert us to a threat so that we can be better equipped to deal with it. But difficulties arise when we are threatened over and over again, or when we are constantly challenged or live in a constant state of emergency. When this happens, what was designed as a protective mechanism begins to be harmful to us. We begin to experience the damaging consequences of stress.
>
> The best way I can illustrate this is to ask you to imagine an

elastic band. If it is stretched between your thumbs and then released, it returns to its normal, relaxed position as soon as the external force is removed. The body's stress response is also 'stretched' whenever it is subjected to an emergency or demand. It ought to return to a normal, relaxed state when the demand is removed. But if the elastic band is stretched and then held in an extended position for a long period of time, it begins to lose its elastic properties, develops hairline cracks, and eventually snaps. Similarly, if our bodies are repeatedly alarmed or held in a constant state of alarm, they soon begin to show damaging consequences. The so-called stress-related disorders—physical and psychological—are the consequence (Hart, 1988, pp. 22-23).

The danger

When we begin to rely upon stress and its associated adrenalin highs to keep us going, we are in danger. Eventually the elastic band will not just remain stretched, but break. And it will break in one of those other areas: like our heart, ulcers, brain or lungs. The fight or flight trigger was meant to get us over the occasional dangerous emergencies of life, not the everyday, ordinary normalities of life.

When pastors who enjoy their work fail to recognize the need for balance and rest, they can easily find the work addictive. Their adrenalin high is required to keep them going. For pastors, an added danger is the temptation to justify workaholism by spiritualizing the addiction as zeal. When this is compounded by the applause that often comes from the parishioners for such addiction, awful consequences for pastors, their families and church inevitably follow.

All this means we do well to obey our body clock.

Obeying our body clock

As I write this chapter, I am conscious that I'm not concentrating as well as I was yesterday. Last night, I was required to give a lecture to social work students as part of a semester's course on ethics. As this was a new experience for me, and a pastoral emergency meant I had to skimp on lecture preparation, I am left somewhat drained of energy.

This is a natural reaction, which Dr Hart calls "adrenalin let-down". It is my body's way of bringing me back to normal after the adrenalin release that enabled me to get to, and then deliver, the lecture. The stretched elastic band is now returning to normal. Thankfully I'm a few days ahead of my own deadline for writing this book, so I'm under no pressure. I can feel my body returning to normal.

Indeed, when I undertook the semester's lecturing at a local university, it was to fill in a gap at very short notice. After consultation with my church leadership and wife, it was decided that it would be a good thing to do, but with two trade-offs in the interest of my self-care. The first was that I would have a week's leave in order to mark the papers, and the second was that I would forgo my evening home group for the duration of the course. This latter move was to ensure that I would able to compensate for the missed family time, and allow time for the adrenalin let-down to occur.

How wise this decision has been. For the first three weeks I just could not have faced being part of a group, because of the emotional drain of lecturing, and presenting new material as a Christian in a secular university. This was despite the fact that I have been part of this same home group for ten years, and derive great joy and support from it. I'm looking forward with great anticipation to rejoining it in a couple of weeks.

To check my current stress levels, yesterday I began wearing a "stress dot"[1] on my hand, which was almost continuously in the more relaxed colour range of temperature 88°F and above. At the moment it is hovering still in the lower range around 84°F.

The process of stress and let-down can be seen from this simple illustration:

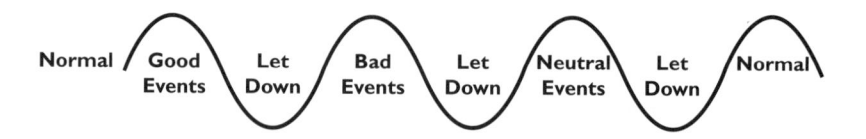

Normal / Good Events \ Let Down / Bad Events \ Let Down / Neutral Events \ Let Down / Normal

The high points represent stressful events. Remember that these can typically be good, bad or indifferent events: the good event like preaching, the bad like a conflict between lay church members, or the indifferent event like a routine monthly church council meeting. Each requires energy from us. Adrenalin is released to enable us to cope and make the best use of these situations. The downward slope represents the time required to return to normal, healthy levels of adrenalin activity. Allowing ourselves time, indeed building in time for this let-down to take place, is vital if we are going to remain fresh for life and ministry.

Hart emphasizes the need for this balance of adrenalin arousal and let-down.

> It would be unfair of me to suggest that all challenge, change, excitement, and fervour for work or play should be avoided because it is stressful. This is not my intention, nor would it be a completely accurate picture.
>
> Life is to be *lived*—and lived to the *fullest*. Being highly motivated to accomplish some task and able to work with enthusiasm is a great blessing. To experience the flood of energy that propels one into action to meet a need, make a deadline, or accomplish a demanding task is what makes life worthwhile. Without such challenges we might as well be dead. Progress in medicine would slow to a snail's pace, the gospel would never reach the unreached, and justice for the oppressed would never get a vote.
>
> Nothing worthwhile can be accomplished without arousal of the stress response system. It is a biological law that we must fight and work for a worthwhile goal. Challenge and fulfilment are important to health and wellbeing. But—and this point is critical—challenges and stress *must* be accompanied by and work in harmony with relaxation and rest (Hart, 1988, p. 50).

This relaxation and rest will take place only when we see that we need it. Many of us who enjoy working hard, think that we don't need to build in times of relaxation and rest. But high adrenalin arousal is a hidden killer doing its work behind the scenes on our weakest link. Hulme makes the point well.

> What actually seems to be happening in the continuous build-up of stress is an acceleration of the body's aging process. The stage of

exhaustion in the body's General Adaptation Syndrome comes sooner rather than later. Stress results in the wear and tear of the body's 'machinery' ... Calcium deposits in the arteries, joints and the crystalline lens of the eye are examples. Blood pressure, which already tends to be high in stressed people, rises even higher to maintain circulation through the increasingly inelastic and narrowing vessels.

The younger person has an abundant supply of remaining healthy tissue with which to cope with these tissue-destroying tendencies. But as we grow older, the reserves get used up (Hulme, 1985, p. 21).

We perceive this high level of adrenalin as being essential to our well being and productivity. How often do we hear it said, "I work best when I'm under pressure"? Meanwhile, the damage will be taking place. In the short term, irritability and addiction to work will replace a calm and healthy commitment. The long-term consequences are depression, premature death or the "4 A's", as we see below.

Let Arch Hart describe the process:

Both roads—stress and burnout—lead ultimately to depression. The depression that comes from stress is due to the exhaustion of the adrenal system. On the other hand, the depression that comes from burnout is the loss of your vision, of your ideals. You become demoralized and you don't care any more.

A fellow from the Harvard Medical School identified the process leading to aberrant behaviour in secular leaders. I see it at work in our Christian world as well. Specifically, the devil uses four A's to lead a minister into big trouble.

The first is *arrogance*. The minister says, "I can do it myself. I don't need anybody else's help". And then he begins to make the rules. He doesn't obey the rules—he makes them.

That leads, secondly, to a sort of adventurous *addiction*. The pastor becomes taken up with what he's doing, very excited and energised by it, and it's an addiction.

Then he begins the third A: *aloneness* sets in. That's the point at which depression is a risk, because he cuts himself off from other people.

Then, finally, there's the danger of *adultery*. The minister turns to sex as the only thing that will give him his kick, as a way to make up for what he has lost, because he has a profound sense of loss.

These four A's are as much a risk for pastors as they are for anyone in the secular world who's striving to be successful. They are the consequences of too much stress (Hart, in London, p. 8).

Practices for pastors
A thoughtful use of your diary is essential

Where possible, we do well to plan for stress-laden activities to be followed by non-stressful ones. Stress management is vital. Hart suggests that those suffering from an increase in blood cholesterol caused by the release of adrenalin from the liver can be helped 13% by diet and 87% by stress management practices. Clearly we cannot anticipate emergency events, but we can usually anticipate regularly-occurring stressful activities.

Our diary can help us manage each day, each week and busy seasons of the year. Hart comments:

> Good stress must have this pattern about it on an hourly, daily and weekly basis: high adrenalin arousal must be allowed when demanded, but then brought back to a state of low arousal afterwards. The pattern should look like a series of hills and valleys. A valley of recuperation should follow every mountain of high arousal. Each day should end with a return to low arousal. Each challenge of the day should end with a calming of the body. And each week of work should end with rest. If you can do this, you will be healthy in body, mind, and spirit—and all your stress will be 'good'. You will be obedient to God's laws for your total person and this will bring you health (Hart, 1988, p. 51).

A tension-filled meeting of church leaders on a Wednesday is better followed on Thursday morning by some preparation, rather than a demanding counselling session. To schedule the counselling for 11 am rather than 9.00 am will be better for all concerned.

Don't take Monday as your day off

The principle is the same. High levels of adrenalin are expended on Sundays. The body is in let-down mode on Mondays. Why give one's spouse the worst time? Why not do some administration, tidying of the desk, and early preparation for next week? Everyone wins. You get administration and preparation done, your spouse gets you much more relaxed on another day, and you'll probably play better golf on Friday than Monday. I reckon I play 4-5 strokes better over 9 holes of golf on Fridays than I used to on Monday mornings.

Enjoy little things each day

- Give yourself time to go for a walk—perhaps at lunch time.
- Smell the roses for five minutes at other times.
- Walk to the shop to post the letters and engage people in 'idle conversation'. It's good for us. It's part of the process of coming back down to earth. These ordinary humdrum aspects of life often provide the opportunity for 'time out' for the body to return to normal. Passing the time of day with others provides the context for humour and non-demanding friendships to emerge.

Build in time for friends

Caring friendships and humour are antidotes to high adrenalin addiction. Friendships need time to be nurtured, and in non-threatening circumstances if trust is to develop. In turn, real friendships will mean that pastors will be less driven to seek importance through achievements, and at the same time will have friends who will help them slow down by encouraging perspective and balance in their ministry. Hart comments "few friends ... will have any more respect for you because you hurry yourself. If anything, most would trust you more if you slowed down" (Hart, 1988, p. 236).

Hulme observes that "interestingly enough, the more a stressful event is shared, the less each person appears to be stressed" (Hulme, p. 52). There are many reasons for this. Friends can help us regain our perspective. Their 'gift of listening' is a positive reminder to us that we are valuable. Their advice and prayer support become God-given gifts that will help relieve our stress. The let-down can run its full course and stressful events are seen in a new light.

Remember: God is in control

When unplanned and unwelcome events that cause us to be stressed come across our path, our worldview or belief system is going to determine how well we cope. Recovery from the initial realization that we are going to have to live and minister in the midst of uncertainty will be made possible, to a greater or lesser extent, by how we understand and are able to accept God's hand in the circumstances. Trust in his sovereignty will help us enormously. Belief in a sovereign God who providentially orders our lives is much more than fate, with its stoical response of 'whatever will be will be'. It is the affirmation of ABC: Adversity Builds Christlikeness. Put another way, Romans 8:29 follows 8:28! The *good* that God works in all things for those who love him and are called (8:28) is none other than to contribute to our growth into Christlikeness (8:29).

Psychologist Dr Pat Cleary affirms this:

> ... remember that our God is sovereign. It helps to remember that nothing can happen (unless we deliberately reject him) that will get between us and our eternal relationship with him. Recall that God is more concerned with our growth than our comfort. He has not abandoned us when we are tempted and tested (Cleary, p. 15).

This is why the apostle Paul is able to say of himself and his team, "We are afflicted in every way, *but not crushed;* perplexed, *but not driven to despair*" (2 Cor 4:8).

Any event that I cannot control will lead me to be more stressed, if I approach it 'as God'. I will then endeavour to control everything, or else give up. *Trust* in God, on the other hand, will enable me to find help and a new perspective, that will in one sense turn the stress into good. Dr Kath Donovan calls this *stress overflow* as opposed to *stress overload* (Donovan, p. 69). With God as sovereign, in control and working for our good, 'stress overflows' contribute to our growth in Christlikeness.

It is because God is in control that we pray. There is no point in praying to a God who is not sovereign. The apostle Paul's deliberate pattern and practice of prayer outlined in Philippians 4:4-6 demonstrate how we may handle and cope with stress.

> Rejoice in the Lord always; again I will say, Rejoice. Let your reasonableness be known to everyone. The Lord is at hand; do not be anxious about anything, but in everything by prayer and supplication with thanksgiving let your requests be made known to God.

Paul's deliberate practice is suggested by such words as *prayer, supplication, thanksgiving* and *requests*. The exhortation he makes is seen as a pattern in his own life and ministry. Prayer has a great effect in our lives, delivering to us God's promised presence and peace. When we pray, we are at our strongest; because we have surrendered the false notion that we are facing a problem as God, and instead finding the blessing of facing it *under God*. No wonder Paul concludes the exhortation with the promise that has brought comfort to countless Christians through the ages " … and the peace of God, which surpasses all understanding, will guard your hearts and your minds in Christ Jesus" (4:7).

Plan ahead

Pastors, like many busy people, have deadlines to meet. Every week, a sermon or sermons, Bible studies, Sunday leaflets and meetings need to be prepared. How can we avoid being stressed? How can we avoid only being able to function when there is a deadline to motivate us? This is the real problem with unmanaged stress. When we are operating at an abnormally high stress level, and need it to be in place so that we can function, we are in deep trouble. This is because:

- we are not at our creative best when we are stressed
- we produce less and take longer to do it, the law of diminishing returns kicks in
- we are less able to reap the benefits of other's insights because we are badly organized and too irritable to converse; hurried and busy people don't have time to listen
- we are setting ourselves up for premature burnout
- we do not get the benefit of reflective, reasoned, prayerful and thoughtful preparation.

The concept of 'early seeding' has been of great benefit to me. Let me illustrate from my sermon preparation. If I leave it to Saturday, I become panicky. Experience tells me that if something unexpected comes along, I'm in trouble. However, if I've begun my preparation early in the week (say Monday morning), begun to make notes, have the passage or topic on my mind, then a number of helpful creative things happen:

- the passage is getting into me, as I think through its meaning and implications
- illustrations from life are suggested by what I see and hear around me
- as different time slots become available during the week, I'm able to use them profitably, by re-reading the passage, consulting the commentaries and books. While this is happening, my note page is growing, an outline or emphasis is beginning to emerge. Early seeding is beginning to bear fruit.

I continually find that the earlier it is in the day, the better I can think creatively. New ideas come easier. If I can jot down an outline or some thoughts, I'm on the way so far as preparation is concerned. Even if I can't come back to flesh it out until a later time, I'm not stressed about it because the outline and ideas are all in place. It goes without saying that I write these ideas down. Someone has said, "one drop of ink is worth a thousand memories".

Hart gives us an explanation:

> There is now abundant evidence that our most inventive and creative state is at low levels of arousal. Contrary to what many people believe, it is when we are minimally aroused by adrenalin that we can do our most innovative and imaginative thinking.
>
> In psychology there is a principle known as the "Yerkes-Dodson Law" (named after those who first formulated it), which states that there is an 'inverted-U' relationship between arousal of the mind and body, and the efficiency with which we can perform certain tasks. The law goes like this:
>
> 1. At low arousal, we are not very effective in action tasks but very good at thinking creatively.
> 2. As arousal increases, we become more effective in action and less effective in creative thinking.
> 3. As arousal becomes very high, our efficiency in both action and thinking drops off again. This is probably the stage of "panic".

> High arousal forces people to move away from creative and innovative responses because in the emergency they are forced back to old, familiar ways of doing things. They tend to panic and act on the reflexes instead of thinking through the alternatives.
>
> Of course, when we have created our ideas or solved our problems at low levels of arousal, we must be able to move to a higher level of arousal to put our thoughts into action. In a sense, therefore, we need both low and medium levels of arousal for effective living. Seldom do we need a very high level of arousal in modern day living (Hart, 1988, p. 198).

Returning to the example of my own sermon preparation: having done the seeding preparation early, I'm then in a position later in the week to do the reaping. On Hart's analogy above, this could be done at medium arousal times, but if it can be done during low arousal creative time all the better. For myself this is often done first thing on a Saturday morning (7 am–10 am), after my day off, and with the prospect of taking the afternoon off. My seeding in terms of preparation notes, plus a mind in tune with the passage (often enhanced by my Tuesday home group where we have already studied the passage), ensures that I am ready to go.

I have found this concept a winner, because my stress is reduced by the creative process, and my mind is refreshed by the opportunity for focused reflection during the week. This process helps me to keep a focus upon the God of Scripture rather than, if I'm always hurried, the task of teaching Scripture.

Watch out for artificial stimulants

Workaholics are often heard to say, "I function best when I'm working", "Resting only gives me a headache". Part of the problem is that they are right. They have managed to trick their body into thinking that every situation is one that requires high adrenalin arousal. Of course resting will give them a headache. This is the body's way of saying "have a really good lie down". Sleep is vital for recovery from stress. Hart comments:

> … to wake up tired, if we have slept long, can be a sign that adrenalin arousal has been reduced to a low level, and this is good news if we are fighting stress disease. After three or four nights of

deep, long sleep, the feeling of tiredness on waking passes off, and we wake up refreshed and replenished in body and spirit (Hart, 1988, p. 157).[2]

Hurried people are short-circuiting the body's mechanisms for keeping us healthy. The commonest way for this to happen, often begun in student days, is to consume large amounts of coffee or other caffeine-based drinks. I heard Dr Hart comment in lectures that caffeine compounds the adrenalin arousal. More than eight cups of coffee a day and you triple your chance of a heart attack. When questioned, Dr Hart commented that the issue was not the coffee, but the tricks it plays on the body's let-down mechanism. It keeps us functioning at an abnormally high level of adrenalin arousal which will then affect our weakest organ, just as "the weakest part of any machine breaks under heavy demand".

The psalmist praises God when he considers the human body.

> For you formed my inward parts; you knitted me together in my mother's womb. I praise you, for I am fearfully and wonderfully made ... in your book were written, every one of them, the days that were formed for me, when as yet there were none of them. How precious to me are your thoughts, O God! (Psalm 139:13, 14, 16, 17).

Stress highlights how God has designed us to cope with the demands of life. That it is a reality which often delivers destructive consequences is a fact of experience and observation. The insights concerning adrenalin arousal and let-down, flowing out of research and provable in our own experience, help us to see the wisdom in allowing ourselves to rest properly. By building in thought and behaviour patterns that enable the let-down to take place regularly we demonstrate how we value our bodies and the work God has entrusted to us.

ENDNOTES
1. Stress dots can be obtained from local Institutes of Management.
2. It is worth buying Hart's book, *Adrenalin and Stress*, for the chapter on sleep alone.

5
Depression doesn't have to be depressing

Depression is the common cold of the emotions.
GARY COLLINS

*... the godliest men and women have been gripped
by profound depression.*
JOHN WHITE

*Depression is no respecter of persons,
and its presence does not deny the power of God or the
earnestness of a pastor's commitment.*
ARCH HART

"THE COMMON COLD of our emotions", is how Christian psychologist Gary Collins describes depression. Many ministers suffer from it. We need to recognize both that depression will be a part of the pastor's experience, and that to be depressed is not necessarily a sign of sin or failure.

My own pilgrimage from naivety to understanding can be plotted:

- Christians shouldn't be depressed
- Christians do get depressed
- Christians I know are depressed
- I get depressed
- Some depression is caused by chemical imbalance
- Much depression is a natural reaction to loss.

As a non-physician who has not had training in psychology, I recognize that I'm treading on difficult ground. However, the ground is not unfamiliar or unrecognizable. I have been very appreciative of a number of people and books that have helped overcome my naivety, which, I trust, keeps me from an unhelpful, simplistic approach to depressed friends. It was Dr John White, speaking at St Alban's Church in Perth, who helped me understand the serious nature of some depressions. Since some of these resulted from biological factors and could be treated very successfully with medication, I was alerted to be neither discouraged when trying to minister to such people, nor afraid to refer them to qualified medical or psychiatric help. White's book *The Masks of Melancholy: A Christian Physician Looks at Depression and Suicide* (1982) is full of good information and wise counsel regarding depression. Dr Arch Hart's books *Coping with Depression in the Ministry and other Helping Professions* (1984) and *Counselling the Depressed* (1987) are both full of helpful insights into understanding the different kinds of depression.

My aim is not to give a detailed explanation of the nature, causes and remedies of depression. I refer pastors and others to the books mentioned above for a more detailed treatment. However, since my aim is to help pastors care for themselves, and to encourage church members to be thoughtful contributors to the pastoral care of their pastors, it might be helpful to offer some of the insights gleaned from these resources.

A working distinction

There are different kinds of depression. The one that I will be discussing is what is called *exogenous* depression. This is depression that is *reactive* to a loss. The following chart will help distinguish the two broad types of depression.

TYPE	CAUSE	TREATMENT	OCCURRENCE
ENDOGENOUS	Biological	Mainly medical	Perhaps 5-8% of population
EXOGENOUS	Reaction to loss	Support, sleep, counselling	All of us, often

How do we distinguish between endogenous and exogenous depression?

- Endogenous depression is often not helped by sleep, whereas sleep helps a person with reactive depression.
- The person with reactive depression can be distracted by humour and other things, but nothing seems to distract a person with endogenous depression.
- When medication takes effect in a person with endogenous depression, the sufferer is aware of this because the depression lifts.

It is obviously important for pastors to be able to distinguish the less common endogenous depression from the common reactive depression, not only since this aids us in our counselling and pastoral ministry, but for our own times of feeling depressed. If we are not responding to rest, or the encouragement of supporting friends or counsel, we may be well advised to have some medical checks lest there be an underlying medical cause to our depression. Even in reactive depression there will be times when we may need a small amount of medication that will prepare us to be more responsive to the rest/friends/counsel triad.

Since we are whole people, we do well to recognize the connection between physical and emotional health. Pastors should have regular physical checkups. Sometimes what is assumed to be a depression caused by external factors can turn out to be a chemical or biological imbalance. Dr Hart suggests that around eight percent of all people experience an endogenous depression, and all of us may have some form of reactive depression each day. It is this reactive depression that is most important for pastors to understand, both for our own health and because it is the most common form of depression we will be called upon to deal with.

Reactive depression

Pastors often deal with situations of loss in ministry. People leave the church, people are not responsive, loved ones die, people move away from Christ. These are all conditions that can provoke depression. I now see most depression as reactive, akin to the grieving process.

"Depression", writes Hart "is, therefore, a process by which the mind and body come to terms with the loss it has suffered ... the greater the loss, the greater the depression" (Hart, 1987, p. 55). In other words, we ought never to see depression as bad or undesirable. If we do, we may well end up making the more serious assumption that life is bad. In Dr Hart's understanding, depression has the important function of bringing healing to our lives. Depression does not have to be depressing!

Viewed in this light, depression can be seen as having a very positive potential; indeed it is part of the way God has made us. It is, in reality, a part of our body's 'early warning system', alerting us to the fact that something is wrong and needs to be dealt with. We may need to slow down, seek medical treatment, turn to God in repentance or allow the grieving process to take its course. Depression may be an agent used by God for our sanity (where the depression is a response to loss), or our sanctification (if there is a sinful act or attitude involved). For every loss situation there is an appropriate amount of depression.

The further insight that "the real problem lies not with the absence of the lost object but with the attachment to it" (Hart, 1987, p. 78) has proved helpful to me personally and in pastoring others. Depression will continue until we have learnt to let go of the loved object. For the pastor, this kind of attachment and loss happens all the time. It can take place in the big or important events like leaving one congregation in order to retire or pastor a new church; but it can also take place when a valued church leader or member dies or, even harder to handle, leaves to attend another church nearby. Unexpected events will cause more depression, because the loss has neither been anticipated nor prepared for.

When I moved parishes some years ago, I came to the new parish with a letter of recommendation from the local community newspaper for which I had written a weekly 'Christian Comment' for over seven years. Though meeting the deadline was sometimes difficult, it was a ministry I thoroughly enjoyed. The new local paper, though inviting me to write on special occasions, was not interested in a weekly column. Apart from the normal loss and consequent feelings of low-grade depression, I was conscious of frustration and even anger at the loss of the weekly column. It wasn't until I realized that I had become attached to the regular column as a real source of my own value, that I could deal with the depression. This loss was in reality the loss of being known and valued by Christians of all denominations. Natural? Yes. Sinful? Yes. The depression was used by God to help my sanity and sanctification, as I came to grips with the fact that my value is not primarily dependent upon being known and valued in the community.

One goal of ministry in the local church is to encourage, by teaching, example and thoughtful management, a deep sense of caring and committed fellowship. Large portions of the epistles are given over to the encouragement and building up of supportive structures between Christian brothers and sisters. Very real losses can be caused by:

- **natural causes**, like death, or moving to another city;
- **Christian obedience and calling**, such as missionary service, response to pastoral call or planting a new church;
- **conscience causes**, for example genuine difficulty with church or denominational teaching or practices;
- **sinful causes**, such as unwillingness to work through differences.

One response is to play safe, and insure against the hurt by keeping others at arm's length. In such a congregation, peace is prized above an honest sorting out of problems, courtesy above genuine care, and politeness above warm, open-hearted relationships. Since loss does cause pain and depression, this is an understandable response. No-one wants to be hurt. But there is another way. It is the way of deep and caring fellowship, when depression is seen not as sinful, but as a way of coming to grips with loss. In this congregation, pastor and people are free to share their hurts and their hearts without fear of being thought unspiritual. To guard against unhealthy introspection or complacency about sin, the expression of one's heart will be seen as a means to an end. Sanity, the restoration of inner joy, and sanctification through dealing with sin, will always be the goal. Where feelings cannot be shared, either because of a misguided view of the place of depression in Christian experience, or an unwillingness (born of laziness and lovelessness) to get involved, we are all robbed of one of God's most wonderful resources for our growth—a caring fellowship of brothers and sisters.

Our Lord's promise of comfort to those who mourn (Matt 5:4) is surely meant to find its fulfilment largely through the thoughtful ministry suggested by Paul: "rejoice with those who rejoice, weep with those who weep" (Rom 12:15). If every loss situation produces an appropriate depression so as to allow a grieving to take place, the application of these verses is clearly much wider than the mourning that follows bereavement.

Two related aspects of the pastor's ministry can be beneficial in the handling of loss. One is a function of the pastor's preaching and teaching ministry, and is *preparative*. The other is a function of pastoring, and is *supportive*. Paul Tournier suggests that we will benefit greatly as we come to experience "a necessary progressive detachment from the world" (quoted in Hart, 1987, p. 80). Here is the paradox: God uses this preparatory "progressive detachment" to help all Christian people cope with loss. The words 'preparatory' and 'cope' are important. It would be inappropriate and unrealistic to have used 'prevent' and 'avoid'. All loss of significant and important people will carry real grief. We do have feelings and will be impoverished if we seek to minimize them by adopting a distant or professional approach to people. Most pastors will want to be able to echo the words of the apostle Paul who, on behalf of his companions, affirmed to the Thessalonian Christians that "we were ready to share with you not only the gospel of God but also our own selves", because " you had become very dear to us" (1 Thess 2:8).

The gospel prepares us for the loss of loved ones in much the same way as it helps us to love them. At the heart of the gospel is the proclamation that "Jesus is Lord". Because he is Lord, the Christian allows Jesus to be the very focus of life. We will learn to value and serve people as he does, but at the same time we will be kept from expecting these people to meet all of our needs. What needs they do meet in our lives we will value and thank God for, and in so doing will be reminded that they are gifts to us from our Lord. When others, even those closest and dearest to us, are viewed like this, we are free to minister to them without expecting them to meet our needs. This will keep us from becoming over-dependent or over-demanding, and will mean our dependence upon the Lord, our Pastor, will grow. At a practical level it will mean that congregational members can be allowed to start a new work, become a missionary, move interstate or even leave to join another church. There will be pain, since such people remain very dear to us; but this pain, once faced, need not turn into bitterness, nor be allowed to develop into a protective remoteness from others, since the Lord Jesus is the one upon whom we are dependent. This will lessen the chance of us either becoming resentful of God, or unmindful of the support available from other Christian people.

As attachment to our Lord grows, we are in fact being prepared to cope with loss. Detachment from the world in this sense does not mean an other-worldliness that is of little or no value to people immersed in the day to day problems of life. It is rather a growing partnership with the Lord, which makes the best of relationships and circumstances. The same paradox is found in Jesus' words, "For whoever would save his life will lose it, but whoever loses his life for my sake will save it" (Luke 9:24). Jesus' statement, whilst not referring to the specific question of depression caused by the loss of a significant person or object in our lives, serves as a general call to be detached from anything that would hold us back from giving our life to him.

Tournier is right to emphasize the element of *progression* in this. Detachment from people or things is a process. It is born and nurtured by a growing commitment to the One who would keep us from losing our lives in the people and things of this passing and changing world. On the other hand, he will give us life as we focus upon him, God the Giver. This will, once again paradoxically, result in an increased enjoyment of the gifts when they are with us and an ability to cope with their loss.

The value of balanced and applied biblical teaching becomes immediately obvious. Preparation against depression is not so much when we are in the midst of it, but systematically accumulated, believed and applied along the way. In short, the learning of contentment and trust in God's sovereignty and faithfulness can help us face loss when it comes, whether through happy or unhappy, expected or unexpected, circumstances. None of this is meant for a moment to downplay the loss of people or things in our lives, but in so far as we are detached from them as reasons for living, and attached to our Lord, we will be better able to face their loss and move through the resultant grieving process. It is at this point that pastoring is required. Dr Hart expresses this well:

> ... depressed people do need to be understood, not judged, not evaluated, not lectured, not pushed, not punished, not

depreciated, and certainly not patronised, but genuinely understood. This brings healing by opening the person to the grieving process and by providing the insights needed to become detached from lost objects. Now while we can never know exactly how another feels, we can help someone to discover how they feel themselves (Hart, 1987, p. 119).

It is a great encouragement for a pastor to find this kind of care from within the church, denominational leadership or peer group. An understanding of the role depression plays in enabling a person to come to grips with a loss is as essential for pastors in their self-care as it is in our ministry to others.

Depression and self-care

In recognizing the following aspects of depression, pastors will find help in their own pastoral care and ministry to others.

1. Recognize that life and ministry are full of situations that can cause loss. This is a given in life, and especially in ministry, with its reliance upon other people, and the unfinished nature of its work.

2. Allow that Christians in general, and pastors in particular, not only experience depression but are allowed to experience depression. Christian psychiatrist John White notes that,

> it seems that the better our grasp of Scripture and of the gospel of God's grace, the better will be our capacity to deal with inner pain. Yet both Scripture and two thousand years of Christian experience warn us that the usual is not the invariable, that thick curtains of darkness may descend over our minds when nothing we can do will bring a ray of light. They may do so with or without any obvious cause. Job, David, Jeremiah, Martin Luther, John Bunyan, William Cowper and Charles Haddon Spurgeon are a few of the more illustrious names among thousands upon thousands of God's people who have suffered such darkness. So thick may be the darkness that prayer dies on our lips. The heavens are sealed. Truth becomes the mockery of meaningless words (White, 1982, p. 23).[1]

Hart would argue, I believe convincingly, that depression must not be seen as being without purpose. If we assume that depression is wrong or bad form amongst Christian pastors, denial rather than cooperation with it can give rise to much harm.

3. Reactive depression gives the depressed person an opportunity for healing to take place. Identifying the loss is the necessary first step in the process. We cannot grieve a loss we cannot or will not identify. Since pastors are very often busy with a number of demands that need to be met every week, it is very hard for 'time out' to be taken. It is often easier to press ahead, and to deny any pain or depression resulting from loss, or to shrug off the hurt and grief. In the short term, this is the less costly option, because life goes on. However, this is usually not very satisfying for anyone. The middle- and long-term price to be paid will range from lethargy and disinterest, to sickness and even premature death.

It is at this stage that support from wise and caring people is most valuable. They can give permission to slow down, take 'time out' or even rest a bit more. Pastors do well to respond to such help. Very often we pastors want it both ways. We expect people to take our advice when we can see their problems, but are often unwilling to receive advice ourselves, especially when it means slowing down. I suspect this has to do with a number of factors including an "I'm indispensable" complex, and often, "What will people think?" if we admit to being depressed and in need of rest or help. It is sobering to remember that even our Messiah has left the work on Earth to others, took 'time out' for rest or to be alone, and found support from friends. Just as our Messiah identified with us by taking our humanity upon himself in his incarnation, it would do our ministry little harm if we were able to identify with our congregations by letting them see our weaknesses. It would appear to be a great foolishness to fight against the process, since if not cooperated with in its early stages, a greater cost will be extracted later on. In other words, depression is built into our response mechanisms so that we can respond to loss in a healthy way.

4. Depression thus becomes an invitation to us to understand the nature of the loss in our life. If this is not allowed to take place, what typically happens is that other things will compound and combine to plunge us into a greater despair.

For example, if a valued congregation member leaves unhappily because of some neglect on our part, we will feel a real sense of loss, anger and uncertainty. For the sake of the example, I won't deal with the rightness or otherwise of the parishioner's response, but we will assume that there was an identifiable neglect of duty that could be attributed to the pastor. Initially, the pastor who owns the problem may feel disappointment, accompanied by a mild depression because of the loss. We may be tempted at this point to increase the workload in an effort to do 'damage control', and thus re-establish integrity. On the other hand, the depression can only be adequately dealt with when the event that triggers it is recognized and dealt with. An attempt at reconciliation through apology, explanation to the leadership or congregation, and of course confession to God would be appropriate. If not dealt with, the feeling of disappointment could easily spiral into disgust, self-condemnation, guilt, anger at self and others, shame and loss of self-esteem. The only way to stop the spiral is to go back to the trigger event.

Hart expresses this in a diagram:

Figure 3

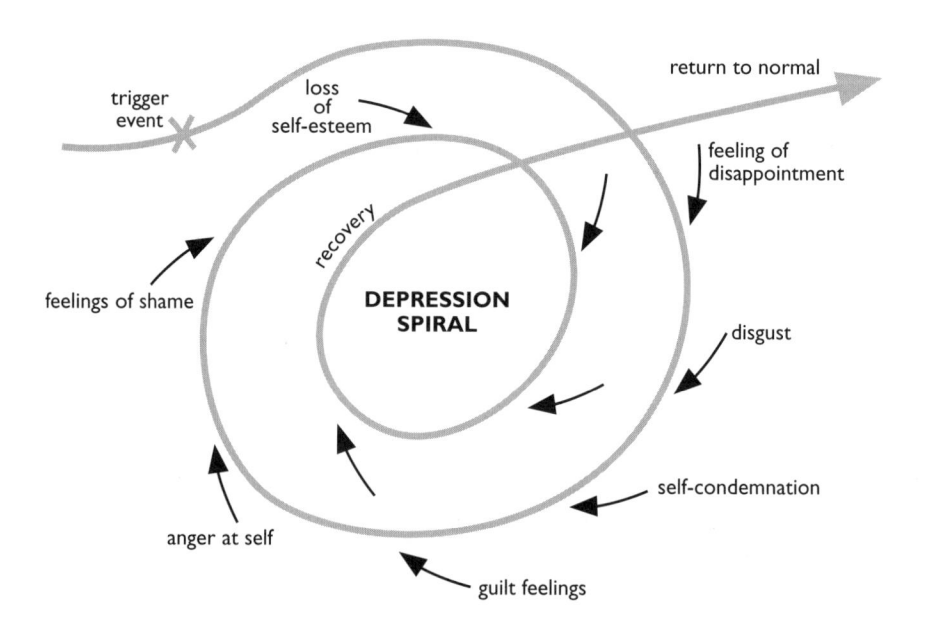

In my own example about the newspaper column, my depression at leaving my previous parish could not be short-circuited, and could not be dealt with until I had understood how dependent I had been on the column. The event had to be understood before I could recover. This took time and teaching. Once understood, a combination of repentance (for it was a misplaced trust on my part), reaffirmation of my value in Christ, and faithfulness where I was, brought recovery.

5. It is good to remember that there is no short cut remedy. Each loss will bring with it an appropriate amount of depression. It is not enough for us to have permission from others to deal with our losses; we must give ourselves permission to deal with it. This is no more a sign of weakness than it is for us to pull into the service station to top up the oil and petrol in our motor vehicle when the appropriate warning light comes on. In fact, it has to do with wisdom.

Losses need to be grieved, and grief takes time. Very often in ministry, as in life, pastors feel that a loss can be compensated for by the gain of something or someone new. This is just another way of short-circuiting the process. Just as parents working through the loss of a daughter in marriage are not greatly comforted by the knowledge that they are gaining a son-in-law, a pastor needs to make an appropriate response to the loss of one church even though he or she is going to another.[2] There will be a sense of loss for the pastor in moving from one church to another, whether the past experience has been happy or unhappy. In fact the loss of leaving a happy experience behind will probably be easier, since the farewell may well have been more affirming and honest, and it will be more natural and expected for some grief to be shown.

When there is a sense of relief by the pastor, and joy on the part of the church, that the pastor is leaving (that is, where the experience has been an unhappy one), there will also be some measure of loss and grief. However it is more likely to be kept inside, and left unexpressed and undealt with. What was expected to be a liberating experience for the pastor, and perhaps even for the former congregation, does not eventuate. There is still a pain, a loss and a low-grade kind of depression in their hearts. Why? Because a sense of failure or frustration has been carried forward. Like the loss from the previous year's accounts, it hangs over the heads of pastor and church alike. The new congregation and new pastor will not prove to be a joy until the grieving over the past loss has been acknowledged, identified, understood and then dealt with.

6. Recovery will only take place after the fullest depths of depression are allowed. In fact, sometimes when a counsellor or friend helps us face up to the causes of our depression, an even deeper depression is experienced. This is understandable, especially when repentance, anger or pride need to be dealt with. However, it usually means the person is coming to grips with their loss, and the end of the road to recovery is closer than before.

Dr Hart's diagram in showing forth this "typical depression cycle" gives us understanding, real hope and assurance that this hurt is leading somewhere good.

Figure 4

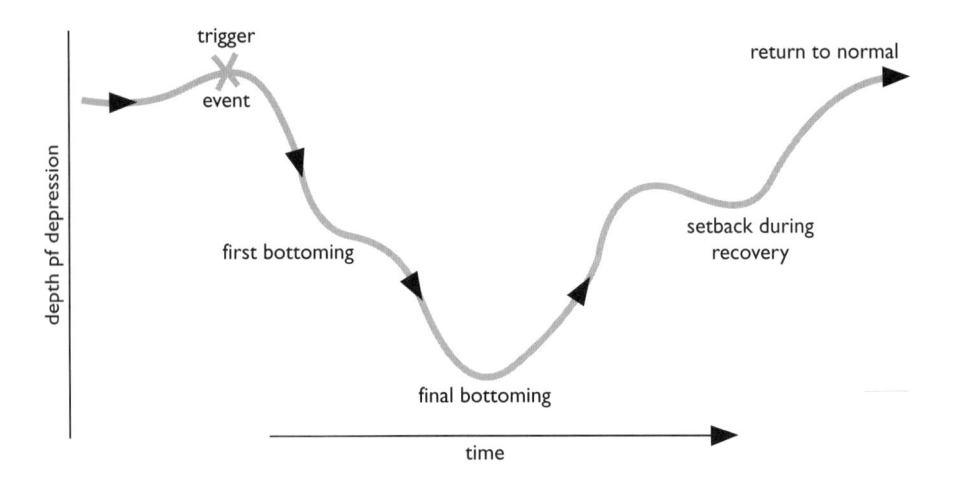

[Graph showing depth of depression over time: trigger event leads to first bottoming, then final bottoming, then setback during recovery, then return to normal]

7. Depression viewed as a part of how we are made will be effective in teaching us valuable lessons. The 'time out' for reflection gives time for a reorientation of our thinking and values, especially in relation to how dependent we have become on people or objects. The ability to view our losses within the wider perspective is particularly valuable. This is so for all people, since there will be many circumstances in life and ministry that bring loss. Each loss situation that is dealt with successfully will prove to be beneficial in dealing with future events that may result in loss.

Listening to each other

Let me make two final comments concerning depression. One is a reminder of the unique resources Christian people have in dealing with depression, and the other a caution against being simplistic in our advice. Theologian Dietrich Bonhoeffer commented that of all the services which all Christians must give one another, listening is the greatest (quoted in Hart, 1984, p. 108). The observation that "God gave us two ears and one mouth", together with the New Testament exhortation that we think highly of one another and bear one another's burdens, makes it plain that we have a mutual responsibility to one another.

We do not need to be an expert in order to help others. It is certainly true that all people are wise to recognize their limitations, and we should refer people on whose problems are beyond our level of competence. However, it is equally true that true friendship and thoughtful ministry, involving careful listening to others, is very powerful.

Dr Lachlan Dunjey, a Christian physician and psychiatrist, wrote in the *WA Baptist Contact* (March 1990) an article offering practical ways we might minister to one another. Called 'The hole of depression', it started with the poem:

> I sit in a hole, I cannot get out.
> Too tired to climb, too frightened to shout,
> The darkness engulfs me, I no longer see
> The light or the hope or the way to be free.
> The pain and the heartache destroying my soul
> Is too much to bear within this black hole.
> Where is the love that would lift me so high
> To heal me within so my spirit could fly?
> All I need is a friend to show that they care.
> Some comfort to give, a joy to share.
> Dear God, if such a friend be
> Please tell them to reach in this hole for me.

How can someone who was normally bright, active, happy and confident write a poem such as this? The answer is depression—a condition that will affect millions of people around the world this year. As Christians, we are committed to caring, but we often fail our brothers and sisters because we don't understand the medical conditions or how to go about helping. Here are some practical comments based on personal experience that could help a friend out of the hole of depression.

- Don't think, "I can't do anything—I haven't any training". You don't have to be a psychologist to say, "I love you".
- Don't think, "I don't have the time to get involved". If seven people give 15 minutes per day each, that's a whole week of helping and caring covered.
- Don't say, "I'm here if you need me" or "let me know if we can help". Some days it is impossibly difficult even to pick up the phone.
- Don't ask, "How are you?" in the church foyer or the shopping centre and expect a truthful answer—you probably won't get one, because of the fear of breaking down.
- Don't assume help is being given. "Everybody thought Somebody was doing it when Nobody was."
- Be prepared to meet depressed people in their own home. They feel safe there and know that you really mean it when you say you want to help.
- Don't try to solve all their problems with good advice. There's time for that when they are well again.
- Don't be offended if they appear rude or angry. It is only an expression of the feelings inside them that have to come out somehow.
- Listen to what is being said. It will give the best indication of how you can help.
- Don't assume that because they are happy and positive one day they won't be suicidal the next. Highs are always followed by lows.
- Don't give up! If you do, they might too, because there is nothing worse than finding out that your friends AREN'T!

Unique resources

As Christians, we share unique resources. Flowing as they do from our relationship to God through our Lord and Saviour, it should not surprise us that they will help us as we relate to our brothers and sisters who find themselves in this hole of depression. These resources include:

- The perspective on life that we have when we consider God's faithfulness and fatherly care.
- A realistic and balanced theology of both failure and forgiveness.
- Forgiveness through the gospel which can release us from much anger.
- The resources of the Bible, prayer, sacraments, God's people and the Holy Spirit's power.
- God's full understanding of us and identification with us.
- The renewal and transformation of our minds.
- The realistic portrayal of men and women in the Bible, and our common lot in life.

As a pastor I need to be constantly reminded of God's truth. When truths are dispensed glibly, I may respond, but it is when they come from one who has sat with me, listened to me and shown that they care for me, that the truths will really prove to be beneficial. The benefit may not be seen or experienced immediately, but truths lovingly, thoughtfully and patiently shared will have the effect of restructuring and reaffirming my solid foundation in Christ.

Many psychiatrists give cautionary warnings about helping a depressed friend, not to deny one another the wonderful benefit of the loving and caring ministry and support of non-medically trained people, but to warn against glib and thoughtless counsel whether from friends, fellow Christians or trained medicos and counsellors. Since depression can be complex and debilitating, a thoughtful and caring approach should be taken when ministering to depressed people, including pastors.

Hart comments, "all types of therapy have been shown to contribute some help", and since the problem is a complex one "a counsellor or therapist must avoid what some have called the tyranny of therapeutic exclusiveness or the tendency to stick with one type of counselling approach" (Hart, 1984, p. 41). John White counsels caution and humility when he notes,

> Depression is not one thing but many, and the way we alleviate it will demand that we develop a profound insight not only into its nature but into the heart of the depressed person. No surgery is so delicate as that of the mind. Unfortunately we too often move into it with clumsy cliches, with subtly damning exhortations, breezy banalities, and the latest idiocy in pop psychology—or else with

unnecessary pills (White, 1982, p. 51).

However, since depression is "the common cold of our emotions", and we all experience loss first hand, all God's people ought to be sharing in this ministry. As Lachlan Dunjey puts it, "be compassionate! There is a good chance that you might be on the receiving end one day".

Considering how to "stir up one another to love and good works" (Heb 10:24), and remembering that the "God of all comfort ... comforts us in all our affliction, so that we may be able to comfort those who are in any affliction" (2 Cor 1:3-4), enables us to see that this ministry of comfort is one in which we can all thoughtfully engage. We all share the benefits.

A willingness on the part of pastors, church members, and local and denominational leaders to take this comforting ministry seriously, could go a long way towards helping to prevent much depression, and at the same time provide the loving and thoughtful support that would help us to cope with depression, and gain the best from it when it comes.

Endnotes

1. On pages 142-146 of this book, White gives a moving account of the darkness of depression experienced by the hymn-writer/poet William Cowper.
2. A very helpful consideration of the leaving of one parish for another is to be found in Robbins (1985). A well defined farewell, and some time in between churches, are important if this sense of loss is to be dealt with adequately.

6

Anger: using it constructively

Pastors are among the angriest people I work with.
A. D. Hart

Anger can destroy perspective.
William D. Hulme

Let every person be quick to hear, slow to speak, slow to anger; for the anger of man does not produce the righteousness that God requires.
James 1:19-20

Be angry and do not sin; do not let the sun go down on your anger.
Ephesians 4:26

ANGER SEEMS TO BE a growing problem in our Western community. Road rage is on the increase; domestic violence and custody anger are a tragic fact of life. And what about pastors? Dr Hart has commented that pastors are amongst the angriest group of people he works with. William Hulme's words are surely correct when he says, "anger can destroy perspective" (Hulme, p. 91). Most of us know this only too well from our own experience.

Unresolved anger is like a time bomb, which can cripple our initiative, sour our relationships, make our preaching negative, cause us to blame and scapegoat others, and render us unable to receive encouragement from God or other people. One of the big problems with anger is that we can sometimes enjoy being angry with others. Perhaps it is because we feel powerful, or that we can get our own back, or that the expression of our anger makes us feel good. If we enjoy this anger, it leaves us in danger not only of leaving a trail of destruction amongst others and of increasing our own guilt within, but most sadly, of not dealing with the reason for our anger.

Since anger is usually produced within us by circumstances, people or blocked goals, there is an opportunity for us to explore what is happening. Our anger, if examined and handled constructively, can help us grow, and in some cases, begin to put things right. When pastors fail to deal with anger, we can scapegoat our spouses and children. This misdirected anger can cause serious damage to our families, not only robbing us of the support of our greatest supporters, but becoming a contributing factor to their disillusionment with both the church and our Lord.

If healthy patterns and strategies for handling anger constructively are not in place, then pastors can either turn the anger inwards, or express it erratically and hurtfully upon others. Without realizing it, many of us become like a terrorist, carrying a time bomb within us. Because it goes where we go, those closest and dearest to us can be destroyed in the process. However, time bombs can be defused. Pastors who want to continue faithfully in ministry need to become skilled 'bomb disposal experts'. Thankfully, many have become just that; in understanding the reasons for their anger they have developed helpful and effective means of short circuiting its painful consequences.

The difficulty for pastors

Anger is a special problem for pastors for at least two reasons. In the first

ANGER: USING IT CONSTRUCTIVELY

place, ministers are not meant to be angry. It is often very hard for church members to handle anger in their minister. This is probably related to the way many Christian people want to invest pastors with a 'halo' image. This is sometimes revealed in the well-meaning, but unrealistic, comments to our spouses—"it must be wonderful to live with someone who is so caring" or "of course you and your husband/wife would never get angry with your children"! Many people seem to consider any kind of expressed anger a bad thing, especially within the ministry.

This is part of a more general view that Christians shouldn't get angry. Perhaps it is these expectations, the fear of the destructive consequences, that cause pastors to become so angry. In other words, we don't deal with anger because we feel it might create a stumbling block for church members, or cause people to speak against or reject our ministry.

Secondly, ministry itself can be the source of much frustration for the pastor. Expectations of church members, competing roles, levels of pay, problems with housing, status within denomination or community, are but a few of the reasons for this frustration.

Another aspect of pastoral ministry in a local church that can be conducive to the unhealthy handling of anger is the voluntary nature of church membership. This is particularly true of the baby boomer generation, where it has been documented that there is a rapidly diminishing commitment to traditional denominational allegiances, with a preference for finding churches that meet current needs. Putting these reasons together, it is not difficult to see why pastors are in a difficult position in the handling of their anger. No-one wants to lose respect in the eyes of church members. No pastor wants to find people going to another church, or worse, going nowhere, because of their anger.

Timely advice

"Be angry and do not sin; do not let the sun go down on your anger and give no opportunity to the devil" (Eph 4:26-27). These words of the apostle are probably the most quoted amongst Christians concerning anger. How helpful they are. They are particularly relevant to pastors, for the context is all about congregational harmony, where Paul is exhorting all Christian people to take responsibility for ensuring that the church grows in a Christlike fashion. Paul is a great realist. He does not rule out anger, but he does warn against its sinful consequences when not dealt with properly.

The New Testament letters deal with the reality of human nature in general, and of Christians in local churches in particular. Even though we put off the old nature when we become Christians, and through the ministry of God the Holy Spirit the new nature grows within us, the fact remains that we are not perfect. There is much more work to be done, and the crucible—the workshop where this sanctifying work must take place—is fellowship with others. Others, like me, are well and truly forgiven, but well and truly sinful. It is one of God's gracious purposes in gathering us into local churches that we must learn the give and take of forgiveness (Eph 4:32), mutual submission (5:21), of speaking truthfully and helpfully (4:25, 29). Unlike the tennis club where the purpose is to provide opportunities for tennis, our purpose as a church is to be a place where:

- Godlike righteousness and holiness may grow (Eph 4:24)
- Christlike self-giving love might flourish (Eph 5:2)
- Holy Spirit joy and ministry can overflow (Eph 5:18)

all in the context of the close relationship of members of the one body (4:25), to which pastors have been given so that it can grow to maturity (4:11-13).

Since we are called to work out our discipleship in these close relationships, it should not surprise us in the least that anger-producing situations will be close at hand as we seek to minister together. Working with people takes time and energy, and the resulting tiredness can easily cause anger. Mutual ministry means that we want people to express their opinions and make their contribution. This too can lead to friction. Since we want to encourage mature participation and not just a group of people who are yes-men (or women), we need to be able to handle anger, not to avoid or discourage people from expressing their opinion.

If anger is considered totally out of place in a Christian community, it will be 'bad form' to express any contrary view, lest it lead to differences of opinion, which may cause anger. 'Arms-length fellowship' is the only possible outcome. In this kind of fellowship, relationships become formal and polite, and superficial fellowship replaces close personal interaction. The source of life and vitality has been removed.

Dealing with anger

Anger needs to be understood, acknowledged and then dealt with. So when Paul in Ephesians 4:31 exhorts us to "get rid of all bitterness, rage and anger, brawling and slander along with every form of malice", he is encouraging us not to allow our anger to be expressed in ways that are sinful. These sinful expressions of anger can be:

- uncontrolled rage, brawling or slander—anger turned outward
- bitterness and malice—anger turned inward.

In line with Paul's 'new for old' method of overcoming ungodly patterns of behaviour, seen so clearly in Ephesians 4:1-5:21, it should not surprise us that 4:32 suggests how we can handle anger constructively. The key is to respond to others in the way God has dealt with us: "be kind to one another, tenderhearted, forgiving one another as God in Christ forgave you". That is, there are two things that will enable us to grow through the anger-producing circumstances:

- kindness and tenderheartedness will remind me to be self-controlled, so that I can understand why you too might be angry
- God's forgiveness of me through Christ will alert me to the fact that, if you have wronged me, forgiveness, not anger, should be my response to you.

This model, expressed in Ephesians 4:26-27, is more conducive to Christian growth and maturity in the handling of anger than is an appeal to Jesus' anger in the temple. This is often cited as an example of 'righteous anger', which it undoubtedly was. However, there are great dangers for us in using Jesus as our justification when it comes to anger. We must remember that he alone is righteous. He alone is without sin. He alone fully understood the motives and reasons behind the behaviour of others. Without denying that there will be times when righteous anger will be demanded of us, we need to recognize the dangers of getting it wrong, of inappropriate expression of our anger and of ensuing self-righteousness. We do well to remember that there were times when our Lord chose not to express his anger when he surely could have. His mistreatment at his trial and crucifixion, when he chose rather to entrust himself to his heavenly Father, reminds us of this (1 Pet 2:23).

The Ephesian exhortation is surely a more healthy and realistic model, since it flows out of the local church context. It clearly focuses our attention upon the holiness and forgiveness of God (4:24,32), the fragrant sacrifice of Christ (5:2), and the work of the Holy Spirit, who will work to change (5:18) and sustain us (4:30) to the end. Dr Louis McBurney, in his book *Counselling Christian Workers*, says:

> I have found it helpful to point out the difference between feeling angry and acting it out destructively. I teach that our anger is a God given emotional response ... when certain stimuli are perceived as threatening, we feel afraid or angry. That response has no moral 'oughtness', but is like our stomach growling when we are hungry.

He goes on to affirm that it is our response which is either right or wrong, constructive or damaging. The event that triggers off our anger then becomes an invitation for understanding amendment or pardon. "Talking it out leads to restoration and that's what redemption is all about" (McBurney, pp. 135, 136).

Thoughtful expression

Ephesians provides a strong encouragement for anger to be recognized and dealt with as soon as possible, so that sinful consequences will not accrue. Great care must be exercised. If we hold in the emotion of anger, feelings of bitterness and malicious strategies can easily become ingrained in our psyche and attitudes. The appropriate expression of anger is especially important for pastors, since we are always dealing with people who can exert much influence over us, and upon whom we are largely dependant to share the work of ministry. Church members can be the people who enable goals and plans to be implemented or blocked.

On the other hand, if anger is thoughtlessly expressed without any regard for others, it will provide a fertile garden for sin to grow and spread like weeds. Satan will be only too glad to foster the growth of such sin. Sadly, the explosive response to anger can grow out of the repressed response to anger. Understanding our anger will equip us to work through it in a constructive fashion. It can be our ally. At the end of the day, all of us, pastors or otherwise, will become angry with some people over some issue or other. The real issue is how we manage our anger.

There are a number of attitudes and actions which can prove helpful in managing our anger. As Neil Warren, in his book *Make Anger Your Ally*, comments: "every person can master his or her own anger ... any person can develop constructive ways of expressing their anger whilst extinguishing destructive old patterns" (Warren, p. 119). After outlining four common strategies for *mis*managing anger—exploding, somatizing (e.g. resentment), self-punishing and underhanding (e.g. gossip)—Warren offers what he calls "a training manual in handling our anger". I have taken his five headings on "anger management principles", and have added insights from other writers including Arch Hart. The combined principles can help us develop constructive ways of managing our anger.

1. We can strengthen ourselves by remembering the central role self-esteem has in our emotional health. "The ability to handle large quantities of anger in a constructive way is one criterion of a strong self" (Warren, p. 122). Since strong self-esteem will help us handle anger—and this in itself will strengthen our self-esteem—we need to have strategies in place for reminding ourselves of who we are. There are two very important resources for this. The first is friends and colleagues who will listen to us, and will help us understand our reason for being angry, as well as affirm us as people. The other resource is what has been called 'self talk'. This enables us to remind ourselves of our value and worth, even if we are angry with ourselves for making a mistake or with others for either blocking us or putting us down. The process is akin to changing the tapes in a tape recorder. We remind ourselves of truths that affirm our value in God's eyes.

2. Clarifying our goals. Anger is very often a result of our goals being blocked. Sometimes we will be angry with others who have sabotaged our efforts, although at times it may have been right that we were blocked. This is especially so when others have had the wisdom to see flaws or shortcomings in our plans. Whilst in theory we may believe this to be an important function of Christian fellowship, it is not always easy to accept in practice, and can easily lead to anger. Very often the anger that flows from constructive criticism, or even from our own failures—such as inadequate preparation and planning—can be wrongly justified by us, and we become entrenched in our position. Sometimes it is because we (and others) have loaded ourselves with expectations of success. A choice needs to be made: either we defend our position (and so anger and resentment will build up), or we can acknowledge the situation, back off and take another look. The second option takes courage, and requires a strong, truthful self-value.

We also need a healthy theology of success and failure. Failure is not sin. Anger and resentment that would blind us to other people's support and suggestions, are sins. "Failure is forced growth", and is in fact "God's nudge to redirect us toward another, better, route" (Hart, lectures). This is very important for pastors to learn, since so much conspires against the average pastor in this regard. Books are usually written by 'successful' pastors. Large churches are usually portrayed as the norm. Most discussion of pastors and churches portray glowing success stories.

It should be borne in mind that pastors are people who are Christians before they are pastors. With pastors, as with all Christian people, God's primary purpose is to build our characters, not our reputations. Very often he uses, and allows, failures—and even situations that may evoke our anger—to facilitate our growth. To 'maintain the rage' may in the end be maintaining anger at God. When this happens, much joy and energy is sapped from the pastor.

3. Reading our inner radar. There are times when we can anticipate situations that might cause us to be angry. David and Vera Mace have a chapter in their book *How to Build a Healthy Marriage* entitled 'Never waste a good argument'. They make two assumptions:

- arguments will happen in a healthy marriage and
- it is our strategies for dealing with it that are most important.

Anger can be profitable if we can call to mind helpful ways of handling it. The strength of this principle is that we will not run away from, or avoid, conflict situations. This is especially tempting if we are still recovering from the pain of previous encounters. However, anger may well still remain and be intensified, and the higher price of avoidance will accrue in the unhealthy consequences of repression. These will inevitably build up and fuel bitterness and resentment. This is a real problem for those of us who tend to procrastinate and put off dealing with situations that cause anger. Warren notes that we can "often end up expressing it destructively in ways less controlled by conscious choice" (Warren, p. 108).[1]

We need to understand ourselves and how we react to situations. There are times when we know we are angry, or when others around us (especially our spouse) know that we are, but we cannot put our finger on its cause. Hart makes the observation that we do well to work at knowing ourselves. We need to understand what causes us to react the way we do, whether we are reacting from ego needs, love needs, security needs or whatever. Sometimes we can do this work ourselves. Often supportive family, friends and church leaders can help us understand what is 'getting at us'. Should the problem remain, healthy self-care and regard for others would encourage appropriate counselling.

4. Thinking. The most constructive approaches to anger appear to me to be cognitive. This should not surprise us, even though anger is largely an emotion. It reminds us of the Christian concept of self-control. Whilst self-control is a fruit of the Spirit, this does not rule out the place of human thought and endeavour in responding to real-life conflict situations. We have already mentioned the role of thinking in establishing our self-value, and in establishing constructive ways of responding to anger. Warren suggests that this thinking process will extend to self-control. He notes, "your challenge is to develop a way of expressing that anger so that the source of your hurt, frustration or fear can be taken care of freely" (Warren, p. 167).

Hart makes an important distinction between anger as a feeling, and anger as behaviour. As a feeling, anger is a valuable sensation that alerts us to the need for a response. It is like an alarm signal that prompts us to make a choice as to how we will behave or respond. We need to have in place ways of knowing what the appropriate choice of behaviour is to be. Very occasionally, a physical response may be required—for example, if someone's life was in danger. Usually, however, an aggressive response will be inappropriate. Here is the place for self-control. To be able to identify and then think carefully about the reason for anger is essential. When this is in place, I can attend to my feelings and to the problem itself. When I simply respond because of my angry feelings, there is every chance that as my feelings of anger increase, other emotions needing attention will be added and the basic problem will remain unattended to.

This can easily be illustrated from marriage. A fight can be carried on (either of the cold or open warfare variety) for hours or even days, and the original issue lost. Where inappropriate physical or verbal methods of hurting each other have been used, further reasons for anger have been opened up. We do well to reflect on how we will deal with the issues, before they arise in a conflict situation.

Here is a list of rules for a fair fight which are as applicable to marriage as to church disputes:

- Identify the issue
- Choose the right time
- Choose the right place
- Give a positive stroke first
- Stick to the issue
- No throwing up the past
- No hitting below the belt
- Take the other seriously
- Express anger verbally and not physically
- No game playing
- No passive aggressiveness
- Avoid "why" questions and blaming
- Avoid labelling and name calling
- Don't get triangled.[2]

Some basic ideas, which we need to have clearly settled if we are to be kept from anger in pastoring, are:

- I'm not perfect. I will make mistakes.
- The congregation is not perfect. They will make mistakes.
- Disagreement or correction doesn't mean I am being put down or devalued as a fellow Christian. Remember Proverbs 27:5: "Better is open rebuke than hidden love".
- My goals may need to be blocked, or at least refined, by correction or advice.
- If my goals are delayed, the process of discussion may mean they will be owned by more people and understood more widely.

5. Leaving your past behind. Forgiveness is the final stage in the process. This does not mean forgiveness is the least important stage (indeed, in some cases it is the only stage available to us), but it recognizes that situations which cause anger can become opportunities for growth through examination and the resolution of problems. Dr Leslie Weatherhead once remarked that "the forgiveness of God is the most powerful therapeutic idea in the world". Jack Winslade, the head of a large

English mental hospital, has been quoted as saying, "I could dismiss half my patients tomorrow if they could be assured of forgiveness" (quoted in Stott, p. 81). Few would deny that forgiveness is at the very heart of Christianity; however the application of forgiveness towards others is not always easy to accomplish. We recognize the call and the logic of our Lord's words in the Lord's Prayer, "forgive us our debts as we also have forgiven our debtors". This is echoed in George Herbert's words, "he who cannot forgive others breaks the bridge over which he himself must pass if he would ever reach heaven; for everyone has need to be forgiven".

If this is true in our general dealings with others, it is also relevant to our discussion on anger, since strong emotions, harsh words, and hidden yet hurtful and sabotaging responses, are sadly commonplace in the church. These are sometimes directed toward the pastor by members, and by pastors toward members and leaders. The following comments may prove helpful in enabling the application of forgiveness to such situations.

(a) Where our anger is in response to a wrong action or word, we need to recognize that we have a right to be hurt and a right to respond—not in a hurtful, vindictive fashion, but in a way that makes right the injustice. Once this right is owned, I can then sacrifice the right, choose to forgive and then take other steps to deal with the situation or person in a gracious and constructive manner.

"Forgiveness is surrendering my right to hurt you back if you hurt me." As such it "is the antidote for anger. There is no other satisfactory solution to our urge to take revenge". These are challenging but realistic words by Dr Hart. The ability to forgive rather than hurt can only become ours as we meditate upon the work of Christ on our behalf. It was he who willingly took upon himself our wrongs. This meditation will issue in real action as the Holy Spirit works within, to enable us to take all available practical steps to be forgiving towards others. As in every area of our sanctification, the more we practice peacemaking the better we become at it.

The art of forgiving is nurtured as we follow Jesus' exhortation and pray for our enemies. It was once said to me many years ago that it is psychologically impossible to hate the people we are praying for.

(b) Forgiveness, then, in the first place, is in order to protect me from myself. It is to ensure that "I do not sin" by a wrong response to anger. In the second place, it is to restore the relationship with another person or persons. I can be prepared to forgive, but that may not restore the relationship, which depends on the response of the others involved.

The apostle Paul's realism is required at this point.

> Repay no one evil for evil, but give thought to do what is honourable in the sight of all. If possible, so far as it depends on you, live peaceably with all. Beloved, never avenge yourselves, but leave it to the wrath of God, for it is written, "Vengeance is mine, I will repay, says the Lord". To the contrary, "if your enemy is hungry, feed him; if he is thirsty, give him something to drink; for by so doing you will heap burning coals on his head". Do not be overcome by evil, but overcome evil with good (Rom 12:17-21).

We need to be realistic. Most people have not responded to God's amazing forgiveness. They may not respond to ours either, but that is not the issue in forgiveness. We cannot determine the other person's response, though by our attitude we may well encourage it. However, we will have done what is right in obeying our Lord's injunctions to forgive and to be a peacemaker. By so doing, not only will we be protected from sinful responses to anger, but in growing more Christlike we will be providing a worthy pattern which will ensure that the church is a reflection of godly ways.

(c) We can leave the punishing up to God. Our part is to do the forgiving. A missionary very wisely remarked after spending years under house arrest, "bitterness is the wasted emotion". He and his wife had every right to feel hurt, and to expect justice rather than their unjust treatment. In choosing to give up this right, and forgiving their captors, they gained much from their ordeal and were able to live through it and beyond with a healthy and stable mindset.

(d) Forgiveness is an act of the will rather than an emotion. For this reason, forgiveness is something that is done in a moment, but needs to be confirmed consistently. Forgiveness is not an emotion or a feeling, but a choice we make. This is important, because if our will and our feelings are not differentiated, we can become confused. The oft repeated advice 'forgive and forget', although catchy, is somewhat misleading. It is misleading because forgiving and forgetting are different. Forgiveness is something we can decide to do, whereas forgetting has to do with our emotions. The problem in the phrase 'forgive and forget' is that it can confuse people who have genuinely forgiven others, but who cannot forget the hurt done to them. Some will be thrown into despair, assuming that since they have not forgotten the hurt they could not have properly forgiven the person involved.

Whilst the choice to forgive takes place in a moment, that choice needs to be lived out and reaffirmed each day. My commitment to God's purposes must overrule my feelings. Dr Larry Crabb suggests that we should be "hypocritical to our feelings rather than our purposes". This does not mean denying our feelings, but having identified the reasons for them, we deal with them appropriately. One appropriate way is to continue to reaffirm the choice we made to forgive. In so doing, we are affirming our purpose to forgive others, as in Christ God has forgiven us.

Forgiveness involves the following three attitudes and actions:

- I will not raise the matter again
- I will not tell others about it
- I will not dwell on the matter myself.

These three aspects of forgiveness, suggested by Eugene Habecker during a leadership course in 1989, have proven practical and personally beneficial to me. It is ever so easy for us to dwell on past hurts, thus enabling anger to raise its ugly head. This is especially so in ministry, in at least three directions:

- inward at ourselves for foolish decisions
- outward to congregational members for their slowness, blocking of goals or lack of appreciation, and
- upward to leaders, whether local or denominational.

Of course Satan loves to have us 'muckrake' over past hurts, especially those which we have dealt with by forgiveness. Since this is a direct attack at the heart of the gospel, it can become unsettling for us. However, it can be easily dealt with as we keep on applying and preaching the gospel to ourselves.

There is a personal and corporate challenge here for all church members and pastors. At the personal level, we must keep reminding ourselves that my forgiveness of another person is not nullified if I remember the hurt, but only if I choose to act in a vengeful manner. As God has kept me from doing so in the past, he can be counted upon to keep me from doing so in the future. This will especially be the case where I have been seeking to act in a godly fashion toward the person who may have hurt me. The gospel that saw forgiveness come to me, at great cost to my saviour, will be the means of my willingness to offer forgiveness and act in a forgiving manner to others. This surely is what lies behind the parable of Matthew 18:21-35 with its contrasting levels of indebtedness.

At the corporate level, we can do ourselves great good by practising this kind of forgiveness regularly in the congregation. The root of bitterness spoken of in Hebrews 12:14-15 will not be allowed to spoil the quality of a church's life and relationships when thorough-going forgiveness is practised by every member. We do each other a disservice when we talk about past hurts publicly, especially if we are wanting to put others down and promote our own goodness. We do each other a greater service when we rejoice in the good and truthful aspects of our life together.

> Finally, brothers, whatever is true, whatever is honourable, whatever is just, whatever is pure, whatever is lovely, whatever is commendable, if there is any excellence, if there is anything worthy of praise, think about these things. What you have learned and received and heard and seen in me—practise these things, and the God of peace will be with you (Phil 4:8-9).

The apostle's challenging words are addressed to us all as brothers and sisters. The call for us to be models one to the other will be all the more effective as we encourage each other in this. God's peaceful presence will surely be the greatest help to us in overcoming the consequences of anger, which can follow unresolved disputes between Christians.

This can be a special ministry pastors offer to each other, since it is ever so easy to speak of problem people or leaders in a disparaging manner. It seems to be a part of our human nature that is easily fuelled by each other. Yet it is destructive to our own Christian growth, and ministry. Several things can combine to help us to encourage each other in the act of forgiveness:

- recognition of the preciousness of the church
- the grace of God to us all in the gospel
- opposing Satan's designs to sow bitterness
- the ongoing nature of forgiveness.

At this point, self-control, and the desire to capitalize on the circumstances leading to our anger, converge. They both contribute to our personal growth, and ability to face future circumstances constructively. Although forgiveness will not be the first step, since the cause of anger must first be faced and dealt with, it will be the key to ensuring that anger does not breed rage, resentment, bitterness or malice.

Anger's benefits

When anger is handled constructively under God, and with his strength, we will experience the following benefits:

- We learn to trust God who knows the circumstances.
- We face the situation *under* God not *as* God. God can be relied upon to deal with injustice caused by others toward us, just as he will deal with us.
- We will mature, knowing that at the end of the day, there is but One person in the grandstand we need to live for. My success does not depend upon everyone agreeing with me, liking me or encouraging me. My status is determined by my response to Christ. I am primarily God's servant not the church's. I serve the church best by serving God.
- Anger that expresses itself as rage is inappropriate. Indignation can drive us to do some of our best work, whether it be seeking reconciliation between disparate parties, writing an article, praying, engaging in self examination or desiring to do it better next time.
- We preach a sermon that will be heard by many every time we handle anger. Done well or badly, it will be seen and remembered. If we do it well, we will be providing a model for others as to how to handle anger in their own families, relationships and the church.
- We affirm clearly that a strong difference of opinion that leads to anger does not mean we do not value or accept another.
- We affirm that even where anger was right, forgiveness, reconciliation and fellowship are at the heart of God's purposes.
- We are enabled to grow in grace every time anger is dealt with well, because we are emulating God in offering grace, and we are reminded that his righteous anger has been dealt with by our saviour.

Endnotes

1. Repression of anger should not be confused with the suppression of anger. Suppressed anger can be healthy when the reason for anger is thought through, and a choice is made not to express one's anger to the person involved. It can be dealt with either by prayer to God, or confidential fellowship with a supportive person.
2. The source was the Fuller Seminary D. Min. course 'Building Strong Families Through the Local Church' with Drs Jack and Judy Balswick, the author unknown.

7

The pastor's family

Ministers who do not give attention to their marriages come to regret it.
DEAN MERRILL

The clergy family lives in the midst of a larger congregational family ... This can be good news or bad news, depending on the quality of the relationship between the two families.
JACK BALSWICK AND CAMERON LEE

BUSY MARRIED PASTORS find themselves with the dual task of building a marriage and a ministry. This creates a tension between two challenges. Not only do pastors and their spouses want their marriages to be stable, joyful and growing, but the church and community, not to mention God himself, have similar expectations.

The words of Paul to Timothy remind us of the close connection between marriage, family and ministry:

> Therefore an overseer must be above reproach, the husband of one wife, sober-minded, self-controlled, respectable, hospitable, able to teach ... He must manage his own household well, with all dignity keeping his children submissive, for if someone does not know how to manage his own household, how will he care for God's church? (1 Tim 3:2-5).

Marriage and family life are the microcosm out of which ministry can grow. Both are vital for the married pastor. To neglect this foundation would make building a ministry well nigh impossible. On the other hand, support from spouse and family provide a marvellous basis for ministry to blossom.

All married Christians want to honour God by being faithful marriage partners, who through serving their spouses, empower them to grow and develop as Christian disciples. We all know that this is God's intention for us, and will be the crucible in which our children can learn love, forgiveness and other-person-centred living based upon our Lord's life and teaching. This in turn will equip them for their own life's journey, relationships and ministry.

'Who is sufficient for this?' is the appropriate and understandable cry of all Christians who are married, with or without children. The added component of a public pastoral ministry renders this joyful call to a marriage and family life a daunting work indeed.

> You are writing a gospel
> a chapter each day
> by the words that you say
> and the works that you do.
> Men read what you write
> disturbing or true.
> What is the gospel
> according to you?

These words of an African Christian are nowhere more challenging than in the area of marriage and family life. These challenges are felt keenly by pastors and their families.

The tension between the ideals of building a healthy marriage and family, together with working hard and faithfully in local church ministry, will always be there. It is a challenge to be met, not an impossible dream to be avoided. The same God who has given us both families—the home and the congregation—can surely be relied upon to grant to us resources to meet the challenge.

Pastors, however, do have to be alert and intentional about giving good time and energy to both families. The promise of God's help is never at the expense of our thoroughgoing adherence to the spiritual and physical laws that experience and Scripture combine to lay before us. This is never so true as in the pastor's marriage and family life. Principles of self-care applied here, reap benefits for all concerned:

- the pastor
- the spouse
- the children
- the congregation
- the community.

Time invested in family should be seen as a wise investment, a building up of marital and familial capital out of which rich dividends will accrue. Where time is not thoughtfully invested in marriage and family, real losses will result. From a purely pragmatic point of view, time will be taken up mending fences rather than building bridges, and putting out fires of discontent and unhappiness rather than fanning into flame warm-hearted faith. Dean Merrill's hard fact "ministers who do not give attention to their marriages come to regret it" (Merrill, p. 55) is true.

However, many pastors do manage to do both well. Marriage, family and church bring real joy to them, their families and others. Often, since we are sinful people living in the real world, this joy grows out of and in the midst of some pain, but there is growth in joy nonetheless.

In chapter nine, I will deal with the special place friends have in the pastor's life. This is true for married and unmarried pastors alike. There will be some special words for the unmarried pastor which I trust will help give them patience as they read this chapter.

The tension

The group of people in my own life who benefit most from my own self-care, and who are the most hurt by my failure to carry out these strategies, are my family. I am the loser, too, if I fail, since when I'm more relaxed I benefit from their care for me. Here is probably the greatest area of tension for pastors. Typically the tension manifests itself in two ways. The first is in terms of *time commitment* and the second is in *preoccupation and tiredness*. Put another way, sometimes it is time spent away from the family that causes problems, whereas at other times, though physically present, the pastor may as well be absent since he/she is emotionally unable to relate. The latter can be worse than the former, since the emotional absence can be expressed in anger and frustration that find a scapegoat in spouse and children. This kind of behaviour can cause short- and long-term problems of resentment and bitterness.

The problem of physical absence can be dealt with by regular family consultation, and a determined use of the diary. Absence of intimacy and care arising out of the problem of preoccupation will need an understanding of the conflicting roles and demands of the pastorate, ourselves and our family.

What God puts together we should not separate. The answer is found in a balance brought about by attention given both to marriage and pastoring, rather than a focus upon either one at the expense of the other.

Which comes first—the family or the church?

A good case can be made that the first church is the family. We are born before we are born again. Creation takes place before regeneration. God is the author of both, so it would be ungodly and therefore unwise to exalt the one or disregard the other. If this is the case, pastors would be wise to keep the balance by maintaining the priority of the family. It is easy to neglect one's biological family in order to invest energies and time in the church family. Sometimes churches can actually promote and applaud the pastor's affair and 'adultery' with the church. This is called "spiritualized adultery" by Paddy Ducklow, which he explains as "the daily reality of the church becoming the paramour" which "seems to lead the list in clergy marriage complaints"—when the pastor loves his work more than his home life. When this happens, says Dr Dennis Guernsey, "the pastor's wife is put in a terrible bind when the church becomes The Other Woman—

but her husband isn't unrighteous for sleeping with her. No one considers this obsession immoral; he's doing God's work"(quoted in Merrill, p. 55).

It is easy to see how all this happens. It is rarely a case of intentional neglect. It tends to be a gradual process that flows out of a desire to be wholehearted in Christian discipleship, and faithful in the pastoral vocation. Ministry is not simply a job, but a call to service, a responsive commitment to the Lordship of Jesus. Graeme Irvine of World Vision reflects upon this commitment that can, for all the best intentions, go sadly wrong:

> I tried to explain my behaviour as immature zeal to serve God but this was yet another spiritual-sounding defence, totally unacceptable. The real issue was whether I loved my work more than I love my wife. The ministry had clearly come between us. I had never imagined that a call could become a seduction that would destroy a marriage. Nor had I been aware of how subtly a ministry can give one an inflated view of one's own importance. How sinister that I could be deluded into believing that it was somehow all right to neglect my wife at a time when her needs for companionship and support were great. What is worse, that I would set her up for spiritual alienation at the same time (quoted in Ducklow, pp. 31-2).

Irvine's experience must serve as an incentive to be constantly monitoring our marriage relationship. Male pastors typically think the relationship is going along better than it is. We do well to be brave, realistic and committed enough to ask our spouses how our marriage is going.

It is not an "either-or" issue, since God is the giver of both marriage and the church. Unless we are called to be single, we need to be faithful to both spouse and church. We need, therefore, to build into our thinking and life, patterns that will equip us for faithfulness in both marriage and ministry.

Ideas that strengthen marriages

John Trent, in 'Taking care of your marriage' suggests the following strategy that will help us give attention and value to our marriages:

- model authenticity in following Christ, not image management.
- take charge of your schedule, and start scheduling for change.
- ask your wife how your marriage is doing.
- be a pioneer, not a settler—move forward and grow your marriage.

- set aside 'recharging' time.
- remember that men and women are different: put in discussion time.
- make these patterns habitual by becoming accountable for them.
- take time to rest.
- turn to Christ for help with your hurts.
- come up with a tangible memorial marker; something to remind you and your spouse each day of your commitment to the strategies which you have agreed are necessary to the growth of your marriage and family (in London, pp 49-61).

It is of paramount importance that every married pastor (as with every Christian) attend to the quality of their family life by their careful and thoughtful attention to the needs of family members.

A helpful model

Some years ago, the wisdom of an Australian Christian leader and his wife was questioned because of his statement that they would put God first and their family second, as they committed themselves to leadership of their denomination. I can understand the concern expressed, since terms like "first" and "second" can signal a wrong message. Knowing the commitment of this leader and his wife to their family, together with their theological framework, I think they were saying "the task we have undertaken is one that God has given us, and we will do it in his way, with his strength and as a matter of paramount priority". Perhaps a clearer way of expressing the relationship between God, our work, our families, and any other commitments, is to move from the "first, second, third ..." way of speaking, and say instead "God is central in my life and he will rule all that I do". This idea is illustrated in the following diagram:

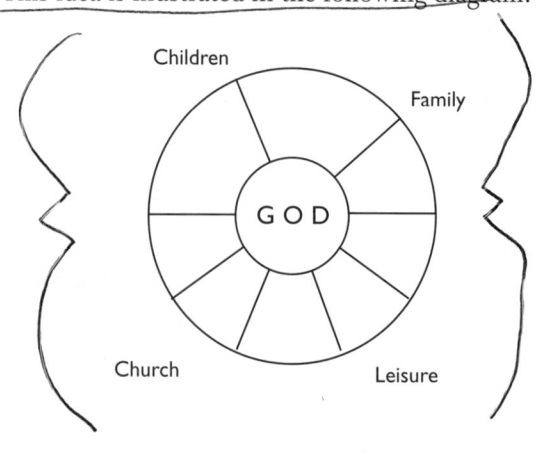

It is interesting to note that the leader mentioned above did not say "church first" and then "family". This would be the source of a grave error, since it sets up a dichotomy that should never exist between family and church.

If God is central to all we do, we will recognize that the way we live as Christians in our family, our work, our church, amongst our friends, and in our hobbies will be important. All will be witness and ministry. Incidentally, we will be saved from the false dichotomy, especially relevant to pastors, that distinguishes between sacred and secular. For the Christian, every aspect of life is as sacred as it is secular. All will be brought under Christ's Lordship. As Abraham Kuyper said in his inaugural address at the opening of the Free University of Amsterdam in 1880, "there is not one inch in the entire area of human life about which Christ, who is Sovereign of all, does not cry out 'mine!'"(quoted in Stott, p. 95).

This theological mindset will always help us to withstand the trio of pressures that work against healthy family life:

- workaholism
- scapegoating
- sublimation.

Workaholism is that drift into a life dominated by work. Family are ignored and relegated to the sidelines, where they are given only the leftover time slots and energy. Pastors share this danger with many within our community, but is often made worse when we rationalize by saying "we are doing God's work". Family and marriage are also surely "God's work".

There are a number of reasons why pastors should not feel guilty about investing quality time and energy into their families. In terms of priorities, the biological responsibility is not over-ridden by the redemptive responsibility. In terms of salvation history, the family came before the church (Adam and Eve were before Abraham and Sarah). In terms of the responsibility of parents to represent God in both caring for and instructing children, we see the priority for pastors to care for their own children. Just as it would be wrong for any Christian to abrogate the responsibility for their children's instruction in the faith by assigning that to school or church, so to it would be a dereliction of duty for pastors to assign this responsibility to others, even their spouse.

Scapegoating is that awful tendency to misdirect frustrations arising from pastoral work on to the ones we love and live with. When workaholism and scapegoating become ingrained habits it is not surprising that sublimation begins to occur within the marriage.

Sublimation is that process where the pastor's spouse (usually the wife), on finding that since she is not receiving real affection nor enjoying thoughtful intimacy with her husband, invests more and more of her time and energies into the children. This is both for self-protection and out of a sense of duty to make up to the children what they are failing to receive from an absent or preoccupied father. If the children have left home, the sublimation may well be into work.

We do well to be reminded that the key Bible text on marriage, Genesis 2:24, affirms that the husband/wife relationship takes priority over the parent/child relationship: "for this reason a man shall leave his father and mother and be united to his wife, and they will become one flesh". The best gift parents can give to their children is a united relationship of mutual service. Since the energy and affection of the pastor's spouse can be sublimated into children, work or relationships, it is vital that both husband and wife work hard to keep their relationship alive and growing. Great losses accrue to all involved when sublimation becomes a substitute for a caring intimate partnership between pastor and spouse. The husband has a special responsibility to make sure this is happening. One Puritan writer described marriage as "a perpetual, friendly fellowship". The process involved in growing such a marriage takes time, intentional initiatives and conviction. But what lasting benefits and joys are given to all in the family (and the church) as a consequence!

Naturally, in any marriage with young children and a busy parish schedule, there will be real tensions in this regard. This is all the more reason to be realistic about the danger caused by an unhealthy and unbiblical distinction between sacred and secular. C. S. Lewis's comment is similar to Kuyper's: "There is no neutral ground in the universe. Every square inch is claimed by God and counter claimed by Satan". If Satan cannot stop pastors by causing us to be lazy and careless, he will be just as happy to make us so busy that the ravages of workaholism, scapegoating and sublimation will exact their toll. However, this is unnecessary and very sad, because God who has given to us all the same amount of time wants us to attend to marriage, family and ministry. In each, God is to be central. When each is attended to in a godly manner, each will benefit from the other and therefore help sustain the other.

Competition, with its attendant anger, strain and frustration, can be transformed into partnership, with its attendant joys and strength.

By attending to the growth of my marriage relationship, I will be offering a model to other church members, providing a witness to others, ministering to my family, and of course reaping the God-given joys of a healthy family relationship.

Pastors and film stars

Pastors are prone to a very special kind of danger if they have not sorted this out. It is magnified if they hold the dichotomy between secular and sacred. According to Dr Arch Hart it is a trap they share with film stars! *It is the danger of living the role.* What this means is that it is easy for the minister to continue to live the role of minister at home, rather than take up the role of husband and father. Dr Hart suggests that the pastor should "play the role (of pastor) not live the role". In other words, I am a husband and father before I am a pastor. Any responsibility to minister to my family arises out of my relationship to them as husband and father, not because I am their pastor. I am to treat them as family, not parishioners. Sometimes we pastors hear the complaint from our families that "church members are treated better than us"!

In suggesting that the pastor needs to learn to play the role rather than live the role, there is no intention of promoting hypocrisy. Indeed the opposite is the case. Every Christian is called to be consistent and thoroughgoing in the application of Christian principles at all times, and in every relationship. To play the role is a way of expressing the truth that the minister needs to relate to his/her family not as the pastor, but as a person. This is especially vital in families, if children are not to grow up resenting the time commitment to the pastorate. If they are to observe an authentic Christian witness from their pastor parent, a practical understanding of playing the role is important. The same must be said about relating to our spouse. In fact, both spouse and children can see only too well any inconsistency and unreal relating within the home.

Perhaps a way of avoiding the misunderstanding arising from the term 'playing the role' would be to say 'work the role'. Put another way, it is the *real self* of the pastor, not the *role self* that needs to be expressed in the home. But it will not only be in the home that this will be appreciated.

When we relate to parishioners as real people rather than role people, we will be much more appreciated. Not surprisingly, what is best for home will be best for church as well.

When I work the role:	When I live the role:
• I am more than a pastor.	• My ego is wrapped up in what I do.
• Relationships are more important to me than roles.	• My esteem is tied to my role.
• Justification by faith is my foundation.	• It defines me totally.
• I am human.	• I tend to workaholism.
• I take responsibility for how I relate to others.	• Relationships with family and friends suffer.

If we want to overcome this tendency of allowing our role to totally define us as people, we need to *demythologize* the role. This can be done in thoughtful ways by:

- The kinds of illustrations we use. We serve neither ourselves nor our congregation well if we only use examples of great missionaries or pastors.
- A proper showing of our humanity from the pulpit and in personal conversation. Our doubts, our struggles, our failures and our disappointments shared in a non-attention-seeking manner will reflect the Scripture's realistic portrayal of the failures and triumphs of the 'great ones'.
- Visiting of parishioners.
- Joining in 'ordinary' not just 'spiritual' activities of the church.

To demythologize the role does not deny that we pastors have a role to play. There are things we ought to do, indeed have been specially trained and set apart to do. I would not want to deny that. But when we can no longer see ourselves as both human and Christian before we are pastors, we will run into relationship difficulties, especially at home.

Lee and Balswick highlight this trap in a chapter 'Perfect Kids: the pressures of the PK'. They tell the story of a young man who, feeling that his pastor dad was treating him like a parishioner, said "I'm not some member of the congregation, I am your son!" They note "in that moment, in failing to respond as a father, the pastor made his son feel brushed aside and depersonalized". J. C. Wynn highlights the incipient tendency for pastors to live the role at home:

> It is ironical that many a clergyman, long trained in the area of social psychology, still handles family relationships as the pulpiteer. Even though he knows full well that behaviour is more effectively altered by relationships that include love and encouragement, he may continue to preach at and preach about his own offspring. He is too likely to get at his own children by means of stern lectures, lengthy precepts and finger-shaking commands. Many a child of the parsonage might well echo what Queen Victoria said of Gladstone: "He insists upon addressing me as if I am a public audience"(in Lee and Balswick, p. 165).

Process or perfection?

We pastors often have unrealistic expectations of ourselves and of our families. When our spouses share these, the pressure on our families can become intolerable. Is it our role to produce perfect children and model a perfect marriage? Or to model a process of how to grow through stresses and pressures? Surely this is more realistic, and in line with the way we see the church portrayed in the New Testament. The apostles never put down errant churches or Christians. They are exhorted, rebuked, encouraged, nurtured, but always called 'brothers and sisters', always referred to as 'saints'. This is consistent with the gospel emphasis on grace. What is amazing is that such ordinary forgiven sinners do achieve so much. When we apply this model to families, we demythologize the ideal (often more in the minds of pastors' families, than in the expectations of church members), into something far more realistic.

Paddy Ducklow distinguishes very helpfully between *processes* that can be modelled, and *perfect outcomes* that prove to be unrealistic. The best family and marriage to model is that which "goes through growth stresses and joys with grace and humility". Pastors' families do not have "to bear an unrealistic standard of perfection for the congregation" (Ducklow, p. 37).

Turnouts

In chapter two, I mentioned 'turnouts' as being that 'time out' period so essential in keeping us from burning out. Nowhere is this more important than with our spouse and families. Built into the routine of life are a number of God-given opportunities for us to 'turnout' from work. Each is designed to give us time for physical and emotional rest, which provide space for good time to be spent with family, friends and spouse. Mealtimes, evenings, a weekly day of rest and annual holidays, well used, can become gracious boons to pastors and their families. The key lies in thoughtful planning, which in turn is dependent on recognition of our responsibility to nurture our spouse and family. Given that pastors never intend to create tension through neglect—and knowing how easily 'practice makes permanent' where bad habits become ingrained—we do well to consider how we can guard turnout times so that all will benefit. This ought to be our concern as we recognize that each of the four turnout opportunities are built into life by either the God-given order (meals and evenings) or orders (Sabbath and holy days). We are wise to cooperate with God's ordinances.

Mealtimes provide time out that gives family members a chance to share the joys and hassles of their day. The food is almost incidental to the real nourishment, derived from mutual interest as communication flows. An ideal? Yes, but where there's a will there's a way. We can deal with some of the 'meal killers'—TV can be turned off, telephones switched off or put onto answering machines, time schedules matched so as to catch as many as possible together. Such positive strategies agreed to as a top priority for all, especially the pastor-parent, signal the shared value these mealtime meetings have. It would be impossible to measure the benefit of mealtimes to families where it remains a regular ritual. The question "which meal grew our family togetherness?" is like asking "which meal made you healthy?". In both cases, a sense of healthy wellbeing grows imperceptibly over time. What saddens me is that my tiredness at the meal table has not proved to be nearly so helpful to the nourishment of our family's life as has the food lovingly prepared by my wife.

Some families find that combined with a mealtime, a monthly family conference has proved beneficial. A family conference is a time planned by the parents where each family member can be heard without the fear of being put down. Some rules that will facilitate a good family conference include: everyone has the right to speak without interruption; everyone's input will be welcome; all concerns will be dealt with. These communicate the truth that we are all committed to each other and the building up of one another through our family.

Such times with one's family and spouse can prevent family disasters. When held regularly, such conferences can help pastor parents and spouses refocus and redress imbalances that have imperceptibly crept in. In my own experience, these times can be painful (as some home truths are expressed). However, the pain is far less than that of the anger, silence or spiritual indifference of a family turned off Christian things by a pastor's absence. It would be my suggestion that God uses the family, and especially the spouse of the pastor, to help keep pastors' expectations of themselves realistic. It is an area where pastors need to "have ears to hear", especially from "the mouths of babes and children". One pastor's wife expressed the heartache of their own children not being involved in the life of the church, because her husband had always put church and church families first. The turnaround for this pastor came when he realized the need to care for himself and his own family. This cry from the heart will be echoed and understood by many pastors and their spouses. Ministry need not be an either/or situation, where biological and church families must compete for the pastor's attention. Everyone will benefit when the pastor spends good and uninterrupted times with his or her family.

Evenings can be busy times for pastors. Intentional discipling, evangelism and the inevitable round of committee meetings highlight the importance of scheduling planned time for spouse and families in the evenings. Ducklow has some wise words about the balance between playfulness and seriousness that good use of the diary can facilitate.

> The capacity of the clergy and their families to be paradoxical, challenging (rather than saving), earthy, sometimes crazy, and even human often can do more to loosen knots in a congregational (or family) relationship system than the most well-meaning "serious" efforts ... Many ministerial types would do well with some marital unseriousness occasionally. Couples can schedule "honeymoons" every six months or year. Some clergy couples have weekly "dates" even if it is just to visit Starbucks and talk about how much you would save if you moved to a small town. Also, weed your evenings weekly from un-good things. Uproot time-wasters, energy-destroyers, anxiety-producers and eros-avoiders (Ducklow p. 39).

Planning is the key. When done in consultation with one's spouse, and perhaps older children, a regular plan of what is a responsible pattern of nights out can be established. I have always found it a very helpful procedure to write into my diary 'night off', or 'CLB' (my wife's initials). This serves to remind me of my commitment, and can help me keep my nerve when consulting my diary in front of a church leader or member seeking an evening to convene a meeting or arrange a visit. On occasions when I've been asked "who is CLB?" or "look, it's a night off, that means you're free", I've been able to explain that it is a night we schedule together or with the family. This means we need to be secure in not having to meet everybody's expectations, and serves as a way of demonstrating our commitment to family as well as church.

Sabbath rest days need to be guarded if we pastors are to relate well to our families and spouses. The actual day will need to be decided upon by pastors, in concert with spouse, and known to church leaders and congregation alike. No doubt it will vary depending upon the age of our children, and whether our spouse is working outside the home. Whilst the primary reason for taking a Sabbath rest is the opportunity afforded for physical refreshment, it should be used as a way of building up relationships with one's spouse, family or friends. Some practical observations concerning this can be made.

Sundays should not be seen as our day off, if we are local church pastors. Much energy is expended in preaching, conducting services and attending to parishioners' needs. This is especially so where there is an evening gathering as well as morning meetings.

Mondays would not usually be a good day off because most pastors suffer 'let-down'.

Where children are in school, Saturday is no doubt the best day to take off, as it allows maximum participation in children's activities and gives ample opportunity for 'knock-around' time.

Taking one full day off every week is an act of faith on the part of pastors. We are saying that we trust what God says about our need for physical rest, and that we will trust him to enable us to do all he wants us to do in six days, not what we feel we could do in seven. As far as our families are concerned, we are teaching them by that most powerful medium—example—that:

- God can be trusted

- our families are important enough to spend good time with
- our bodies matter
- work is important; so much so that God wants us to rest from it so we can do it well.

Holidays. What wonderful times of refreshment and family time these bring to us. How important it is that they are taken regularly. Conventional wisdom varies as to what are the best ways of dividing up the four weeks generally granted to pastors. Some prefer two by two, others four weeks in a row, others three weeks with a one-week break midway, and some four separate weeks. Generally I think the last one is to be avoided, since it takes, on average, a week to wind down when on leave. Some pastors report that it takes up to two weeks for them to relax before they get full benefit from their time away.

The value to families is obvious:

- time spent away from the demands of that 'other family'
- their pastor parent all to themselves
- memories that are made, as activities and time are spent without the ever present clock and diary.

Pastors need to guard holiday times carefully. A question that I ask pastors' groups to clarify the issue is, "Would you come back for the funeral of a church member if you were on holidays?" To my amazement, pastors are equally divided on this one. This amazes me for a number of reasons. For one, congregational members don't expect us to. When I asked this question at a meeting of over 100 lay people in Perth, not one expected their minister to return to conduct the funeral. Whose expectations are we pastors fulfilling? If we return for one person's funeral, for example, an elder's or the organist's husband, we must come back for everyone's funeral in the future. Our spouses and families have it confirmed that they are not as important as the church family. Others can take funerals. Surely the best thing is to have arrangements in place before we go. Where someone is close to dying, specific arrangements made with families will convey our care and discharge our pastoral responsibility. The opportunity to minister to the dying has been taken, and ministry to the grieving will still be available on our return. Why should the situation be any different whether holidaying just 50 kilometres away, or being interstate or overseas with no possibility of returning?

My own view is that it is better that we are not contacted for anything to do with church when away. Then we don't have to be put on the spot to make decisions. When church leadership endorses this plan, we are in a position of freedom rather than bondage to messages, or daily phone calls back to base.

Holidays should be times when families can receive and give real, uninterrupted loving attention to each other. When our actions show how important this time is, our spouses and children will understand their true value to us, and we will be fulfilling our parenting and modelling role to them.

Family life, I often say, is a means of grace. As we learn to sacrifice our self interest, as we ask for and offer forgiveness, as we learn to be patient with each other's foibles, temperaments and inconsistencies, we learn a little of how kind God is toward us. One pastor, quoted by Cameron Lee and Jack Balswick, wrote:

> I have learned more about the practice of forgiveness from my long-suffering, understanding children than they have ever gained from me. And I now understand more about the doctrine of the grace of God through family life that I have ever understood from books in theology (Balswick, p. 168).

Don't take each other for granted

How grateful I am to my wife and four children, who have been very patient with their pastor husband and father, who was sometimes physically absent and (I fear) more recently preoccupied and tired. They have encouraged me, been the source of much love, and given me much support through companionship and caring interaction. My great danger in all of this is that it is easy for me to presume upon their high level of commitment to me. I did not, and still do not, set out to do this. However, it can easily happen. When complaints are made about "caring more for parishioners than us", it is easy to put the problem right for a week or so and then slip back into old habits. We need to attend to comments made. Take each one seriously. Talk, clarify and work to understand what is being said. Discuss children's comments with your spouse, and take their comments very seriously.

Quantity and quality time

We need to give both *quantity* and *quality* time to spouse and children. Very often when I hear people say "we don't have much time together, but what we have is quality time", I know what they are affirming. All of us should think carefully about, and then make good use of, the time we have, especially if we are busy. However, we must be careful that this does not become an excuse to justify our busyness or, even worse, our unwillingness to spend quantity time engaging with spouse and children. My own experience as a husband and a dad is that *quality time requires quantity time*. This is especially important for me as a male, since we are typically more generous in our estimates of how long we spend in meaningful interaction with our spouses and families than the reality of time actually spent. Quantity time will enable the relaxed atmosphere for quality engagement to take place. Certainly this is the case with teenage children, who will often spend a good deal of time getting around to the issues on their heart. Sometimes this is because they need time to build confidence in raising the issue, but mostly I think it is necessary for them to know that we care enough to just 'muck around' together. Perhaps there is an element of testing the water to see what kind of mood we are in. Is Dad snappy? Is he listening to the ordinary stuff that is being spoken about? Can he be trusted with the intimate sharing that is about to come? All this is perfectly natural when we think about it, especially if our usual reaction is a "quick fix" of dispensed advice.

The same applies to time with our spouses. Quality time can only really occur when we are relaxed and simply doing things that demonstrate our desire to be with the person we married, and not merely to solve a problem. Very few couples have the luxury of unlimited time together, but we can plan to give to our marriage partners good quantities of time that reflect how much we simply want to be with them as friends. When this is built in and kept in place, the opportunities for quality conversations are going to occur much more naturally than if we only meet to resolve a crisis. The strength of the quality time concept is that we guard, cherish and then make the most of each opportunity when it comes. The strength of spending quantity time with our spouse or children is that we will be more relaxed, and thereby demonstrate that we want to spend time with each other. This then means that we affirm our love by giving value to the unique friendship and support that our spouses and children bring to us.

Don't break promises

We must determine not to break promises made to our families. Very often it is not the amount of time pastors work that families and spouses resent, but the promises broken by interruptions or demands of churches. Real resentment comes when the regular day off or the long awaited family outing must be delayed or even abandoned by a pressing demand, or worse, by the pastor's remembering that a phone call needs to be made or parishioner visited.

How I hate the phone ringing just as we are packing the car! We need to remember that 99% of church crises can wait until tomorrow. Most have been weeks, if not years, in coming to the surface. Another day, another week, will not be a problem. So if the phone call is from an elder suggesting a visit to an aggrieved member, a simple thank you for the message, and "I will call them tomorrow, or perhaps you could arrange a meeting for next …" should suffice. We must never assume that silence from our families when we allow interruptions to intrude on family times (be they family nights, days off or holidays) indicates acceptance. It is more likely the evidence of helplessness, and an anger that is being repressed and turned into a resigned bitterness and resentment. Promises made to families are every bit as important as commitments made to church members. We need to consider what it would take for us to break our commitment to lead the service or preach on a Sunday morning. Why should it be different for the 'family congregation' outing?

Spend time with children

As pastors we have opportunities to spend special times with our children. By having a midweek day off, we can sometimes attend a special event or arrange our schedule to spend some time at activities other parents may not be able to attend.

It is all too easy for pastors to give ourselves too much time off, and this needs to be guarded against. However, a way of building relationships with our children, especially if we are out at night, can be to carve out special times just for them. One colleague in Perth shared how he would give each of his children one hour of his diary and $2 of his money. I did this for a while, and with four children it meant that once every four weeks each child could come out with me after school. This was valuable one-on-one time together. Other people had time slots in my diary; so did my children. This was good time just to be together and talk if they wanted to.

We should never fall into the trap of teaching our children that they are junior pastors. This expectation is hard enough to handle when church members make comments like "you shouldn't do that because you are the pastor's son" or "as the minister's daughter you will be wanting to give a good example". We should not add to these unrealistic expectations and pressures. Of course we want them to follow Christ and experience the joys of service, but that will come much more naturally as our children choose this for themselves.

Whilst being careful not to add this expectation upon our children, it is good from time to time for us to be able to remind them of some of the benefits clergy kids enjoy. Meeting and entertaining Christians from other cultures, and having Christian missionaries and leaders around the meal table, are privileges that other Christian children don't always have. Knowing that there are church members who are quietly praying for them is especially powerful when church members, in an unobtrusive manner, take the time to talk and enquire after school, sport and other interests with our children.

Spending time with our families benefits more than just the family. Our Christianity must never become compartmentalized, but rather be that which transforms every aspect of our lives. The way Christ transforms and enriches relationships within our homes will provide a model to a watching church and community. It will establish the concept of Christ being central to all the Christian seeks to do, and will hopefully provide a model that will help others who are tempted to invest their energy and time into career, sport or church.

Wise pastors will rejoice in the encouragement and support of their families. Not only is this God's design for husbands and wives, but in itself is a way a marriage will grow and be enriched. In other words, our spouses will be encouraged when we find strength and wisdom from their counsel and comfort. This does not mean the sharing of every detail of every pastoral situation, but it does mean that praying together about joys and fears, concerns and ideas, will be a means of growing the relationship. In this way our spouses are treated as equals. They know that they and their advice are welcomed and valuable. They consider themselves part of the team, and in touch with us. All this will contribute to a fellowship that will enable our families to pull together, and keep our spouses from living in ways that can become substitutes for mutual companionship and consideration. Such companionship and consideration can provide us with a fellowship of support that will enable church work to be seen in a healthy context. Where the work is hard, and there seem to be many 'knock-backs' and opposition, we can count on the love and acceptance of our home base. Where there is success, and the temptation to work even harder, or to become somewhat arrogant about our achievements, the home base can call us back to prior responsibilities and down-to-earth relationships.

Value your family immensely

The relationships of common grace (marriage, family life and friendships) are not obliterated by the special 'grace relationships' brought into being through the gospel. From a pragmatic perspective, our spouses and families will be with us after our ministry, whether it be after this particular job or after our retirement. For many pastors these days, spouses and children were there before they embarked on ordained ministry. Pastors, along with all fellow Christians, must attend to serving their spouses and nurturing that relationship for its own sake, for the church's sake and as a way of honouring God. We are wise indeed to attend to our marriage and family responsibilities carefully. God has not only joined husbands and wives together, but has given us a ministry to the 'first church', the family, and our 'other church', the congregation.

My wife and our four children are wonderful gifts of God to me. They have been consistent channels of God's grace, comforting me and at the same time reminding me of my own frailty. Both are needed. I often find that I want the comforting means of grace, but not those means which would strengthen and correct me through humility. My family has proved to be such a means of grace in both ways. I know they accept and love me, even though I often try and test that love by my insensitivity. They also bring me down to earth, as I am reminded of some home truths about my own selfishness and forgetfulness. I show how much I value them, as I respond to their criticism by seeking their forgiveness, and God's wisdom and strength, along with their advice as to how I can put things right. The idea of 'process rather than perfection' is vital here. No one, least of all our spouses and families, who know us so well, expect us to be perfect (that's why they get so angry and disillusioned when we try to pretend we are), but they do expect us to model the process of growth. Ducklow comments:

> The everyday practice of the eight most important words in marriage (or, for that matter church politics) help in the depedestalizing of the minister:
>
> 'I'm sorry'
> 'Please forgive me'
> 'It's my fault'
>
> Just the occasional saying of this phrase is liberating for the leader and his followers (Ducklow, p. 40).

Since our families, like the other means of grace, are God's provision for us to grow in Christlikeness, we do well to thank God for them regularly, but especially when their ministry has brought us to our senses. Our families are like a crucible where impurity can be extracted, and much grace can result through the interplay and interaction of parents together and with their children. Perhaps the most fruitful self-care strategy of any married pastor will be to make sure good time is given and thoughtful strategies are in place for this interplay to happen.

Whose servant are we?

Dr Ray Anderson's question "whose servant are we as pastors, God's or the churches?" is a great help in clarifying this issue and mobilizing us to focussed action. If we assume we are the church's servants, we will find ourselves with a master we cannot possibly please. How can we serve a master who speaks with many and varied voices? The old saying is apt: "you can please some of the people all the time, and all the people some of the time, but you cannot please all of the people all of the time". Clearly we serve God and we belong to him, and have been called and commissioned by him to be his servants. We will serve the church best by serving him. If this is the case, then our service of the church can never be at the expense of the service we owe to our spouses and children. The apostle Paul's words to Timothy demonstrate the clear link between family *and* church for the pastor:

> ... if someone does not know how to manage his own household, how will he care for God's church? ... Let deacons each be the husband of one wife, managing their children and their own households well ... I hope to come to you soon, but I am writing these things to you so that, if I delay, you may know how one ought to behave in the household of God, which is the church of the living God (1 Timothy 3:5, 12, 14-15).

When this is taken with the general link made by Paul in Ephesians 5:21-6:4 between church and marriage/family, we see that pastors are responsible to serve their families and the church. The God who calls us to marriage and to ministry will not want us to neglect either in favour of the other. Rather he will want each to benefit from the support and ministry of the other. This balance will gain its motivation and keep its focus when we recognize that we are primarily servants of God. In serving him we will then be enabled to properly serve both our family and our church.

Regrets?

As forgiven sinners living in a world of sinners, some forgiven, others hardened or indifferent to God, there will always be regrets. None of us will be perfect parents, none of us will have perfect children, nor will our pastoring performance or church communities be perfect.

Yet how do we handle our feelings when we see our failures? How can we do it, especially when as pastors we are convinced that our pastoral busyness has contributed greatly to either our spouse's or child's resentment of us, indifference to the church, or rejection of Christ? Assuming that we have repented before God of our known part, and apologized to family members concerned, what can we do?

- Remember that God's grace is sufficient and available to us in all situations. (Heb 4:14-16; 2 Cor 12:9).
- Failure is not final in God's purposes. Our response is what matters and may be the finest, longest and most difficult sermon we ever preach. Remember that *process* and not *perfection* is the key. The way we respond to hurtful comments, to inner pangs of guilt, to

rebuilding relationships and restoring trust and love will speak volumes about the quality of our commitment to loved ones.
- Remember that God's 'agape' love is primarily about attitude and actions, and only secondarily about emotions. Feelings of love will follow our commitment to showing love in a whole range of practical ways.
- We do no-one any good by flogging ourselves about past failures, by remorsefully interrogating ourselves or blaming ourselves for unexplained defections from the faith. Where we know we were wrong, and have repented, we are forgiven. Where we don't understand or do not feel responsible, we serve no useful purpose by engaging in either self-recrimination, coolness in relationships or blame. We pray for our children when they wander off the path or reject our Lord, we do all we can to show God's love, and then we must leave them with God.
- If they are adults, we remember that at the end of the day it is their choice to turn from the Lord. At the same time, whilst praying confidently for their return, we know that we sought to give them an example and teaching about our Lord which was not all bad.
- We may do well to seek out a fellow church member or pastor who has a similar experience, enlisting their prayer support. Many people know first hand the sadness of seeing children wander from the path of Christian discipleship.
- We know that God understands our broken hearts, since he watches over many who turn their back on his love.
- We commend them and ourselves to God's grace knowing that the heartache we are experiencing is fully known by God the Father (Jer 2:11-13), God the Son (Luke 19:41) and God the Holy Spirit (Eph 4:30). God understands the cries of his children when their children are wandering from him.

8

Sexual temptation in the ministry

If you do not understand transference and counter transference in the ministry you are dead in the water.
A. D. Hart

*Let your fountain be blessed, and rejoice in
the wife of your youth, a lovely deer, a graceful doe.
Let her breasts fill you at all times with delight;
be intoxicated always in her love.*
Proverbs 5:18-19

*Treat younger men like brothers, older women like
mothers, younger women like sisters, in all purity.*
1 Timothy 5:1-2

"THE TWO GREATEST DANGERS for the missionary and pastor are sex and money." These words came as a great surprise to me, a recently converted Christian still in my teenage years. The words of Bishop Alfred Stanway, a former missionary leader and theological educator, no longer surprise me, but remain as a timely warning to all. They have been borne out time and time again in my own observation of fellow pastors, of Christian leaders worldwide, from the data of surveys, and from my own experience. Indeed the words of Bishop Stanway were repeated by Mr Michael Griffiths in the mid 1970s, as he led a frank discussion among a group of male missionaries about their struggle to remain sexually pure, and the attraction of women other than their wives. One younger missionary confided in Griffiths how encouraged and relieved he was to learn that the other missionaries, many of whom he looked up to, were also struggling with sexual temptation. He had thought he was alone, abnormal and therefore an abysmal failure as a Christian, even though he loved and had remained faithful to his wife.

Temptation is not the only problem for the pastor in the area of sexuality. Pastors are only too aware of the consequences of sexual sin. It is important for the term 'sin' to be used in this context, for it highlights the key issue for Christian pastors. Pastors know that, unlike their accountant, if they sin sexually or leave their marriage, they will almost certainly lose their work and credibility. The stakes are very high for the pastor who commits sexual sin. Pastors do well to understand these implications, but also to learn to recognize the warning signs so that attraction will not lead into a temptation that may in turn lead to sin.

The pastor's example

"Let marriage be held in honour among all, and let the marriage bed be undefiled, for God will judge the sexually immoral and adulterous" (Heb 13:4). This is one of the most succinct and clearest exhortations regarding sexual purity. A few verses later, the author adds, "Remember your leaders, those who spoke to you the word of God. Consider the outcome of their way of life, and imitate their faith" (13:7).

Sexual integrity will be one of the ways in which Christian leaders direct, teach and demonstrate real discipleship. Being an example (1 Pet 5:3) and a model (Phil 4:9) goes with the job. Sexuality mirrors what it means to be made in God's image (Gen 1:26-27), and to live in community (Eph 5:21-33). Christians in general, and pastors in particular, who live within the biblical boundaries for sexual expression will be giving a clear lead to church and community alike.

The awful consequences of failure through pastoral sexual misconduct are devastating and obvious. Stanley Grenz, in an article called 'When the Pastor Fails: sexual misconduct as a betrayal of trust', concludes with these sobering words:

> What happens when a pastor fails? He/she denigrates the integrity of the pastorate. He/she violates the trust between pastor and people—a sacred trust that stands at the foundation of ministry. He/she betrays a power trust, a sexual trust and the divine image. In short, he/she has failed to live up to his/her ordination vow. Left unbridled, sexual misconduct in the pastorate will bring disastrous results. It will confirm the scepticism of critics, turn seekers away from the doorway of the church and leave the faithful disillusioned. It will stop the ears, dull the conscience, silence the Spirit and, from the human perspective, make the death of Christ irrelevant. We dare not allow this to happen! (Grenz, 1995).

In 1985, *Christianity Today*, through its magazine *Leadership* and its Leadership Library series, provided pastors with a helpful publication called *Sins of the Body—Ministry in a Sexual Society* (edited by T. C. Muck). This publication is very helpful, dealing openly with the problem of sexual misconduct among pastors. It is sad that there is an issue to deal with, but it is good that it is being faced in a real way. One suspects that if some of the realities had been addressed in earlier years, some of the heartache of pastors, spouses, families and churches may have been prevented. The case of the missionary who thought he was alone and abnormal would not be an uncommon one. This feeling obviously made it very difficult for him to find real help and encouragement. On the other hand, it would probably be true to say that many pastors would assume that sexual misconduct would not be their problem. This assumption may be based upon a good track record and a happy marriage relationship. These should not be allowed to blind us to our own vulnerability.

Hart confirms this vulnerability, even for the happily married pastor:

Although a minister's personal, family and married life is a basic deterrent to deliberately searching for an illicit affair, it does not guarantee safety in the counselling room or the more subtle encounters of committee or project work. I have always believed, despite protests from unsuspecting pastors, that a minister's vulnerability has nothing to do with his marital happiness. For many centuries Scripture has warned us to be on guard when we feel most safe! Sexual attraction can occur as easily when one is happily married as when one is not. You may more deliberately seek out an affair when you are not happy, but you are not necessarily safe when all is bliss at home (Hart, in Muck (ed.), p. 88).

The advice given by the apostle Paul is as true now as when it was written to the Corinthian Christians:

> Therefore let anyone who thinks that he stands take heed lest he fall. No temptation has overtaken you that is not common to man. God is faithful, and he will not let you be tempted beyond your ability, but with the temptation he will also provide the way of escape, that you may be able to endure it (1 Cor 10:12-13).

To claim and profit from this promise, it seems clear that we do well to be realistic about our own vulnerability. We should neither assume that we are beyond temptation or vulnerability to this sin, nor that we are the only ones facing this area of temptation. The former will keep us from pride, and the latter from a lonely despair. Both should drive us to our knees in confident prayer, and to a healthy reliance upon our spouses or trusted fellow Christians to aid us in our quest for faithfulness.

God understands the problem

God made us sexual beings. The strong attraction between a man and a woman is God's creation, and we can be sure he understands it. Our problem is that we live outside the Garden of Eden, after the Fall, having to do battle with wrong ideas about our sexual feelings and God-created sexual attraction. The starting point in the handling of sexual attraction is to be convinced of the biblical guidelines for the purpose and expression of our sexuality. Without a commitment to the biblical framework, and to the wisdom of God who has lovingly and clearly made known his framework, faithfulness would be an uncertain proposition.

A brief yet simple framework for the proper expression of sexuality can be expressed in the following way.

- The sexual gift is a good God-given gift.
- God has revealed the context in which sexual intercourse is to take place, namely:
  – between a man and a woman
  – between a man and a woman who are married to each other
  – between a married couple with consideration for one another.
- Sex is not essential to living a full and complete life. To be single is not inferior or superior to being married—both are gifts from God.
- God can be relied upon to give grace and strength to help a person to live within God's ways.
- When a person sincerely repents of behaviour that is outside God's revealed ways, he grants pardon and grace to live according to his ways.
- Obedience to God's ways will result in an ongoing joyful experience of his goodness, whereas persistent disobedience will only deliver a growing alienation from God and others.

With such a conviction the Christian pastor will be quickly reminded of his or her commitment to be godly. This is one way to stand firm. It ought to be inherent in our thinking as described by Bill Hallsted,

> ... a devotional pattern that places us starkly in awe before a fearsome God. A God-angled view of sin and its consequences. A habit of escaping the pressures of Christian work for relaxation and renewal—activities that don't violate the holiness of God. Easy? Not at all, but necessary (Hallsted, in Muck (ed.), p. 46).

Hallsted argues that since we are so familiar with the things of God, we need to give our minds a rest from our work. Yet here lies the temptation concerning sex. Since so many of the amusements in our society are sexually based (e.g. television, magazines, 'health club' style exercise and the like), we can be in danger of leaving God out as we escape into amusements. At this point his exhortation to consider the 'fear of God' is timely.

One pastor writes that it was our Lord's statement "blessed are the pure in heart" that helped him to progress from an addiction to sexual temptation, in which he nurtured the temptation in unhelpful and inappropriate ways, to freedom from such bondage. The apostle Paul in 1 Thessalonians 4:1-8 makes this same point when one of the eight reasons given for sexual purity among Christians is the powerful motivation of God's punishment: "the Lord is an avenger in all these things, as we told you beforehand and solemnly warned you" (v. 6). Whilst punishment is not the only, nor the most compelling, reason for behaving rightly, it is nevertheless an extremely powerful motive for Christians and pastors alike to have clearly factored into their thinking. Sin, especially for those of us who deal in the things of God for a living, can be so deceitful and easily rationalized. This being the case, if God's love toward us will not draw obedience out of us, I for one am grateful that the truth of God's judgement is a powerful incentive to obedience. I find the prayer of preparation in the Anglican Communion Service a very powerful reminder of my obligation to God and his purifying love toward me. It is as applicable in the area of sexual purity as in every other area of life.

> Almighty God,
> to whom all hearts are open,
> all desires known,
> and from whom no secrets are hidden:
> cleanse the thoughts of our hearts
> by the inspiration of your Holy Spirit,
> that we may perfectly love you,
> and worthily magnify your holy name,
> through Christ our Lord. Amen.

The eight reasons given by the apostle Paul in 1 Thessalonians 4:1-8 provide a powerful motivation to godly conduct, and remind us of God's good purpose for the sexual gift, and the privilege of belonging to him.

> Finally, then, brothers, we ask and urge you in the Lord Jesus, that as you received from us how you ought to live and to please God, just as you are doing, that you do so more and more. For you know what instructions we gave you through the Lord Jesus. For this is the will of God, your sanctification: that you abstain from sexual immorality; that each one of you know how to control his own body in holiness and honour, not in the passion of lust like the Gentiles who do not know God; that no one transgress and wrong

his brother in this matter, because the Lord is an avenger in all these things, as we told you beforehand and solemnly warned you. For God has not called us for impurity, but in holiness. Therefore whoever disregards this, disregards not man but God, who gives his Holy Spirit to you. Now concerning brotherly love you have no need for anyone to write to you, for you yourselves have been taught by God to love one another, for that indeed is what you are doing to all the brothers throughout Macedonia. But we urge you, brothers, to do this more and more (1 Thess 4:1-10).

Here are the eight reasons for sexual purity:

1. Jesus' command (v. 2)
2. God's will (v. 3)
3. Self-control (v. 4)
4. Distinctive witness to those who don't know God (v. 5)
5. For the sake of other people—that we do not wrong them (v. 6)
6. God's judgement (v. 6)
7. God's call to holiness of life (v. 7)
8. Because God the Holy Spirit lives within the believer (v. 8).

This clear passage of the Bible is a powerful reminder to be faithful.

It is important if we are to stand firm against temptation in this area to maintain a clear biblical theology of sexuality and marriage, and an experiential, daily, devotional dependence upon God. G. K. Chesterton remarked that "there are many angles by which we can fall, but only one by which we can remain upright". Modern theology, in overthrowing orthodox teaching concerning human sexuality, has already contributed to much confusion in this area. Churches which embrace this teaching should not be at all surprised should their pastors be unfaithful to their marriage partners. Orthodox teaching, coupled with a devotional pattern that takes seriously both the love and fear of God, is more likely to result in faithful behaviour. However, we also need the help of others in this aspect of our sanctification.

People helpers

As we begin to recognize the resources available, we can develop patterns of behaviour and thinking that will provide a preventative pattern to help with the problem of sexual temptation. Scripture and experience combine to tell us that we should never consider ourselves above temptation. The failure of others must always bring sadness and a warning to us. "They too were dedicated, ethical and caring pastors." But before we move to note how other people can prove to be God's helpers in our lives, we will briefly consider the lifestyle patterns that can make pastors vulnerable.

Dr Hart has suggested that pastors who are arrogant, alone, and addicted to their work are especially vulnerable to sexual temptation. The *arrogant* pastor will not consider the danger. He or she may also, by being focused upon his or her position, invite temptation by giving an impression of greatness in the eyes of others. Such a pastor will very often be removed from the friendship of pastoral peers, and isolated from or above any church or denominational accountability structures. Neither of these informal (friends) or formal (leadership) structures will be able to act as a sobering or balancing corrective. If intimacy and friendship are not found through these diverse relationships, it may be easier to seek intimacy in an affair. Arrogant leaders often have a strong need for affirmation. If this does not come from normal working relationships (and it will diminish if leadership becomes remote through arrogance), it can easily be sought through an affair. It should be noted that the reason is not primarily for sexual satisfaction, or even intimacy, but in order to meet diminishing ego needs. Domination will very often be the pattern.

Many pastors are not arrogant, but do feel very much *alone*. Irrespective of the reasons behind this 'aloneness', it is at this level that pastors and church members need to be alert. The pastor needs to see the importance of having a variety of friendships. Congregations should encourage their pastor to take time to nurture friendships, and to recognize that friendship with some church members need not be a sign of playing favourites. A wide range of friendships can help to meet the pastor's emotional needs. When these needs are being met in the normal round of pastoral life, ministry and friendship, it is less likely that loneliness will trigger off an affair with someone whom the pastor thinks may take away the loneliness.

Pastors who are *addicted* to work are very much in a high-risk category. Not only will the high workload tend to take them away from their spouses and families, it will contribute to a cycle of diminishing family and marital happiness. The less satisfaction at home, the more partners are driven away from each other emotionally, thus causing them to invest their energies in other people who will respond emotionally. Typically, the wife invests energy in children, work or hobbies and the pastor in work. It is at this point that churches, and especially leadership, must take some responsibility for the problem, but more importantly for its cure. Very often churches encourage their pastors to be unfaithful to their spouses, by expecting and applauding hard work expressed in long hours away from family.

Dean Merrill recognizes this tension, and suggests a healthy way to achieve a balanced work style.

> Hard fact No. 1: The ministry never has been and never will be a nine to five job.
>
> Hard fact No. 2: Ministers who do not give attention to their marriages come to regret it.
>
> These two facts, of course, do not mesh very well. Both are true; both are acknowledged by husbands as well as wives. Neither fact is going to change. Pastoral couples simply have to accept them (Merrill p. 55).

'Acceptance' does not mean 'do nothing'. Rather, it requires work to achieve a balanced pattern. There needs to be a three-way consultation: pastor and spouse, pastor and local church leaders, pastor and denominational leaders. There is great sorrow when a work-addicted pastor finds that after growing away from his wife, family and friends, understanding and nurture is sought in an affair. On the other hand, the rewards are high for both pastor and church if the pastor models a healthy and balanced set of work and family priorities. For this reason, it is in our best interest if we heed the exhortation and follow the example of caring church members who encourage us to take days off and enjoy good family time. Congregations will benefit greatly as its members understand that their pastor has a responsibility and obligation to rest physically and, if married, spend good time (in terms of quantity as well as quality) with spouse and family.

Realism is called for

In what ways can we remain faithful and able to overcome sexual temptation in ministry? Firstly, we need to understand that as human beings, temptation can come our way. Secondly, we need to understand that the work and role of ministry will bring temptation to us especially easily.

It is important for pastors to consider the possibility that there may be one or two occasions during their ministry when a person may come along for whom they would surrender all; even their faith, family and work. This is a hard concept, but I suspect it has real validity. It really says more about the nature of our humanity, and the peculiar temptations of pastoral ministry, than about the sexual make-up of pastors. It has to do with being realistic about our humanity and our ministry. There are bound to be a number of people to whom we are attracted. This attraction will be as much to personality, competence or spiritual maturity, as to physique. Within the Christian church, this attractiveness will be heightened since we are a fellowship of men and women who are encouraged to grow in our commitment to each other and to grow in Christian character, which is itself attractive. It is hardly surprising that pastors who come into contact with so many people might find themselves attracted to others, and others attracted to them. The church in general, and ministry in particular, provides many venues for initial attraction and its nurture. What begins publicly can be pursued privately, given that counselling and home visits are normal in pastoral ministry. The recognition that into our lives can come one for whom we may be prepared 'to sacrifice all' is therefore healthy and realistic. When this proposition is recognized in advance by pastors and their spouses, a very important safety net comes into place.

Pastors who find themselves in this situation will do well to enlist the help of their most powerful allies, their spouses. Single pastors do well to have a trusted friend with whom they can share. The strength of temptation is greatly reduced once it has been spoken about. Since temptation is most likely to thrive on the secrecy or forbidden nature of a possible affair, the sharing of it will make it much easier to deal with. Needless to say, such sharing should take place immediately, which means temptation has less time to grow into sin. Louis McBurney reminds us that our wives have the ability to see what we male pastors do not, or perhaps, will not see. He adds,

> Wives are one of our most important protective screens ... we may be oblivious to some of the early non-verbal signs, or they may just be flattering enough that we do not want them to stop. If we learn to listen to our wives, they may save us from becoming too involved in a potentially destructive relationship (Louis McBurney, in Muck (ed.), p. 105).

Paul Tournier shares much the same wisdom:

> The best protection against sexual temptations is to be able to speak honestly of them and to find in the wife's understanding, without any trace of complicity whatsoever, effective and affective help needed to overcome them (Paul Tournier quoted by A. D. Hart, in Muck (ed.), p. 95).

Clearly, for this to be effective, discussion before the problem arises will maximize the potential help of the pastor's spouse.

Pastors should realize that in most cases it is their role, not their person, that others are attracted to. Pastors sometimes need this humbling reminder—especially (I suspect) the male of the species! Idealization is very common in churches. The pastor is seen up front, speaking caringly and helpfully from God's word. On top of this, the pastor very often has time to listen; indeed makes time to listen. This is often in stark contrast to the real life situation of church members and others in the community, whose own spouses may be absent, thoughtless, harsh, have no time, and show little or no inclination to listen. It is this *idealization* that the wise pastor will keep in mind, and work at demythologizing the role as a matter of course in normal ministry. If we remember that it is the role to which another person is attracted, not to us in particular, it can help in keeping the attraction, be it one-sided or mutual, in perspective. The truth is, if someone else were the pastor, the attraction would be towards them. This is a sober and realistic way of defusing the situation.

Transference

Transference and counter-transference are closely related to the issue of idealization. Dr Hart commented at a clergy school in Perth, "If you do not understand transference and counter-transference in the ministry you are dead in the water". The very qualities required of pastors set us up for idealization. There is an expectation that we can meet the needs of people. So when a person comes to the pastor, that person may be idealizing the pastor by attributing idealized and imaginary qualities to him or her. You may know that you are not always patient or understanding towards your spouse, but the counsellee may think otherwise.

Hart explains transference and counter-transference in the following way.

> If you were hungry for love, wouldn't it be nice to find someone who was well-educated, mannerly, articulate but also a good listener, respected in the community, occupationally powerful, yet unselfish, and willing to spend time alone with you for free?
>
> Numbers of counsellees think so. They come to a church office and find themselves in the presence of the kindest, most receptive, admirable, gentle, wise person they've met in a long time. The solution to their turmoil, they gradually realize, is not so much what the pastor is saying as the pastor himself.
>
> In my classes for working clergy who are pursuing the D. Min. degree, I talk about this hazard, technically known as transference. (The client is projecting feelings and desires into the counselling relationship that belong somewhere else.) Each term the students write a paper on how the course has related to their situations. Every time, 20 to 25 percent of them report transference as a problem they have faced in their ministries.
>
> Counter-transference, the even more distressing corollary, is when the counsellor projects into the mix feelings and desires that belong elsewhere (Hart, in Muck (ed.), p. 85).

The fact that this is usually unconscious makes it important for pastors to understand what may be going on in counselling and other church relationships.

There are many counsellors who recognize that counselling can only really take place when transference and counter-transference are understood and capitalized upon. It has been said that transference and counter-transference are the stuff of which the counselling relationship is made. However, this dynamic of the counselling relationship should be recognized as a potential minefield, especially when the counsellor begins to share inappropriate information about themselves. Danger signs are the sharing of personal information by the counsellee far too quickly, and when affection, attraction and dependence upon the pastor begin to take place. If at the same time the pastor is experiencing a developing attraction, and is inappropriately sharing his or her own personal, intimate information and feelings with the counsellee, decisive action must be taken. Apart from sharing this with one's spouse, the pastor in these circumstances would be very wise to refer his counsellee on to another counsellor. This will prove beneficial to everyone.

We pastors need to be very tough and realistic with ourselves. It is folly to believe it only happens to other pastors, and that we can keep the sexual temptation under control whilst flirting at an emotional level. Transference is about a growing relationship. If not understood or checked, this can lead to disaster. Hart notes the potential for growth from emotions to sexual action, and at the same time warns pastors to be realistic.

> 'I've been lonely', wrote one pastor, 'and I cannot communicate with my wife. She doesn't understand how I feel. All she wants to talk about are the kids and her mother. I want to explore ideas, thoughts, and feelings. So I began to spend time with a woman after we finished our counselling sessions. She understands me. I can share myself with her. I hope this doesn't go further; I'd hate to have to decide whether to leave my wife or not.' This pastor is kidding himself. The relationship will go further if he does nothing to stop it. All sexual affairs begin in this benign way. Although most liaisons emerge out of counselling relationships, some start when a minister has to work closely with someone on a committee or project. Since more and more younger women have assumed church responsibilities in recent years, male ministers are now in close working relationships with women where feelings of warmth and affection can easily arise. Sometimes the relationship develops with a secretary or other work colleague.
>
> Male pastors are typically attracted to younger women, although it is not unusual for ministers to be attracted to older ones as well. And attraction does not require extensive contact. Glances from the pulpit to someone hardly known, or a chance encounter in a corridor or on a hospital visit can find the pastor obsessed with a strong attraction to someone else (Hart, in Muck (ed.), p. 86).

Some authors have written concerning the special case of the seductive female who might for a variety of reasons—conscious or unconscious—find a particular reason or source of pleasure in orchestrating an affair with a pastor. Louis McBurney outlines the problem:

> From my experience, I'd identify yet another danger—the angry seductress. Some women cherish a deep, inner hatred for men and compulsion to gain control over them. Frequently they were rejected or abused by their fathers. Often they learned in childhood and adolescence that sensuality is their most effective weapon. Consciously or unconsciously, they form a pattern of conquests while they appear to be helpless women who need a strong man to care for them (L. McBurney, in Muck (ed.) pp. 98-9).

Andre Bustandy, whose article about 'Counselling the seductive female' gives excellent advice, notes that

> no safeguards will work if we do not come to terms with our counter-transference, if we allow our own affection for the counsellee to go in a wrong direction and lead to improper behaviour. Having come to terms with our own sexuality, however, we can establish a professional relationship with the counsellee (A. Bustandy, in Muck (ed.), p. 169).

I am not aware of evidence that would support the case for some men seeking out female pastors in the same way. The above quotations are not meant to suggest that *only* women or *all* women act like this. I expect that as time goes on and the number of female pastors increases there may also be men who will act like this. The key is to be aware.

Those who seek out pastors for counselling have needs, and pastors must assume that those who come are seeking healing and relief. The fact that some have established self-defeating patterns of behaviour in seeking to combat their difficulties, should not lessen but rather strengthen our resolve to minister to such people. Greater help will be given by pastors who recognize their vulnerability in sexual temptation, than by those who refuse to acknowledge their vulnerability. A healthy acceptance of this vulnerability, and having wise steps in place to understand and minimize the dangers, will be to the long-term benefit of pastors, their families, their churches and those who seek their counsel.

A number of positive steps in combating sexual temptation have been mentioned above. This approach could be described as both anticipatory and cognitive. Our beliefs should come from Scripture, which gives us direct commands, exhortations, warnings and examples that are both wholesome and tragic. All this is grounded in the Creator's loving good purposes, so it should not surprise us at all that observable and experiential confirmation of the fruits of obedience and disobedience are held before us. A healthy belief system, based on Scripture, and confirmed in our experience by daily obedience, will go a long way towards helping us stand firm when sexual temptation threatens.

The following general comments are offered in order to show the role that our biblical belief system, combined with God's grace, can play in keeping us on track.

Larry Crabb's reminder that "I'm to be hypocritical to my feelings, not to my purposes" is applicable in every area of my life, but is most appropriate sexually. Feelings must be controlled by godly purposes. Louis McBurney shows us our need to allow God's Scripture and Spirit to control us when he comments: "A common path to sexual sin is the notion that feelings are not only all important, but also totally uncontrollable—they just happen to you" (McBurney, in Muck (ed.), p. 95).

- This is advice all need to hear, even when things are *going well*. We see this in 1 Thessalonians 4:1—"just as you are doing ... do so more and more". Ours is a sex-saturated society, as was the New Testament era. Timely reminders from God's word will keep us focussed on God's ways.
- *The apostle's instructions are Jesus' instructions*. It is sometimes said that Jesus did not speak much about sexuality in general, and not at all about homosexuality. That we do not have Jesus' thinking recorded in the Gospels does not mean we do not know his mind on these issues since the apostle(s) clearly spoke with his authority.
- *Sanctification is God's will for us*. Our salvation from sin's penalty took place when we believed the gospel (Rom 5:1). But as Romans 6 and 7 demonstrate, this was for the purpose of our sanctification, that steady gradual growth into Christlikeness. This must take place in every aspect of our life, including our sexuality. Sanctification is for our good, for witness to the world

and for love of our brothers and sisters in the church.
- Since sanctification is God's will for us, *we can rely upon him to enable us to obey*. This becomes clear as we take responsibility for obeying his exhortations. We are actively to avoid sexual immorality, and embrace God's way of self-controlled, other-person-centred, Christlike love. But we are not alone when we obey. God has given us his Holy Spirit to help us become holy in practice (1 Thess 4:8). The giving of his Spirit took place at our conversion. Active disobedience will render the Spirit's work ineffective, whereas by implication ongoing obedience ensures a constant leading by the Spirit of God. Paul applies the same teaching to our sexual fidelity as he does in Ephesians to congregational fidelity, where we can either grieve or be filled with the Holy Spirit (Eph 4:30; 5:18).
- The apostle's call in 1 Thessalonians 4:4, "that each one of you know how to control his own body" reminds us of the Holy Spirit, whose fruits include self-control. The fact that we are to learn self-control shows us that we do not have to allow our feelings to dominate us. Progress can be made. The old hymn reminds us of this progression when it says, "each victory will help you some other to win".
- *Our beliefs* are therefore not simply based upon commandments and warnings, though these abound, but upon the flowering of that one and only, eternal and all-fulfilling relationship; the one we enjoy with God the Father on the basis of his Son's death and resurrection, and made real to us by the Holy Spirit.
- Sex is not to be the central focus of our lives. This can be seen by the way Paul moves straight into an exhortation about *brotherly love* in 1 Thessalonians 4:9-10. We must not become obsessed or focused upon sex as the means to fulfilment or enjoyment. This is in stark contrast to Western culture's preoccupation with sex, as the only possible way to intimacy. The apostle sets these verses after the section on sexuality, as does Hebrews, whose key verse on sexuality (13:4) is found immediately after those on love within the Christian community (13:1-3). Nurturing a wide range of friendships within the congregation and wider Christian community will always serve to ensure our real needs for intimacy

and companionship are met. Where the congregation is working well in this regard, the need to meet our needs in sexual relationships that are off-limits is far less likely. We do have the privilege and responsibility of being our brother's keeper in this, as in every area of our sanctification. Here is a challenge to marrieds and unmarrieds alike, as to the quality of our congregational life.

The unmarried

Much of what has been said is equally relevant to those who are unmarried. Some of the advice needs to be supplemented with some special words for those who are single. Nonetheless words for singles will be equally relevant to marrieds, since everyone is single once in their life, and almost half of us will be single twice.

Close, caring and trusted friends will have a special place in the lives of those who are unmarried. This will be nowhere more needful than in guarding against the danger of secretiveness in allowing sexual attractions and their attendant thoughts to flourish. To break the power of secretiveness, a close trusted friend will be much valued. Since the majority of people within society and the church are married, it is very difficult, even for the happily single members of our churches, not to feel the full force of the bombardment of messages that suggest we must be in a sexual relationship if we are to be normal and happy. Of course, nothing could be further from the truth. Though a trusting and committed sexual relationship may be our desire, it is not a necessity in order to achieve either full humanity or full happiness.

Since the war is often waged in the mind, let me offer the following suggestions.

- The most fully human, happy person was surely Jesus of Nazareth, our Lord and Saviour. He enjoyed a whole range of friendships but was neither married nor engaged in sexual relationships.
- As the Scriptures unfold, we see that the words of Genesis 2:18 ("it is not good that the man should be alone") find expression in a whole range of relationships. Marriage is but one; it is essential for procreation, but not for providing companionship and friendship.
- The words "male and female he created them" are preceded by

"God created man in his own image". In other words, each person is a full personality created in God's image (Gen 1:27).
- Biblical mathematics when it comes to marriage is not as is sometimes supposed 1/2 + 1/2 = 1, but 1 + 1 = 1 (Gen 2:24). Each person is a full person. The two come together, not to complete each other, but to find companionship and to form a complete partnership. But each person has needs, to be sure. These needs can be met as lives are shared, but not completely or fully by one other person. That is to expect too much of our marriage partner, and not enough of God, ourselves, our community and our church.
- It has been said that a person is not really ready to be married until they are happy to be single. In other words, if I marry because I'm unhappy in myself, or feel insecure or incomplete, I'm very likely to contribute to an unhealthy marriage. Someone who enters marriage thinking 'you must meet my needs' has already sown seeds that will quickly grow into selfishness.
- Intimacy is not dependent on sex. What it does depend upon is a committed and caring friendship. This joining of minds can be nurtured by talking and listening, sharing pursuits and interests, thoughtful interaction and helpfulness, all on the bedrock of mutual trust, respect and care. Sex will not deliver intimacy when these are not present, and where they abound, sex is not essential for intimacy. What a married couple enjoys in the sexual act is more dependent upon this bedrock than on the bed itself. Every thoughtful married couple knows that. But we could be excused for forgetting it, since sex is seen as the be-all-and-end-all of relationships.
- It is for this reason that God's word forbids sex before and outside of the marriage relationship, as well as an inconsiderate relationship within marriage.
- I believe that God places prohibitions on non-married sex so that the things that make for real intimacy can be pursued without the powerful pull of sex. When the relationship is grown on the basis of companionship, thoughtfulness, listening, shared pursuits, hopes and thoughts, a realistic basis for an ongoing committed marriage relationship can be formed.

Decisions about marriage can be made upon the firm basis of self-giving, other-person-centred *agape* love rather than the more self-focused *eros* attraction or lust. This, when expressed in a committed marriage relationship grounded upon the bedrock of Christlike love, can be purged of its false and self-interested passions and given and received in the joyful manner God intended it to be.
- The pursuit of intimacy, especially that available to all Christian people within the congregation, can deliver much joy, and it is essential to single and married pastors alike.

Congregations with single pastors do well to remember the possible loneliness experienced by their unmarried pastors. This will be especially so for those who may not have chosen their singleness. Inclusion in home groups, mealtime hospitality, family evenings, barbecues and outings will prove to be a wonderful gift and expression of brotherly love.

9
Friendship

*Better is open rebuke than hidden love.
Faithful are the wounds of a friend.*
PROVERBS 27:5-6

*Death and life are in the power of the tongue,
and those who love it will eat its fruits ... there is
a friend who sticks closer than a brother.*
PROVERBS 18:21, 24

Iron sharpens iron, and one man sharpens another.
PROVERBS 27:17

*And though a man might prevail against
one who is alone, two will withstand him—
a threefold cord is not quickly broken.*
ECCLESIASTES 4:12

WE ALL KNOW THE JOYS of friendship, but building friendships takes time. If they don't appear to be productive, at least in the short-term, we can be tempted to skip the necessary time commitment to their growth. We experience a friendship deficit syndrome. We retreat more and more into ourselves. But it wasn't meant to be like this. The truth of the words "it is not good for man to be alone" are known only too well by us all. Given the wide range of friendship examples in the Old and New Testaments, I am convinced that these verses find fulfillment in a much wider context than marriage.

Since we are made in the image of the triune God, it is little wonder that we long for and thrive on committed friendships. Relationships matter to all people; pastors are no exception. Whether we are married or single, we grow through our friendships. As we give and receive in friendships, we find growth.

We see the important place friendships have in God's purposes for us from the intersecting lines of Scripture.

- "It is not good that the man should be alone" (Gen 2:18).
- David, Jonathan and Mephibosheth.
- The teaching of Proverbs.
- Our Lord's example as the "friend of sinners" and his circles of friends.
- Barnabas and Paul.
- Paul, Priscilla and Aquila.
- The 35 brothers and sisters mentioned in Romans 16.
- The "one another" passages of the New Testament.

Friendship is clearly important to the whole life of ministry. Some would say that friendship *is* ministry. We become Jesus' friends, we follow him, and as we form friendships in our local churches, others, thirsty for friendship, find Jesus.

Dale Hansen's book *The Art of Pastoring* has many fresh and honest insights into pastoral work. In his chapter on friendship he says,

> When Jesus befriended sinners, they followed him. When the disciples befriended sinners, they followed Jesus. When the 'enacted parable' of Jesus' life of friendship was taken over by his disciples, they became enacted parables of Jesus. Jesus fully intended his disciples to spend the rest of their lives befriending sinners (Hansen, p. 118).

Yet the fact remains that many pastors are lonely, many of us have few friends, and some have been actively taught that they shouldn't have friends in the congregation they serve. Why is this so?

A number of factors combine. Mother Teresa, when asked what she thought was the worst disease, answered: "it is not AIDS, leprosy or cancer, but loneliness". In other words, it is a problem we all share in a busy and often fearful society. In our mobile society, many people suffer the loss of friendships formed through shared school, community, sport or professional contacts. Pastors, however, may find it particularly difficult to develop friendships if people idolize them. This happens when they are put on a pedestal. The 'tools of trade'—prayer, preparation and proclamation—whilst essential, can tend to isolate pastors from people. The clothes of office can be unhelpful, fostering a 'them-us' mentality.

It is to overcome this problem that Hansen develops his paradigm of the pastor being a parable of Jesus Christ, not a symbol of God. He writes:

> Pastors as parables of Jesus bring Christ to people, and then as quickly as possible become unimportant, unnecessary, superfluous to the important thing: the parishioners' relationships with Jesus ... It is tempting to extend our effect on people long enough to get adulation and to create the appearance that we are necessary to people. We can wave like a flag, but we always end up hanging ourselves. Rather, pastors need to allow their personal effect on people to be powerful, but light-handed and brief. This is what it means for a pastor to be humble (Hansen, pp. 132-3).

Once we can allow ourselves to minister *under* God, not *as* God, we will be able to open the door to those who want to build friendships with us, recognizing our need for the support friends can bring to us. London and Wiseman suggest,

> ... many others [pastors] keep themselves emotionally isolated because they fear being upstaged. They are troubled that someone might see this weakness if they get too close. Therefore they keep their distance from others because the facts are not as good as people think. None of this sounds like the relational pattern of Jesus (London and Wiseman, 1993, p. 50).

This is sad, because God would refresh us greatly through the ministry of friends.

How helpful is the old conventional wisdom that we shouldn't have friends within the congregation? My own view is that it is almost impossible to exercise a New Testament ministry without friendships emerging. The gospel will, under God's gracious influence, bring people into God's family as we become sons and daughters who are no longer enemies but friends of God. When we align ourselves with Jesus as disciples and servants under his Lordship, we are brought into a relationship that can be described as friendship. Our Lord encouraged his disciples with these words:

> As the Father has loved me, so have I loved you. Abide in my love. If you keep my commandments, you will abide in my love, just as I have kept my Father's commandments and abide in his love. These things I have spoken to you, that my joy may be in you, and that your joy may be full. This is my commandment, that you love one another as I have loved you. Greater love has no one than this, that someone lays down his life for his friends. You are my friends if you do what I command you. No longer do I call you servants, for the servant does not know what his master is doing; but I have called you friends, for all that I have heard from my Father I have made known to you. You did not choose me, but I chose you and appointed you that you should go and bear fruit and that your fruit should abide, so that whatever you ask the Father in my name, he may give it to you. These things I command you, so that you will love one another (John 15: 9-17).

Of course there is a danger of taking the friendship theme too far in our relationship with the risen Lord. Complacency born of familiarity will be kept at bay when we take note that we are to do what he commands, and remember it was he who chose us. Yet friendship with Jesus remains a powerful reminder to us of the intimate relationship we enjoy with our Lord.

This security is the joy of all Christians, pastors included. We fail in our role as fellow Christians, and in our ministry of leadership, if we do not model this friendship with one another. Yes, there are dangers. Favouritism, manipulation and cronyism are all possibilities. However, they need not be a problem where friendships are built for the good of each other.

The dangers can be surely minimized when it is recognized that:

- the pastor needs friends
- the pastor cannot be a friend to everyone

- those who can form friendships with the pastor are exercising a ministry to the pastor on behalf of the congregation
- everyone will then benefit, in that the pastor's loneliness will be minimized and refreshment maximized
- there are different levels of friendship and all members of an average size congregation can engage in friendship at one level or another. Failure to build friendships leads to a church of formal and arms-length relationships.

Different kinds of friends

Gordon MacDonald has identified six kinds of special friends that a pastor needs.

The sponsor

> The sponsor ... is another name for mentor or discipler. We have already looked at the role of the sponsor in another context when we thought about VRP's, the very resourceful people who pour energy of passion into us rather than drain it away.
>
> But let's take a second look at this role now in the context of the special-friend team.
>
> The sponsor is that Very Resourceful Person (the VRP) who ushers us into opportunity and possibility. He or she is usually close by and can be drawn upon, when courage, guidance, or assurance is needed that a path chosen is the right one (McDonald, p. 319).

This person will be especially important to the pastor early in their ministry. Indeed, we may be in ministry because somebody saw our potential. Ideally this is the way a person should seek ordination or missionary work. They are seen exercising faithful ministry, and observed to be a keen disciple of Jesus in daily work and conduct. A sponsor will be one who encourages a person to keep growing, and to keep serving others under God and for God. We need sponsors all of our life, but during mid-life, they come into their own. This can be a time of doubt or disappointment for pastors, especially when invitations to go to other churches begin to dry up. One who can draw alongside to encourage will be providing a great ministry to the pastor, and to the many others who reap the rewards of a refreshed and mature ministry.

The affirmer

The affirmer has to be the second person in our address book of special friends: he or she is the one who moves alongside and inspires us as we act out our destiny. The affirmer takes up where the sponsor leaves off. The affirmer takes note of what we are doing and what we are becoming and attaches value to it (McDonald, p. 322).

Some church cultures, and certainly the Australian ethos, downplay encouragement. Somehow we feel that it might go to a person's head, or it might not be giving God the honour, if we give praise or thanks for something done well. Affirmation is totally different to "the empty compliments and plaudits that are carelessly tossed about in human relationships" (McDonald, p. 323). Affirmation is not flattery, "it is not given with the motive of obtaining reciprocal favour".

Affirmation is genuine appreciation, expressed quietly to another person, for what they have done. It is standing alongside someone who has been criticized. If the criticism was deserved, affirmation lets them know that you still believe in them; and if not, that they should ignore it and confidently get on with life. Affirmation is that thoughtful word, expressed in person, on the phone or by letter, that demonstrates how helped you were by your brother or sister.

The proverb reminds us of the power of words to build up or tear down: "Death and life are in the power of the tongue, and those who love it will eat its fruits" (Prov 18:21). Here is a ministry that every pastor can exercise toward church members, and one that can be lovingly and thoughtfully returned as the opportunity arises. An affirmer must have a special mind-set. Like Barnabas, the affirmer will want to encourage because he or she has seen and experienced the value of affirmation.

This thoughtfulness is expressed in Hebrews 10: "And let us consider how to stir up one another to love and good works". How often? The next verse would suggest every time we meet!

The affirmer helps put out the fires of cynicism and thoughtless speech, whilst at the same time offering a tonic to a weary, lonely or discouraged pastor. It is a ministry we should all be exercising as the church of "one another" (1 Thess 4:18, 5:11).

The rebuker

It takes courage to include the rebuker on the team. For what he or she says often hurts and leaves bruises on the spirit. *But we may be talking about the most important member among our special friends.* We all need truth-tellers, even if we don't really want them. Pass them up or avoid them, and spiritual passion may be in great jeopardy.

The writers of the book of Proverbs put a great premium on the position of the rebuker: "Better is open rebuke than hidden love. Faithful are the wounds of a friend; profuse are the kisses of an enemy" (Prov 27:5-6) (McDonald, p. 325).

No-one likes to be a rebuker. We naturally and rightly do not seek this special ministry to each other. It can be fraught with dangers, and whilst Scripture has its own warnings (not least our Lord's in Matt 7:1-5), it also teaches us to do this for one another.

A few texts make plain the value of exercising this thoughtful ministry of rebuke and therefore the responsibility we have to do so:

The ear that listens to life-giving reproof will dwell among the wise (Prov 15:31).

A rebuke goes deeper into a man of understanding than a hundred blows into a fool (Prov 17:10).

Reprove a man of understanding, and he will gain knowledge (Prov 19:25).

Jesus said, "If your brother sins, rebuke him, and if he repents, forgive him " (Luke 17:3).

Do not rebuke an older man but encourage him as you would a father (1 Tim 5:1).

Preach the word; be ready in season and out of season; reprove, rebuke, and exhort, with complete patience and teaching (2 Tim 4:2).

... exhort and rebuke with all authority (Titus 2:15).

Our capacity to benefit from a word of rebuke will be increased if certain conditions are met. It will greatly help if the word of rebuke comes from someone who has demonstrated that they really care for you as a person. Some of the passages quoted above combine encouragement and rebuke.

Jesus says rebuke a "brother". In other words, we will refuse to engage in the cheap shot of criticism designed to hurt. When I personally have been rebuked by those whom I know really care for me as a brother (care demonstrated by encouragement and preparedness to rebuke), I have been able to handle the rebuke as an expression of their love.

If I am rebuked, it doesn't mean I'm useless, a failure or unappreciated. If a loving fellow Christian is thoughtful and caring enough to rebuke me, my self-esteem ought not to be destroyed. My self-esteem is based on my relationship with God through Christ, not my performance. Though my faithfulness and my friends' acceptance will help me feel good and value myself, I should not be totally tied to their affirmation. Indeed, their thoughtful rebuke will be a sign to me of God's love (in sending them) and of their commitment to me and my growth. Had they not said anything, they would only be committed to my mediocrity or my folly. Rebuke over a specific issue is just that—a specific issue needs to be addressed. Rebuke given prayerfully, out of a demonstrated caring relationship, is a gift—an unwanted one perhaps, but necessary to our future growth and possibly saving us from much heartache and hurt if left ignored. Seneca knew what he was saying when he said, "He who excuses present evils transmits them to posterity". The old hymn invites us to rebuke one another in the words:

> Tell me the old, old story,
> when you have cause to fear,
> that this world's empty glory
> is costing me too dear.

The intercessor

If I am to gain spiritual passion from my special friends, among them will be those who play the position of the *intercessor*. Intercessors are those who have accepted the responsibility for holding me up to God in prayer (McDonald, p. 331).

The apostle frequently invited people to pray for him and his team. It was not uncommon for Paul to thank those who did. In turn, he was regularly at prayer for distant fellow Christians. On many occasions, he wrote his prayer for them to read.

Any congregational member can exercise this friendship ministry towards their pastor. Prayer for the pastor, that he would be faithful in prayer, preparation, preaching, evangelism and pastoring, is essential to his ministry and the life of the church. Pastors always value prayer for their growth as Christians, for their families and for daily wisdom.

Sometimes we pastors are a little slow to receive this ministry. We shouldn't be, and we would do well to encourage those who want to join us for prayer or who ask us how they might pray. Whether personal prayer requests are shared or not, all members can profitably be intercessory friends to their pastor. I am always grateful if friends use Paul's prayer for the Philippian Christians as a model when praying for me.

> And it is my prayer that your love may abound more and more, with knowledge and all discernment, so that you may approve what is excellent, and so be pure and blameless for the day of Christ, filled with the fruit of righteousness that comes through Jesus Christ, to the glory and praise of God (Phil 1:9-11).

By personalizing the pronouns, this can easily become a real prayer for our pastors. For example, "Gracious Lord, this is my prayer for our pastor John: that his love may abound more and more, especially to those he is seeking to minister to in the high school ... give him ... knowledge and depth of insight today as he prepares for Sunday's sermon and as he chairs the parish council tonight ...".

We do well to remember that as Christians we are engaged in a warfare. Not only has Satan blinded peoples' eyes and hardened their hearts to the gospel, but he loves to cause divisions in churches, which divert and dilute our energies for the great commission and for living out the great commandment. Intercessory prayer provides a great ministry in seeking God's blessing and power, but also takes away the possibility of idolizing our pastors, or expecting them to do it all. It has a great purifying effect not only in the answer but in the praying. Dietrich Bonhoeffer puts it so well when he says, "A Christian fellowship lives and exists by the intercession of its members for one another, or it collapses".

The partner

Another player on our team of special friends is the generalist, the roving fielder if you please. That player is the partner. The restoration and maintenance of spiritual passion frequently depends upon the process of partnership with one or more who share the load. In fact, I am not sure that most of us can ever reach the full extent of our energies if we are not in partnership with someone else (McDonald, p. 335).

When Jesus sent out the team of evangelists on their training run, they went out two by two (Luke 10). Certainly as we follow through Paul's method of ministry we see the way he valued team members. This is evident from the partnerships he forged with Barnabas, Silas, Timothy and many others whom he called fellow soldiers, brothers or yokefellows. "Iron sharpens iron; and one man sharpens another." We do well to value friends who will sharpen us. Discussion of a book, the sharing of a meal where listening is the main menu item, and the thoughtful acts of service that ease the load, are just a few of the tools in the partner's kit. The list in Romans 16 of the 35 people or groups that Paul is in touch with, demonstrates the value of partnership friends. These are not all people like Barnabas who spent much time with and were well known to Paul, but they were people whose paths had crossed his. The quality of these relationships and Paul's own model as an affirmer is worthy of close study. We note how partners work:

- they are fellow workers, like Priscilla and Aquila
- they work hard in the Lord, like the three women Tryphena, Tryphosa and Persis
- they have shared prison, like Andronicus and Junia
- they open their homes for church, like Priscilla, Aquila and Gaius
- they are family to Paul, like Rufus and his mother
- they are warm in sending greetings and showing affection.

The pastor

There is one more player on the team of special friends—the *pastor*. This is the tender person, the person who comes alongside in the moment of exhaustion. The pastor—and I'm not necessarily talking about ordained ministers—is the one who helps make sense out of life when all has become confusing (McDonald, pp. 315-16).

Pastors are people who will pray for us, and be especially gentle to us when we are finding the going tough. They will catch the sense of lowness in our voice, as an older lady in our congregation did when I called her about a mundane matter, and then say, "Are you all right? Why don't you just go and do something for yourself for the rest of the day?" It was a tonic to me that she cared. I didn't have to go and do something for myself. She had done it for me.

The old saying "to have a friend you need to be a friend" has some relevance here. As pastors, we need to take some special responsibility in seeking friendships, and making time in our diaries for them to grow. Friends will help us keep our spiritual passion alive, so long as they each recognize that this is a special ministry that comes as God's gift to us.

A danger

Sadly, pastors themselves can miss the opportunities of friendship by failing to capture the moment. Much time can be wasted in criticism of denominational leadership, on unhealthy comparison with others or a failure to consider the needs of one another. I have been guilty of each one, and have no desire to hold the high ground whilst criticizing my peers. My own part in it has been unhelpful to me, as I'm sure it has been for others. Bonhoeffer's words about prayer, quoted above, are a great antidote to this poison. As pastors, we might do well to draw up a covenant with each other, based on Hebrews 10:24, that would enable us to make the very best of the times we meet. The friendship of pastors for one another can be of a very special kind, or an occasional one, but there is no doubt that we can do much to encourage each other given the common nature of our work and experience.

Mentoring

Mentoring has a long history within and outside the church. MacDonald's six styles of friendship could be summarized by the concept of mentoring. John Mallison, a long time mentor to many Christians, defines mentoring as "a dynamic, intentional relationship of trust in which one person enables another to maximize the grace of God in their life and service". Mallison suggests that there are three overlapping ways that any Christian can be involved in mentoring others. Mentoring will involve a *receiving relationship* with a more mature person who has been faithful over a long period of time. A *sharing relationship* is where two people, peers of similar age decide to make their normal friendship more intentional. It will still be an informal arrangement but one which gives a high priority to each other. The informal context will ensure that the friendship will remain a delight but its intentionality will make it a truly loving and caring time together. A *giving relationship* is where we develop a mentoring friendship with a younger or less experienced pastor. This will involve much listening but will provide a real means of support and strength.

To be a good Christian mentor, we need:

- an adequate idea of God
- a sane estimate of ourselves and others
- the ability to ask good questions
- active listening skills
- to know our limitations and be able to set boundaries
- to understand how adults learn
- to have the time to give
- belief in the power of prayer
- familiarity with the Bible, and above all
- a living relationship with God (Ducklow, p. 34).

Intentional friendships will be an essential aspect of the pastor's self-care. In the Perth survey, all but one of the married clergy answered 'my wife' to the question, 'Who is your greatest support in ministry (apart from God)?' Whilst there is a very positive aspect to this home support, it can become a pressure point, placing real strains on the marriage and family life. A diffused structure of support lessens the pressure and can certainly help minimize marriage tension and family stresses.

Friendships can be intentional especially where an agreement is entered into to provide thoughtful and prayerful support. H. B. London offers the following suggestion for how a friendship covenant can be engaged in for one another's benefit. The advice, which he has adapted from "Creative Love" by Lewis Evans Jnr, makes good sense. Far from turning a friendship into a rigid or formal relationship, it could prove to be the very means of keeping pastors from the destructive and poisonous criticisms mentioned above.

FRIENDSHIP

Covenant love — *good for cohort?!*

In a covenant relationship, each person is to grow into "the fullness of Christ" (Eph 4:13). To encourage that growth in another person, we can promise before God and to them, to the best of our ability, that we will:

1. **Affirm** one another—there is nothing that the other(s) can do or say that will make you stop loving them, even if you disagree with their actions.

2. **Be available** to one another—you will offer your time, energy, possessions, prayer and insights to them, within the limits of your known resources.

3. **Pray** for one another—you will set aside a regular time to bring their concerns before the Lord.

4. **Be open** with one another—you will endeavour to be as open as you are able with your feelings, struggles, hurts, fears and joys.

5. **Be honest** with one another—you will commit yourself to be as open as you are able to "speak the truth in love", even when it is difficult (Eph 4:15).

6. **Be sensitive** to one another—you will do your best to listen, observe and sense their real needs.

7. **Be confidential** with one another—you will promise to guard what is shared within the confines of your spiritual partnership.

8. **Be accountable** to one another—you will be responsible to them to become the fullness of God's design for spiritual growth and nurture.

> I/We hereby agree to be committed to this spiritual partnership. It is my/our intent to faithfully fulfil these privileges and responsibilities. It is my/our hope that this relationship will be a means of spiritual accountability in my growing faith in Jesus Christ.

The words, "I will pray for you" are some of the most powerful and comforting words in the language of man. Here is what it means:

> I covenant to pray for you in some regular fashion, believing

that our caring Father wishes his children to pray for one another and ask him for the blessings they need.

Why?

- You find a person whom you believe in, and enter into a covenant to pray for one another.
- The length of the covenant should be determined after you have entered into the prayer agreement.
- The prayer covenant is between two people (can be more) who are seeking a special release of God's power in and on their lives.
- One never enters a prayer agreement with an air of superiority ("I don't need anything thank you, but you do ..."), but in a feeling of mutual need.

Particulars

- The prayer covenant should be between those of the same sex.
- You agree to pray for one another each time you pray.
- Where possible you meet together face to face for at least one half hour per week.
- You attempt to make contact with your covenant partner at least twice more each week through the telephone, short visits, or letter.
- You are never judgemental or condemning; always supportive and helpful in true Christian honesty (Ja 5:16).

How?

In a covenant/intercessory prayer relationship, we release the grace of God to a loved one in a way that is not possible through any other method. It is through intercessory prayer that God turns loose powers and strength that are not otherwise available.

Evidence and observation reveal the great tragedy that many pastors are lonely. The primary responsibility for our self-care must come from the pastor. An intentional friendship, once initiated and formed, can go a long way in overcoming the debilitating effects of loneliness. Perhaps the covenant approach above will prove a helpful means of initiating a friendship. Its initial touch of formality could prove to be a blessing as it will provide both an opening and a framework out of which friendship can grow.

Thoughtful questions

Both Mallison and London suggest that good and thoughtful questions can be a great means of expressing, confirming and working at the mutual commitment of mentoring friends. London suggests 26 such questions that 'accountability friends' ask one another (London, 1996). Here are twelve:

> How is your relationship with God right now?
> What have you read in the Bible in the past week?
> What has God said to you in this reading?
> Where do you find yourself resisting him these days?
> What specific things are you praying for in regard to yourself?
> What are the specific tasks you are facing right now that you consider incomplete?
> What general reading are you doing?
> How are you doing with your spouse? Kids?
> Are there any unresolved conflicts in your circle of relationships right now?
> What would you say are your fears at this present time?
> What are your greatest confusions about your relationship with God?
> What have you done to play?

We need friendships

"The friendlessness of the ministry", writes Paddy Ducklow, is

> a most common complaint of clergy couples and it relates to *where you kick off your psychological and spiritual shoes*. It relates to who can you talk to, confess to, shoot the breeze with, unload upon, even when it's about your spouse. Friendlessness is an important variable in marital depression and is a reliable predictor of things going wrong in the relationship of family and church (Ducklow, p. 34).

Whether single or married, we need good friendships. They may be found within the congregation, from previous churches, pastors or spouses groups, or from pastors or Christian friends from our formative years. But we need them. They become another gift of God to us—a gift of creation (Gen 2:18) and a fruit of our redemption (Gal 3:26-28 and 6:2). Like all God's gifts, they need to be received and then attended to. Gratitude to God, service to others and our own self-care can combine in granting us the wisdom to set time aside for cultivating such friendships. None of us can mentor or support everyone else. We cannot, nor do we have to, but opportunities abound for us to slow down long enough in order to consider how we could strengthen a fellow pastor's hand. This ministry is open to all of God's people. As pastors minister to church members so church members can exercise wonderful ministry through friendship with their pastors. My own experience has been that I have been given my strongest support from lay people within the churches I've been pastoring.

All who exercise this ministry will be doing a great service to pastors, their families and congregations, since a pastor with friends will be more likely to be spiritually alive, passionate for the word and equipped for the work. Friends who mentor us will be conveying to us three messages: "It can be done! You're not alone! I believe in you!" These words of Larry Crabb convey to us the awesome power of thoughtful friendship. Each of these affirmations, whether given in the context of building us up, comforting, encouraging, rebuking or teaching is needed if we are to run the race joyfully to completion. When they have come to me in the form of words, attitudes or gifts, they have lifted me from despair, enabled me to fight off Satan's darts of doubts, to sort out criticism that needs to be ignored from what must be attended to, and above all to recall that God is faithful. I thank God for my friends. I'm sad that I've not always made time to build friendships. But I am convinced that they are essential to my growth as a person, as a Christian and especially in my work as a pastor.

10

Principles and strategies of self-care

*In the gospels I read about a man called Jesus
who went about doing good. My problem is
why I am content with just going about.*
KAGAWA

*Do you not know that your body is a temple of the
Holy Spirit within you, whom you have from God?
You are not your own, for you were bought with a price.
So glorify God in your body.*
1 CORINTHIANS 6:19-20

INTENTIONAL SELF-CARE IS a means by which we keep ourselves refreshed for the work of ministry. The strategies we develop, and put in place in our lives, show that we value spiritual renewal and refreshment so much that we will plan for it to happen.

In this chapter, I want to outline some principles of self-care that flow out of our Lord's example and training of his apostles and evangelists. This will highlight the proposition that the God who commissions us has built into our work the means of renewing us. Then I want to share the 'top ten' strategies employed by the Perth Anglican clergy whom I surveyed in 1992. This will demonstrate the wisdom of having self-care strategies in place, together with the struggle it takes to keep them going.

In the following chapter I want to offer a plan, a maintenance contract, which will help us implement and then keep the strategies going. Such 'pitstops' are for the purpose of keeping the engine of our bodies well tuned, rather than having to deal with costly blow-outs through neglect and over-heating due to excessive patterns of wear.

Our Lord's example

Since God is the Creator of people, it would be unusual and unexpected if our response to his Son would entail, on our part, actions that would run against either our wellbeing or the spread of the gospel. The gospel needs to be taught and lived out in a fallen world. This means that our bodies do wear out, that gospel ministry will attract opposition, and that even amongst Christians there will be problems that need dealing with. All of these will impinge upon the pastor's health, both of mind and body. It is not surprising, then, that within Scripture itself there are principles that emerge which will contribute to the self-care of pastors. Eight principles in particular will enable Christians, lay and pastors, to follow Jesus in a life of sacrificial service. Each will contribute to self-care and health.

1. The Sabbath rest

Whilst we see Jesus healing on the Sabbath and being very critical of those who made it a burdensome day, he never derides the command to keep it. The main purpose of the Sabbath rest seems to be for physical refreshment. Work is a good and proper task for people, but bodies and minds need refreshment if that creative activity is going to be effective over a sustained period of time. God clearly cared enough to establish the pattern of rest into the Ten Commandments. Physically rested people are better able to remember God, reflect upon his goodness and purposes and then serve others through their work.

Here, of course, the local church pastor, most chaplains and denominational leaders have a problem. On the traditional Sabbath day—Sunday—there are sermons to be preached, services to be conducted and people to be pastored. The feeling that these activities are not really 'work' needs to be dealt with. Put another way, most pastors enjoy what they are doing on Sundays, and have become pastors because they did this 'work' as lay people on Sundays before they were ordained.

There are differences of course. There is the expectation on the pastor to be there and to be up front preaching or leading worship. This means the pastor is 'on duty', and therefore open to requests. One of my problems as a full-time minister has been to accept the fact that work includes non-physical work. Listening, speaking, preparing and spending time with people in a pastoral setting is work that can be emotionally and spiritually draining. Where a pastor is involved in morning and evening services, even though these may be enjoyable and spiritually refreshing, there is a big drain emotionally. The anguish caused by members absent again, the uncertainty caused by one church member's critical and thoughtless response to another, and the desire to welcome the new or less popular church members all combine to promote tiredness. There is little doubt in my mind that we do well to obey the fourth commandment by making certain that we guard our day off and take it regularly. Failure to do so, whilst reflecting a desire to serve the Lord wholeheartedly, will inevitably invite the law of diminishing returns to do its devastating work.

In keeping a Sabbath, we provide a model of obedience for others, and a pattern that will enable ministry to flourish in a refreshing manner. When a self-employed person keeps the Sabbath principle, they act in faith by relying upon God to supply their needs with six days' income rather than seven. So too pastors, who keep the command, are demonstrating faith that God will enable us to complete our work, and indeed to be happy with what has been accomplished, in the six days.

The reality is that in ministry, as in many other relationship-building vocations, more could always be done. Sermons and services could always benefit from more preparation, more people could be followed up and cared for, and more prayer could always be offered for more people. To be able to take a day off for refreshment reveals a faith that God understands, knows and cares about what has been accomplished. The undone can be left with him. The Sabbath in one sense is a reminder that he cares for, the person more than the work they have been called to do. The reality, of course, is that in caring for us, God is caring for our work and those we serve.

The next six principles can be found in chapter ten of Luke's gospel. This is the account of the 72 whom Jesus sent out two by two.

2. Partnership, or network

"Two by two" meant that each disciple had a running partner. Self-care can be doubly effective if others are involved with us in the work of pastoring. This principle, although requiring work to sustain the partnership, can be applied in many different ways. Whether it be team ministries, husband and wife working together, pastors and lay people, pastors who meet regularly with fellow pastors, denominational leaders and pastors or any combination, it is a principle worth pursuing. There is real benefit in working together, for "a threefold cord is not quickly broken" (Eccl 4:12). In "bearing one another's burdens" (Gal 6:2), other people can be very helpful in enabling pastors to keep a clear perspective on things.

3. Realism

Jesus warned that some towns and people would welcome the messengers, but others would not (Luke 10:5-10). This principle must not overthrow our obligation to seek out the lost, to pursue the careless and to work hard at urging the non-believer to repent. However, it is a healthy reminder of the existence of unbelief in the world. Jesus and the apostles applied this principle in their own ministries, because they knew time was limited, and that when God's Spirit creates hunger and thirst for the truth it was wise to keep nurturing that receptive ground. This of course raises the doctrinal questions of human sinfulness and the sovereignty of God in regeneration. The principle is simply an acknowledgment that God gives the growth and brings about conversion, that the pastor is used by God to spread the gospel seed, and by careful nurture, to encourage growth and maturity. This realism will assist greatly in the care of the pastor, especially in churches where there is great pressure applied to measure success in terms of new converts and congregational size.

4. Your names are written in heaven

Allied to the third principle is the fourth one. "Do not rejoice in this, that the spirits are subject to you, but rejoice that your names are written in heaven" (Luke 10:20). This is very important. Often a pastor can be extremely faithful and happy in ministry. Then comparisons are made with other pastors whose work is painted in a more splendid light. Sometimes this comparison is made only by pastors in their own minds, the result of a conference, a book they've read or a passing remark. At other times, it is pointedly made by church members, another pastor or a denominational leader. Whether the comparison is real or imagined, nothing is quite as powerful in throwing pastors off the healthy and happy balance they previously enjoyed in ministry. On the other hand, success can easily breed pride in the mind of the pastor, especially if this is fuelled by flattering commendations of their ministry. This too can throw the pastor off balance, and discontent can creep in. Thoughts like "perhaps a bigger church with a more prominent ministry would be appropriate in my case", will inevitably breed restlessness and affect the pastors equilibrium and joy.

Our Lord's remedy in Luke 10:20 is as powerful as it is simple. In effect, he says, "Do not rejoice in what I have chosen to do through you, but rejoice in what I have done for you in making you my child". Neither a deflated self-image, nor a swollen head, is conducive to personal care and health. Both spell unhappiness for pastors, and if allowed to continue open up a veritable can of worms in terms of unhealthy thoughts and practices. These words of our Lord, it appears to me, were designed to both bring down to earth those tempted to think their performance made them better than others, and to exalt those whose performance may not have been as spectacular as others. The health that flows from the knowledge that who we are as pastors depends primarily upon God's gracious calling of us to be Christians ("your names are written in heaven"), and not from what we achieve in God's work through our ministry, has far reaching benefits. The value of knowing that God has accepted the person whose trust is in Christ, quite independently of anything they have done or will do, provides a solid basis for self-care in ministry.

5. It is God's work

The fifth principle follows naturally from the previous two. In Luke 10:21-22 Jesus makes it plain that God is at work to draw people to himself. This truth is not introduced to run counter to the obvious fact that the gospel needs to be preached, seen in the sending out of the 72, but to emphasize that behind all evangelistic and pastoral activity is God. He is the Great Shepherd and 'Bishop' of the sheep (1 Pet 2:25); the rest of us are employed in his service. J. I. Packer's book *Evangelism and the Sovereignty of God* is most helpful in the application of these doctrines to evangelism and ministry. Many breakdowns in ministry (and watering down of the gospel) have been avoided by pastors who hold in balance the sinfulness of humanity, our free will and the sovereignty of God in conversion. As we would expect, balanced doctrinal views will contribute to balanced pastoral health. He will do his great work through us; all we are called to do is ours.

6. Find hospitality

Both Jesus and his messengers were to find hospitality with people. Here is a sixth principle for self-care. On finding people who welcomed their message of the kingdom, the messengers were to stay in their home and enjoy their hospitality (Luke 10:5-8). This advice was not to encourage laziness through sponging off these "sons of peace", but to enable the gospel to be adequately taught and its implications explained to enquirers and new converts. Such ministry brings health and care for a pastor in a way that hardly anything else can. Nurturing people who are born again, and helping them to come alive to God's promises in both understanding and commitment, involves careful attention and thoughtful conversation, which brings its own joy. The joy might be likened to that of the midwife who shares with the mother the joy of the new baby; or the cook whose long hours over the stove are rewarded by the enthusiastic response of the guests to a meal. Jesus himself spent time with people who were described as his friends. Where care is taken not to allow friendships to cause favours to be given or received, they can and indeed ought to provide a warm context for the care of pastors.

7. Take action in taking time

The seventh and eighth principles are clear. Time for learning requires deliberate action. Good things need to be laid aside at times in order that the better may be pursued. Jesus' words to the unhappy Martha make this principle clear (Luke 10:41-42). There is a real need for pastors, especially those who work alone, to take 'time out' for study and reflection. This needs to be intentional, since a dozen good things will inevitably crowd it out. This is simply the nature of things in Christian ministry. It sometimes strikes me as ironic that we pastors, who expect our church members to be disciplined in marking out time for church, home groups and prayer, are slow to be intentional about marking out and planning times for our own learning and growth.

8. Prayer

The same can be said of prayer, which goes together with learning from God's word. In Luke's Gospel, Jesus' response to his disciples' request to teach them to pray comes immediately after the Mary and Martha incident (Luke 11:1-13). Some pastors are very intentional about their need to make time for regular study and prayer. They have developed a habit of marking in their diary:

- the first hour of every day
- one day every week
- one extra day every month
- and one week of every year

for personal Bible reading, prayer, preparation and evaluation.

Here is a way that denominational leaders and local church members can help their pastors. Just by giving them permission to set aside this time as "work" will be a great encouragement, and in its own way a means of exhorting pastors to care for themselves. There is little doubt that everyone benefits when the pastor is exercising self-care in this intentional way. Denominations often make courses, retreats or training days available. These can set the tone and provide the much-needed stimulus to set up opportunities for refreshment.

Two Australian Christian leaders encouraged me not only to give time, but to adopt a realistic strategy, for keeping prayer and learning high on my agenda. Michael Challen remarked once that he had three desks, "a work desk, a study desk and a prayer desk". It was not because each was a separate activity—indeed they are intertwined and are dependant on each other—but the danger is that each can crowd the other out. Prayer is usually the loser, since as a "secret" activity it is easily neglected. Such realism about Satan's ability to deflect us by any means, whether laziness or earnestness, provides a stimulus to adopt any strategy that would keep distractions away.

On another occasion, Paul Barnett suggested that ministers should read the Bible for three purposes—for personal edification, for preparation and professionally. Once again, it is not to keep these purposes separate, but so that we are well balanced in our study of Scripture. Every time we read the Bible we should be seeking to apply it personally, but the trap is that we can become so busy that we only read it because we need to prepare. Experience has shown me that I must constantly view myself as a human person before I'm a Christian (this will help me to rest and respect my body), and as a Christian before I'm a pastor. As I do this, I will want to sustain myself from God's word and by prayer. When I fail to do this, the pressure and anxieties of ministry can rob me of the basic joy of being a child of God, with my name written in heaven. Reading Scripture, meditating upon it, applying it and praying it, personally keeps the joy and sheer privilege of belonging to the Lord alive.

We must remember that the pace of life was slower in Jesus' day, with no electronic communication to rob us of times of quiet, no electric light or television to rob us of sleep, no motorized transport to rob us of exercise or the opportunities of observing creation first hand.

Perth's top ten

We see a remarkable similarity between what has gone before, and the top ten strategies employed by Perth clergy—strategies that have been demonstrated to work.

1. Maintaining a regular day off.

PRINCIPLES AND STRATEGIES OF SELF-CARE

2. Regular prayer and Bible reading.
3. Pursuit of hobbies and other interests.
4. Physical exercise.
5. Spiritual direction.
6. Wife and family.
7. Support groups.
8. Reading and courses.
9. Regular holidays.
10. Careful use of diary.

We have seen the value of many of these strategies in different parts of the book so far. Each one makes sense in itself, and most need to be included in our self-care plan. Each one needs to be intentionally planned for, and vigorously maintained. Some are easier to maintain than others, and some people are better at keeping them going than others. Certainly local church members and leadership can play a big part in encouraging their pastors. I remember with gratitude my friend Norm, who made sure I played golf with him every fortnight at his club. Most of us need to guard the time necessary for these strategies with our life! And that, in the end, is what is at stake.

Just a few comments regarding these strategies, born of my own experience and from conversation with fellow pastors, may prove helpful.

Regular days off must be guarded and kept. This will be easiest when the congregation knows which day it is. Most church members will help you keep it, since they know its value to you and to them. Why not have a retired pastor on call to take funerals that must take place on your day off? Funerals of church members can usually be arranged for another day. If the day must be intruded upon for some exceptional reason, substitute another that week. Remembering to keep a Sabbath shows that we trust God. Allowing intrusions, no matter how good in themselves, is to say, "God, I can do it alone".

Regular prayer and Bible reading. Remember the words 'Satan trembles when he sees the weakest saint upon his knees'. The reason is simple; this is God's indispensable means of grace for all believers. Planning and guarding our time for these essentials are simply expressions of our love for God. We can relate to God 'on the run', but it must never become a substitute for times set aside where we can drink deeply from the wells of living water he has so graciously provided for us.

The words of the translators of the Authorised Version (1611) have proven true in my own experience day after day (except of course in the days where I've been too rushed to take it in, or even worse when I have neglected reading the word):

> If we be ignorant, they will instruct us
> if we be out of the way, they will bring us home
> if we be out of order, they will reform us
> if in heaviness, they will comfort us
> if dull, quicken us
> if cold, enflame us.

Hobbies and other interests help to refresh us by taking us out of our preoccupation with work. Needless to say, they will need to be pursuits that will not be morally wrong, put us under financial pressure or take us away from our family responsibilities. They may be a regular sporting engagement, bush walk, swim or jog; or an irregular yet consistent interest like painting, woodwork, stamp collecting or cooking. The key is that we have something else in our life that will help relax and refresh us. Something that does not depend upon church cooperation will be therapeutic medicine indeed.

Physical exercise is the one that I find hardest to keep up. At the moment I am facing the realization that I'm not very fit. I joke with my family that "I'm practically fit"—that I can do all I have to do, like mow the lawns. However my body is not in as good a shape as it could be. I discovered this on a day when my arm was sore after bowling a few balls to my son in the park the day before. Something needs to be done. A partner to help, or an appointment at a gym, will often keep us at this one. This is a great ministry church members can have with their pastor. Everybody wins when we are in reasonably good shape. A regular walk with our spouses or children can work wonders for our physical and relational fitness.

Spiritual directors are mentors whose value we saw in the previous chapter on friends. These mentoring kinds of friendships can be maintained by phone, email and letter. Their value is largely in being remembered, and in knowing we have someone with whom we can talk openly and in a friendly fashion.

Wife and family. Many women are in paid Christian ministry, so this could as easily be 'spouse and family'. We saw the importance of these relationships in chapter seven. Partnerships need nurture, and nurture requires time. Time requires planning. We can survive with 'on the run' communication, so long as it doesn't become the habitual norm. When good quantities of time are regularly marked out for our spouses, children and friends, our life and ministry will be the richer.

Support groups are of great value. My research confirmed my experience that voluntary groups of pastors who shared a common view of ministry were valued greatly. Group times which were planned for, were of greatest value to country pastors who often set aside the whole day to travel and attend. Groups that had a focus on sharing for prayer, together with a study of Scripture or a shared pastoral issue, tended to meet the support needs of pastors better than business meetings or those that tended to become joint 'gripe' sessions.

Reading and courses were valued by pastors and congregational leaders alike in my survey. In fact, the lay leaders suggested that if a course related to their pastor's ministry, they would be happy for their pastor to attend for one to two weeks each year (not as annual leave) and that the church should contribute towards the cost. However, many of the ministers didn't feel they could ask either for the time or the money. Here is a real opportunity for local and denominational leaders to proactively inform and encourage their pastor of this provision. Similarly, provision of a book allowance would signal to their pastor affection and permission to keep fresh and up-to-date by reading and training. We would expect our doctor, our accountant and our mechanic to be up-to-date by attending courses and reading—why not our pastors?

Regular holidays, as we have seen earlier, provide ideal uninterrupted times of refreshment for pastors. Pastors living on site would sometimes like to spend a holiday at home. Where this happens, the support of the church in not intruding can speak volumes in terms of support and care. If family finances are tight, the loan of a holiday home by a parishioner or friends could provide a well-needed tonic. If holidays derive from the Old Testament festivals and holy days then we can see the God given nature of these concentrated Sabbaths for our wellbeing and refreshment. We would be wise indeed to take them regularly.

The careful use of your diary really undergirds every strategy we might put in place. It has been quipped that "pastors have an infallible book"—their diary! Since time is limited and opportunities abound, we must all choose to give time to what is important and essential in our lives. Careful use of our diary will not only save us from embarrassing mistakes, but also ensure that essential strategies for self-care actually take place. When this happens we will remain fresh, less likely to burn out and more likely to run well. My car has a maintenance schedule in the owner's manual, and on the top of the windscreen there is a reminder "20,000 km or 23 February". We should be at least as careful with ourselves. I'm a wise person never to forget that the God who made me has built in ways for me to remain fresh for the work he has entrusted to me. We have seen some principles from his Manual. Our diary, like the reminder note from the mechanic, will help ensure that regular servicing keeps me running effectively for as long as possible.

11
Where the rubber hits the road— a maintenance plan

Plans are nothing, planning is everything.
Dwight Eisenhower

Plan your work and work your plan.
Anonymous

I am busy because I am lazy.
Eugene Peterson

The saying "when all is said and done there are more things said than done" is ever so true in my own life. I bring together now a number of issues under the theme of 'planning'. In doing so, I want to acknowledge that it is difficult to break out of a routine long enough to put in place work practices that will contribute to renewal and refreshment. As a practitioner, I am still learning and need much encouragement and many reminders to implement my plans. I know the principles are true, for when tried they have delivered benefits to me which have refreshed me in the work of pastoring which I love. Conversely, I know that when I'm either too lazy or too stubborn to take the time to put them into practice, my work is less effective and I'm less joyful.

Eugene Peterson suggests that "we are busy because we are lazy". He explains:

> I indolently let other people decide what I will do instead of resolutely deciding myself. I let people who do not understand the work of the pastor write the agenda for my day's work because I am too slipshod to write it myself. But these people don't know what a pastor is supposed to do. The pastor is a shadow figure in their minds, a marginal person vaguely connected with matters of God and good will. Anything remotely religious or somehow well-intentioned can be properly assigned to the pastor. Because these assignments to pastoral service are made sincerely, I lazily go along with them (Peterson, p. 140).

A pastor's plan will gain maximum strength and return its full potential if it is worked through with other interested parties. If Dwight Eisenhower was right in suggesting that "plans are nothing, planning is everything", then the pastor who is married is wise to encourage the participation of his or her spouse in the establishment of a maintenance plan. The process will raise many issues, some painful, but the resulting plan will certainly be enhanced by the wisdom and support of the pastor's greatest ally in ministry.

A pastor will also be wise to seek help from local church leaders in the establishment of a maintenance plan. I believe that the best time to involve church leaders is after the plan is formulated. This is a matter of taking the lead in what is essentially a personal plan to exercise ministry fully and faithfully. I share my plan with leaders to inform them, and gain their goodwill and understanding, in such areas as study and rest. Since the time spent in both of these areas can be easily misunderstood, one way of defusing possible misunderstanding is to make known the whole plan. Given my own propensity to lapse into workaholism and a haphazard schedule (both of which are unhelpful to me and the congregation), making myself accountable to one or two leaders is beneficial. Sharing the plan could begin this process.

The other obvious benefit of sharing the plan with church leaders is that they may well have insights from their own experience that will help to make your plan work. This is essential, since there is no benefit in having a plan that proves to be unrealistic and therefore unworkable. On the other hand, the very act of sharing your own plan might well be an example to others who need to take stock, and to plan for their own self-care.

God has already provided his contract or covenant with us. "I will be with you always", was the promise of Jesus to his apostles as they went about their task of disciple-making. Through his Spirit this promise is kept. The apostle Paul makes this clear. (He was writing in a different context, but his words can be applied to the pastor's self-care.)

> Or do you not know that your body is a temple of the Holy Spirit within you, whom you have from God? You are not your own, for you were bought with a price. So glorify God in your body (1 Cor 6:19-20).

As with every aspect of our sanctification, the work of God's Spirit must be matched with our thoughtful obedience. With this in mind, time taken out to plan and maintain ways of using our time, bodies, minds and strength wisely will be well spent.

1. Plan to work

Pastoring is going to involve work; work that is hard and often trying. The nature of the work is such that there will always be more to do, and the results are not immediately evident or encouraging. For any plan to work, it must take into account the word of God, our church program, local context, agreed priorities, the pastor's gifts and time available. To be workable it will need to be specific, in terms of hours to be worked each week and each day. Since the basic structures of most pastoral ministries are daily and weekly, it is a good idea to work around them. How the structure shapes up is individual, and will vary according to personality and responsibilities. For some it will mean a day for this and a day for that. For others the mornings might be spent in prayer, reading and preparation, time after lunch for administration, and the afternoons and selected evenings for visiting or discipling. There is no one structure, and even for each pastor it may change from year to year or even month to month. What is unchangeable is the need to 'plan our work and to work our plan'.

Planning our work will not give us more hours each day, but will ensure that the hours we have available will be used most effectively. A simple example: I find that if I plan my administrative duties so that I can spend 'prime time' (for me, in the early mornings) in preparation of Sunday's sermon, everybody wins. I gain because my thinking is clearer and I am rarely interrupted. Others gain in that my sermon is better, and I can give quality time to people because I am not preoccupied with thoughts and overwhelmed with anxiety about Sunday's sermon. My family gains because they do not have to live with an anxious and preoccupied husband and father still scratching around for a sermon. The parish gains because administration is attended to.

A plan of work is vital if I'm to do anything other than keep the machinery oiled. There is usually enough of the urgent to easily occupy the average pastor. Sunday quickly comes and provides enough to occupy us in the week to come. Very often, important work is left undone through failure to plan. A plan will keep the pastor from despair and panic. Much of a pastor's work is cumulative and brings results slowly, especially at the beginning. The work plan will provide the stimulus to keep going in the face of personal discouragement and opposition from others. Although it can be threatening, it is worth the effort since it causes us to ask questions about intention and goals. It is a way of holding us accountable for what we actually do each day and week. It can also prove to be liberating, with many benefits derived from being purposeful and organized. Whilst being hard to measure, the benefits are easily verifiable in our experience.

2. Plan to plan

Once we decide that our work is best driven by our purposes, and not the urgent demands that can easily fill up a week, we will appreciate the value of planning. But planning takes time! Time is valuable! I am busy!

I cannot afford the time to plan! It becomes a vicious circle. Being in this spiral is like being a pilot in a plane out of control. This is exactly what happens to many of us. We burn out or change planes in the hope that a change will provide an escape. The solution, however, is to take control. Planning is a means of taking control.

What this means is that each year, each month, each week and each day will be useful in direct proportion to the amount of planning we give to it. As an example, would a week of planning at the beginning of each year (or perhaps toward the end of the previous year, prior to annual holidays), a day at the beginning of each month, an hour at the beginning of each week and 15 minutes at the beginning of each day reap rich dividends? Simple arithmetic shows us that this would mean that approximately 28 days would be spent each year in planning. This is the equivalent of 1 hour per day spread over the year. I suspect that more than one hour of each day is lost when there is no real plan in place. The loss takes place through worry and preoccupation with the question, "What will we do next week, next month, next Easter?" A plan to plan is a willingness to take control, to exercise leadership and to be true to goals and ideals rather than be preoccupied with less important, and often trivial, pursuits.

Once again this can be illustrated from the issue of sermon preparation and selection. If deciding a sermon schedule was part of the pre-year preparation week, where the broad themes and passages were established, then countless hours lost through concern over which passage, theme or topic, could be immediately converted into fruitful preparation of the already-decided passage. Putting aside time for planning will always reap benefits for the pastor and congregation. Again, the pastor is much more likely to gain objective help from congregation leaders in determining the sermon program if it is done as part of a planning process, than if it is a week-by-week decision.

A plan to plan is a way of building in times of reflection and assessment, that when combined with prayer, can prove to be beneficial in clarifying the mind, thus establishing a regular means of spiritual health care.

3. Plan to rest

Perhaps this is the key to the work of pastoring. It could be said that the value we give to resting is an indication of the value we give to our work, to our family, to ourselves and to God.

It is very easy for pastors to keep on working. It is very tempting to allow work time to encroach upon days off, family evenings and even holiday times. This is why rest needs to be planned and scheduled. It is easily neglected by pastors, and misunderstood or abused by others.

The significance of rest time is that it is time built into our daily routine (especially nights, Sundays and holy days) by a gracious God, so that we can function effectively in our daily vocations (whatever they be). If the commandment to rest was given originally to ensure that materialistic masters would not extract seven days labour out of their people, it is a weekly reminder to us of God's graciousness and our need to be saved from workaholism where we allow work to master us.

Our plan to rest, while including a commitment to at least one clear day off each week and to regular amounts of good sleep, should also take into account peak times of stress. For example, a members' meeting about a potentially divisive issue can be counted upon to be stressful. It would be wise to plan to follow it with stress free, simple administration rather than other stressful activities such as counselling sessions.

Plans to rest will take into account any desire to exercise or play sport. My own experience has been that if I want to exercise, I need to write it into my diary if it is to continue for more than a few weeks. Many of us see rest as non-productive time, because we are not at our desks or with people. The truth is that it is possibly our most productive time in that it is really a necessary prerequisite to fruitful preparation and leadership. We cannot separate our bodies from our emotional and spiritual lives. Times of rest give opportunity for each aspect of our nature to be fed and nurtured.

4. Plan to study

The need for a pastor to study is likened to exercise and training for the sports person. Study is preparation for ministry. Most churches still call the pastor's office a 'study', which carries with it the implication that our principal means of working is not by officiating (office) but through thoughtful and prayerful study. Pastors tend towards activism, meeting the expectations of church members, and a pietism that downplays systematic study and preparation. These alert us to the importance of planning study time into the weekly schedule. This plan will need to be practical and achievable, and must take into account the ease with which study time can be neglected. Study, because it does not mean visibility for the pastor and is often hard work, needs to be planned. However, for both of these reasons, having the full support of church leadership can be of great value. If leaders value a pastor who spends time in thoughtful study, they will answer others who criticize the pastor who takes study seriously. For example, they will soon recognize and appreciate the link between thoughtful, prayerful study and well thought-out, edifying sermons, and thus provide a reasoned defence to any critics.

Study needs to be planned in three areas.

(a) **Time for personal study.** This will include Bible reading and reflection together with personal reading designed to meet our own spiritual needs. This is best if it is unrelated to a specific teaching/preaching program, thus avoiding the trap of being done because it has to be done. Along with all Christian people, pastors do well to make time to be alone with God, having no other agenda than to meditate upon God's word and to respond in prayer.

(b) **Time for preparation study.** This will be reading specifically for teaching and leadership responsibilities. Each pastor knows the value of this preparation for his or her own edification. Sadly, they also know the struggle to keep this kind of preparation from being mechanical or minimal.

(c) **Time for professional study.** From time to time each pastor will gain benefit from a conference, or the like, with other pastors. Church leaders can provide great stimulation to their pastors by encouraging them to set aside time (not during holidays) for professional study. When the church also makes funds available for this kind of study, the pastor is greatly affirmed. This kind of balanced study schedule will enable, as far as is humanly possible, the ongoing edification of the pastor. It is usually acknowledged that we can only give out what we have received. The plan to study recognizes this truth. In taking steps to build this into the daily, weekly and annual program, you will ensure a healthy growth that will keep up with the demands of pastoring.

5. *Plan to be a spouse and parent*

It is easy to assume that those closest to us will understand our busyness. Next week, next month, next year become excuses, and sadly, reasons for disappointment and disillusionment in our spouse and children. The song 'Cat's in the Cradle' by Harry Chapin is a poignant reminder of how becoming distanced from our loved ones rarely happens in a moment, but bit by bit, gradually, insidiously, over time. Pastors know this only too well. God does not give us immunity from the consequences of neglected duties because we are "doing the Lord's work". Planned time is the only remedy I know to overcome the pain caused by pastors who are too busy for their family.

There is of course no dichotomy between pastoring and giving good time (agreed upon together in advance) to one's family. Since the essence of love is commitment, it is a loving action on the part of pastors to set aside time for their spouse and children. The notion of scheduling time for spouse and family sounds to some unromantic, and not spontaneous enough. However, scheduling of time actually enables spontaneous interaction to take place, because real time is required to allow relaxed relating to occur. Clearly, this will vary according to the ages and number of children, or whether the pastor's spouse works outside the home or church. When families are given good time, they will rarely feel neglected by their pastoral spouse or parent, nor grow to resent the people in the church who have a call on the pastor's time.

6. *Plan to remain humble*

Ministry can sometimes cause a pastor to become proud, and on other occasions to despair. Both have the tendency to move God out of the pastor's focus. Despair can lead to an introspection that will ensure defeat. Pride can easily lead to an arrogance that results in a disregard for other people, and a shallow dependence upon God. Humility is the key.

Just prior to my ordination in 1974, our chaplain at theological college shared a simple three-point saying that sums this up well: "Don't whine, don't shine, don't recline".[1] Humility is best experienced, and is most surely nurtured, through prayer to our heavenly Father. He is the one who can help us keep a clear perspective, keeping us from whining, from needing to shine or from reclining on the job. Since each of these things can easily come upon the pastor, it is good to take large doses of the preventative medicine of a humble reliance upon God.

The attitudes expressed by whining, shining and reclining can easily become habitual. Unhealthy habits are best broken by replacing them with healthy ones. Prayer borne out of humility, being such a health-giving habit, deserves a place in our intentional plans. We can plan to be humble by attending to this vertical aspect of our ministry constantly.

The words of the hymn—take time to be holy, speak oft with thy Lord—remind us of this. The second verse reminds us of the need consciously to make time for prayer:

> Take time to be holy,
> the world rushes on;
> spend much time in secret
> with Jesus alone—
> by looking to Jesus,
> like him thou shalt be!
> Thy friends in thy conduct
> His likeness shall see.

The "world rushes on", and often even prayer seems to be an unnecessary intrusion. There is no doubt that time taken "in secret with Jesus alone" is the primary duty of the pastor, and the essence of faithfulness and healthy nourishment.

The plan shows our determination to make it a reality and thus ensure that we are regular recipients of the divine medicine administered through a humility nourished by prayer.

7. Plan to be accountable

Just as this maintenance plan is best constructed in consultation between pastor and spouse, and shared with leadership, so too is the discipline of accountability. Indeed a maintenance plan and contract, such as the one suggested here, could form the basis for a healthy relationship between the pastor and local or denominational leadership. Most accountability structures within the church sadly (and unnecessarily) resemble emergency room treatment. Big doses of medicine, either of rebuke or encouragement, are dispensed, so it seems, to make up for the neglect of regular support, care and nourishment. Very often the emergency would not have arisen if a healthy accountability relationship were in place. Accountability will be welcomed and cooperated with when the goal is to uphold the welfare of the individual pastor, rather than the name, interests or welfare of the denomination or local church. Here is the challenge to denominational leadership. For this kind of accountability to work, both the initiative and genuine concern for the pastor's well-being must come from the leadership down.

However, pastors can also seek out congregational members and leaders to whom they are accountable. It may be in the area of sermon preparation, or prayer, where a lay person is invited to become a partner. Given the propensity for pastors to become isolated by their success, a friendship structure with either a church member or fellow pastor (or both) could be very therapeutic. Similarly, the pastor who is finding the going very hard and whose work is not deemed to be successful, would find real strength in regular meeting, dialogue and prayer with a fellow pastor to whom he or she is accountable.

The value of accountability is two-fold. First, meetings can easily be crowded out and second, it is easy for isolated or discouraged people to avoid meeting with others. My own experience confirms the value of accountability. On almost every occasion that I have felt discouraged, and therefore unwilling to meet with peers, the accountability factor has forced me to meet, and has brought about a healthy refocussing and encouragement. The analogy of church attendance is helpful. There have been many times since becoming a pastor when I have not really felt like going to church. However, I am accountable at this point. I am expected to be there, and there has never been a time when I have been sorry that I have honoured my commitment. So too with a supportive friend. It does not matter whether that person is a fellow pastor, a member of the congregation, a denominational leader or a group with whom we meet. What matters is that each person is accountable to another; accountable to keep the appointment and accountable for the welfare of each other. Such accountability knows nothing of superiority or inferiority, only mutual concern and trust.

Since this takes time, time out of the urgent, it must be planned. The planning will bear fruit and reap rich dividends for all concerned. An encouraged pastor will result in an encouraging ministry, which will ultimately lead to an encouraged church.

WHERE THE RUBBER HITS THE ROAD: A MAINTENANCE PLAN

A suggested maintenance contract

1. Plan to work

A simple grid like this is helpful in determining a weekly plan.

(a) WEEKLY TIMETABLE

	SUNDAY	MONDAY	TUESDAY	WEDNESDAY	THURSDAY	FRIDAY	SATURDAY
Morning							
Afternoon							
Evening							

(b) DAILY WORKSHEET (example)

DATE	TASKS TO BE DONE
8.00 am	Preparation
9.00	
10.00	
11.00	Phone Calls
12.00	
1.00 pm	Letters
2.00	
3.00	Visits
4.00	
5.00	Other
6.00	
7.00	
8.00	

- Mark in plan from weekly timetable
- Schedule tasks into appropriate time slots or transfer to other days.
- Tick off completed tasks.

2. Plan to plan

- Mark times for forward planning in your yearly planner.
- Mark days (or whatever is appropriate) for monthly planning.
- Mark time for each week's planning in your weekly timetable.
- Mark time for each day's planning in your daily timetable.

3. Plan to rest

- Decide which day(s) off are appropriate each week. Mark these in your weekly timetable.
- Each week, identify and highlight 'high stress' times and schedule 'low stress/recovery' activities to follow.
- Mark in time with your spouse and family (if applicable) to determine appropriate ways of spending time off.

4. Plan to study

- Schedule time for daily personal reading. Mark it in your weekly timetable and diary.
- Schedule time for preparation study. Mark it in your weekly timetable and diary.
- Consider the possibilities, and talk with church leadership about professional study.

5. Plan to be a spouse and a parent

Have you talked with your spouse about expectations in this area? Set some guidelines as to:

- nights at home mid-week
- use of weekend
- presence at children's lessons/sports
- talk to children about activities you can do together
- use your diary—place initials of your spouse and children into times agreed to.

6. Plan to pray

- Find a place to pray where you are not easily interrupted.
- Make time to pray regularly.
- Mark times for prayer into your diary.

7. Plan to be accountable

- Plan to share this contract idea with church leadership, a trusted peer or a fellow Christian.
- Seek to set up a regular meeting time.
- Mark this in your diary.

This contract is a suggested model only. It can be improved upon and tailored to each person's situation and needs. However, it is a start. Since procrastination is an ongoing problem for many, and no-one is demanding that such a contract be produced, this is offered as a catalyst and an encouragement to take self-care seriously.

There is more than one party to a contract. A contract like this may be entered into between the pastor and God. In other words, it will be prepared and carried out thoughtfully and prayerfully. Other witnesses, such as church leaders, spouses or friends, will be real partners in fulfilling the contract. Since good self-care is going to honour God, enhance ministry in the home and church, and bring many benefits to each person whose life is touched by the pastor, it makes good sense for a maintenance contract to be in place. For the same reasons, a pastor's family, friends, peers and leaders can contribute in a powerful way by encouraging its preparation and application.

ENDNOTE

1. It was Dr Bill (W. J.) Dumbrell who shared this with us. These words were also spoken by Bishop Clive Kerle to his graduating class in 1956, and have been exemplified in the lives of both men, who have served God's people in their respective fields, Kerle as a well-loved and respected bishop, and Dumbrell as theological educator, biblical scholar and author.

12
A word for local church members

Obey your leaders and submit to them, for they are keeping watch over your souls, as those who will have to give an account. Let them do this with joy and not with groaning, for that would be of no advantage to you.
Hebrews 13:17

Let the elders who rule well be considered worthy of double honour, especially those who labour in preaching and teaching.
1 Timothy 5:17

One who is taught the word must share all good things with the one who teaches.
Galatians 6:6

The Christian leader's chief occupational hazards are depression and discouragement.
John Stott

My purpose in writing this chapter is to encourage Christian men and women to care for their pastors. However, I am very conscious that many pastors, myself included, have not encouraged or allowed church members to exercise this ministry of loving care.

There is often remarkable goodwill and love built up between church members and their pastors, yet this love is not always understood or received by pastors. At other times, church members are not sure how to convey their appreciation.

My own conviction is that all Christians are ministers, all are priests, all are called and all have a unique work to do for God. I am personally very uneasy about distinctions being made that denigrate one Christian or exalt another. The truth is that we are all 'laity' (people of God) and all 'clergy' (called by God). Yet the Scriptures teach us that some are called to the work of pastor/teacher and positions of leadership described in the interchangeable terms of bishops and elders (Eph 4:11, 1 Tim 3:1-10; Tit 1:5-7; 1 Pet 5:1-4; Acts 20:17-28). Others are called deacons (1 Tim 3:11-13). Some of these people are to be paid for the work they were called, gifted and set apart to do (1 Tim 5:17).

The pastor's role may be different, and whilst this does not convey extra status to the pastor it puts him or her into a position of leadership which entails varied responsibilities. For this reason, respect (1 Thess 5:12), honour (1 Tim 5:17), and even obedience (Heb 13:17) are enjoined upon church members. The dangers of idealization or idolization on the part of church members, or harshness and carelessness on the part of pastors, are kept in check by the reminder that we are all children of God through faith in Christ, all servants, all priests under the Great Shepherd. This balanced reminder could not be clearer than from the pen of the apostle Peter:

> So I exhort the elders among you, as a fellow elder and a witness of the sufferings of Christ, as well as a partaker in the glory that is going to be revealed: shepherd the flock of God that is among you, exercising oversight, not under compulsion, but willingly, as God would have you; not for shameful gain, but eagerly; not domineering over those in your charge, but being examples to the flock. And when the chief Shepherd appears, you will receive the unfading crown of glory (1 Pet 5:1-4).

The balance and corrective of Christlike service is clearly expressed by

A WORD FOR LOCAL CHURCH MEMBERS

Charles Colson:

> The attitude Christ modelled for us is one that should typify every Christian, whether in pulpit or pew, whether leader of a vast organization or solitary prayer warrior. Not puffed up with self-importance but poured out for others (London & Wiseman, 1996, p. 36).

What follows are some thoughts from one who counts it a great joy and privilege to be a pastor-teacher among God's people who gather week by week. However, I still consider myself first and foremost a Christian layman who has enjoyed greatly, indeed been sustained by, the ministry of church members all my life. These words are designed to encourage church members to continue to give support, and pastors to receive it gladly. Some ways of expressing support that are practical, achievable, powerful and effective in sustaining pastors will be suggested.

Recognize our joint standing

The worst possible thing church members can do for pastors is to set us upon a pedestal. It can only lead us to pride or despair—pride if we are tempted to believe that our ordination either adds anything to our status or makes us especially holy; despair because we can neither live up to your expectations or do everything ourselves. We are not (despite the way we sometimes act) omnipotent. There are three words used to describe all Christians in the New Testament that we do well to think about. We are priests, ministers and people.

- As *priests* we are to pray for each other.
- As *ministers* we are to serve one another.
- As *people* who are saints we are to remember each other's weaknesses and status.

All priests

The priesthood of all believers is taught clearly by the apostle Peter:

> As you come to him, a living stone rejected by men but in the sight of God chosen and precious, you yourselves like living stones are

being built up as a spiritual house, to be a holy priesthood, to offer spiritual sacrifices acceptable to God through Jesus Christ ... But you are a chosen race, a royal priesthood, a holy nation, a people for his own possession, that you may proclaim the excellencies of him who called you out of darkness into his marvelous light. Once you were not a people, but now you are God's people; once you had not received mercy, but now you have received mercy (1 Pet 2:4-10).

The Old Testament priesthood, having been fulfilled in Jesus who is our great High Priest, no longer resides in a special tribe of Israel but in all believers. Those Old Testament priests represented God to the people, and the people to God. Jesus fully represents God to us, and makes it possible for us to enter into God's presence. We Christians are able to bring each other to God in prayer. Here is a unique ministry church members have for each other in general, and their pastors in particular. Pastors experience some unique pressures. Consider the following:

- projected anger from someone who is angry with God
- sermons to be prepared each week
- a community that sees pastors as non-productive
- 'behind the back' criticism from congregational members
- the daily anguish of observing the first three responses of the parable of the sower
- personal, family and financial issues
- sadness when members leave
- Satan's desire to deflect and discourage pastors, and divide or deceive congregations
- issues that cannot always be shared with members
- days of great emotional drain such as when a funeral, family counselling, business meeting, and the resignation of a key children's worker all happen within a few short hours.

As priests, all church members can be great sources of encouragement to us when they pray. William Chapman says it plainly: "Church members have much more to do than go to church as curious, idle spectators, to be amused and entertained. It is their business to pray mightily that the Holy Spirit will clothe the preacher and make his words like dynamite".

Should you offer to pray with your pastor? Why not ask? Your pastor may have a group already, but if not, he may value greatly your offer, perhaps with one or two others, to pray regularly. Remember, however, that this is not a time for placing personal demands upon the minister, or for parish chatter, but to pray. Mostly though, this will be a ministry you engage in secretly. Your pastor will know that you are praying for him or her because those who pray convey their loving partnership in countless ways.

Should you ask for specific requests? Yes, this is a good way of expressing your support, but once again don't be put off if your pastor is happy for you to pray generally for leadership, wisdom and especially for Sunday preaching.

All ministers

The ministry of all believers is most clearly taught in Ephesians 4:11-13:

> And he gave the apostles, the prophets, the evangelists, the pastors and teachers, to equip the saints for the work of ministry, for building up the body of Christ, until we all attain to the unity of the faith and of the knowledge of the Son of God, to mature manhood, to the measure of the stature of the fullness of Christ.

The implications are straightforward. We must all seek ways of ministering. The pastor/teacher is to equip God's people for ministry, who should seek help from their pastors so they can be better equipped. When all Christians work in concert, more is achieved more joyfully. The health of the body of believers will, I believe, contribute greatly to the health of the pastor. An example of this healthy growth is seen in Ephesians 4:16:

> [Christ,] from whom the whole body, joined and held together by every joint with which it is equipped, when each part is working properly, makes the body grow so that it builds itself up in love.

The body builds itself when it is healthy. There is no greater gift church members can give to their pastor and one another, than this "each part working properly" growth. Another gift is the way newcomers are welcomed. Often a person comes along to church through the pastor's ministry, only to be frozen out by the church members. Whether intentional or through neglect, this diminishes everyone and brings enormous despair and discouragement to pastors.

All are saints

The New Testament speaks of all Christian people as saints. The word 'saints' speaks of our new status in Christ, and as such is closely linked with justification by faith. Ordinary people (the Greek word is the one from which 'laity' is derived) are called by God (the Greek word is the one from which 'clergy' comes) to become saints. All are laity, and all are clergy, because there is no other basis for standing with God than that of faith in Jesus Christ. So pastors are ordinary people, because they are human, and are ordinary people along with their fellow church members. A number of practical things follow. We have friendship needs. We have cares and worries. We need support. Many years ago I remember reading a letter in a church newspaper headed "whoever heard of the sheep ministering to the shepherd!" It was a sad response to the issue of members ministering to their pastor. For sure, pastors have sometimes been hurt by betrayal of confidence, but so have church members from pastors and one another. That doesn't stop the pursuit of the ideal. Don't excuse our sinful attitudes and behaviour, but do be quick to forgive us and afford us the understanding due to us as fellow forgiven sinners. We have foibles just like you. Remember we are people; it will encourage us, and keep us mindful of and sympathetic to your needs.

But we are also saints *together*. What a joyful privilege this is. Outwardly our church may be small and imperfect in its performance, but in Christ we are accepted by God. Our personalities may differ, even clash, but we are saints together. What a difference this makes to the way we see ourselves and each other. Coupled with this is the observation that every New Testament usage of the word 'saints' is plural. Indeed, of the 62 usages, the only time it is singular it reads "every saint greets you"! The implication is that ordinary people as a called people are a very special people, together.

Recognize the unique hazards of the ministry

It has been said, "in choosing ministry one chooses to command an outpost of unequalled danger which threatens from without and within". Add to this the diminished standing of local church pastors in the community, and the pastor's need for affirmation from the local church becomes obvious. Pastors who have a profile in the community are usually those involved in social service kinds of ministry. Those who work away, year after year, at the word-based ministries of evangelism and preaching are not viewed highly by society. A recently received local government publication, in asking for nominations for awards, listed over 25 different categories of potential recipients; not one included pastors. It is not that we want rewards. My point is simply that since the community won't affirm pastors (we should not expect it to), the local church should be quietly recognizing them. Dr Rowland Croucher, who directs John Mark Ministries, a group dedicated to the support and nurture of ex-pastors, estimates that there are 10,000 remunerated local church pastors in Australia, but there are also 10,000 ex-pastors.

The opportunities for affirmation and encouragement from local church members to their pastor are numerous, and reap huge dividends by maintaining the passion and the hopes of pastors. Perhaps this is why Paul urged the Christians in Thessalonica "to respect those who labour among you and are over you in the Lord and admonish you, and to esteem them very highly in love because of their work" (1 Thess 5:12-13).

The work is important and unique. Eternal destinies and earthly happiness hang in the balance. If the work is important, so too is the worker. Church members can help show appropriate respect, by understanding two ministry hazards. Pastors are what I call "one track people": our work becomes our life. Put another way, our church involvement is both our life and work. Though it is true that every Christian is a minister as they go to their work, working church members have another focus of attention. This focus, their work, is often one that delivers a significant degree of contentment, and contributes to their sense of worth and value. In addition they derive much joy and a sense of value and purpose from Christian ministry in their church.

This needs to be remembered when pastors are not always enthusiastic about sharing some of their core tasks, like preaching, with church members. Given what has been noted above about the priesthood and ministry of all believers, this may not always be a right response, but it needs to be understood by church members. This is especially so in churches where the expectation is that the pastor will preach, and where the pastor feels that this is his principal role, key gift and great joy.

Sometimes the expectations of church members upon paid staff can be very discouraging. I'm at a parish meeting and a new project is keenly endorsed by the meeting. Lasting for six weeks it will involve me, the pastor, for four Wednesday nights. Everyone's assumption is that I will be there playing my part. This is a recipe for discouragement and possible resentment (especially at home since Wednesday is family night). Why? Because of presumption. It makes a world of difference if at the meeting someone asks, "Peter, we would value your presence very much but realize this is not a night you usually work. We would be happy for you to forego your attendance at Tuesday evening meetings if it would mean you could come on Wednesdays, but if you can't change your plans that will be all right as well". Here is a recipe for encouragement. I am now free to give my time should I choose. No longer am I expected to, but I can choose to attend. It makes all the difference not to be presumed upon.

Recognize how resistant churches can be

Few people welcome change. Churches want pastors to lead, but leadership will inevitably involve change. I'm certainly not advocating change for change's sake, nor change because the pastor says we need it. But when change is required, there can be attitudes which will make it easier or more difficult. Attitudes that will prove helpful and encouraging are:

- Speak up publicly or talk about your problems with your pastor personally. Resist building factions and murmuring behind the scenes. Your objections, if valid, will probably be endorsed by others. If not, you may be wrong.
- When a decision is made in concert after thoughtful discussion and prayer but which is different to your way of seeing things, trust the judgement of the body and run with them.
- If time proves you right don't tell them, "I told you so". Grow in grace and put your shoulder to the wheel to get it back on track.
- If time shows they were right and you were wrong, rejoice in the communal wisdom and move on with the change.
- Seek to be positive and look for the strengths and opportunities. Never play the 'devil's advocate', because others may not know whether you are serious or not.
- Be prayerfully excited about change. It shows that your pastor and leaders don't want the church, or the people in the community, to die. Remember that a rut is like a grave; it just has different dimensions!

- Remember that your pastor is probably scared about change as well. But if he is advocating and seeking to bring change about, it's because the consequences of maintaining the status quo are even more frightening.
- Unity of direction and commitment to Jesus and his people are more important than waiting for a uniformity of agreement on every issue or detail. Inertia is always easier than initiative, but it rarely produces results.
- When initiative that leads to change is welcomed, leadership is affirmed. Initiative ignored, discouraged or quenched can only lead to pastors who leave the ministry, go to another church or become stifled and uncreative.

We do well to remember these simple New Testament truths that will help us to be positive and supportive when it comes to change:

- Repentance is fundamental to our relationship with God as individuals and churches. Changes involving churches are ideally a repentance for either doing nothing, or doing wrong things, or doing the right things badly. Leaders are meant to aid this growth. Continuous resistance will amount to disobedience that renders the body ineffective.
- We belong to each other as a body (Rom 12:4-5). Change that is initiated by one member, or seen to be vital by a number of members, will be for everyone's good, but can only happen properly when all are actively engaged.
- Great truths of Scripture regarding doctrine and ethics will never change—they are 'givens'—but the epistles are always calling upon Christians to change in response to these lasting truths. If repentance is vital in leaving wrong practices behind, faith demands that churches explore new and stretching ways of reaching out with the unchanging gospel.

Pastors are called to lead by teaching. This has been described as "comforting the disturbed and disturbing the comfortable". We love to affirm the former, but we also do well to see that once the disturbed are comforted, the only way for our comfort not to degenerate into complacency is for the disturbing gospel call to be relentlessly applied, year in, year out. Encourage pastors who do this by listening, engaging in the process, fine-tuning the needed changes and then running with them to make the changes a living reality.

Recognize the power of thoughtfulness

"Let us *consider* how to stir up one another to love and good works" (Heb 10:24). Congregational growth just doesn't happen. The most natural attitude is for men and women to take each other for granted. Christians are not immune to this poison. We should be considerate towards one another, if for no other reason than that our Lord and Saviour showed and continues to show much gracious consideration to us.

One of the reasons that Christians need to be considerate to each other is that we are such a varied bunch of people whom God lumps together. The place for his grace to be worked out in practice is the local congregation. As we do, we show Christlikeness of attitude (Phil 2:1-10), thus providing a demonstration to the world of Christlike love (John 13:34-35).

As in families where we cannot choose our relatives, we cannot always choose the other members of our church. Here is the opportunity for grace to triumph, but only when we are prepared to be thoughtful. We are to think about how we can stir up one another to love and good deeds. Revolutions of the best kind would take place within our churches if we demonstrated our obedience to this exhortation by giving our energy to this 'prayerful consideration'. Congregations can minister greatly to their pastors by thoughtful displays of appreciation. One minister in Perth said that he kept in his desk drawer an appreciation file where he kept notes and cards from people who had expressed their thanks for his ministry. He went on to say that he got it out from time to time, especially when there was criticism in the air or he felt down about ministry.

H. B. London and Neil B. Wiseman describe how we can come alongside our ministry team "to facilitate spiritual restoration and renewal". They give many practical examples of how church members and local church leaders can affirm their pastors. Though appreciation is best when it comes unrehearsed, they note that people need to be encouraged to build it into their thinking if it is to take place. Why is this? We often take each other for granted. Others genuinely believe that we don't have to give or receive thanks. Some even think that praise is bad to give, feeling that the person praised might get a big head. Others express a false spirituality and piety saying, "We give God thanks for our pastor and would not want him to grow to depend upon our praise, since he knows their praise is from God".

One pastor expressed what I think is a balanced view: "We are not living our days waiting for recognition or to be placed on a high pedestal,

but it is nice and comforting to have a congregation saying 'thank you'".
London and Wiseman comment:

> Businesses, large and small, are discovering how much CEOs, vice presidents, janitors, and all workers in between need the big A's—affirmation, appreciation and admiration ... Affirmation, appreciation, and admiration all work well and are greatly needed in the church. In many congregational settings, insightful lay church leaders wish a "three A's" climate existed or could be cultivated, but they don't know how to start. Others don't miss it because they have never experienced it, but they will like it when they do. Though many people realize how important the three A's are, for some strange reason we find it hard to build strong acceptance and love into our church relationships, especially in communication to spiritual leaders from lay leaders (London and Wiseman, pp. 113-14).

My own experience confirms that words of appreciation provide me with the energy that I need. Indeed, I have found during the past twenty years that God's timing is exquisite in the way he brings these affirming words and actions. That God uses people to build us up is in no way contradictory to our trusting him. Of course at the end of the day, and in the sometimes lonely hours of the ministry, it is God who is the chief sustainer of all Christians. His affirmation is all that matters. Yet since we belong to one another, since we are like running partners, it is hardly surprising that God chooses to bring encouragement to us through fellow believers.

Any talk of "stirring up one another" must be tempered with the words "to love and good works". It is often seen as a mark of Australian masculinity to stir others up by criticisms. Sometimes it is harmless, but it is mostly thoughtless, and is often a way of pulling people down. Many have been hurt by insensitivity, and priceless opportunities for real encouragement are missed as a result.

Pastors are often vulnerable when:

- we are compared to our predecessor
- our church is criticized
- another church's programs are praised in such a way as to put ours in a bad light
- we are blamed for a project that didn't get off the ground.

Affirmation and appreciation are not the same as flattery. As we saw in the chapter on friendships, affirmation does not exclude correction. However, affirmation can properly be given even if we have some differences of opinion. Being a pastor is a little like playing fullback in rugby. Everyone sees your bad moves as well as your good ones. Sadly though, church members sometimes remember only the pastor's bad moves.

The three A's—affirmation, appreciation and admiration—are needed by all Christians, not just between members and their pastor. A way to build up this affirmation reservoir in the church is to start with the pastor. To do so will result in a more encouraged pastor who, together with the church, will be better able to offer affirmation one to the other.

This 'flow-on' principle is expressed in a slightly different context in the Anglican Morning Prayer service. In response to the petition "clothe your ministers with righteousness" the congregation says "and make your chosen people joyful". The "chosen people" who will be joyful are not the ministers (pastors) but the whole people of God, who will benefit greatly from righteous ministers.

London and Wiseman suggest 49 ways church members can show love for their pastors. Let me suggest some that are easily implemented, and which will speak volumes to the hearts of your pastors and (if married) their families.

- Offer thanks quietly when you have been challenged or helped by your pastor's ministry.
- Make a phone call, send a card, a fax, but better still a handwritten letter, conveying thanks, inquiring about how things are going or promising prayer support.
- Remember and celebrate an anniversary of the pastor's ministry.
- Endorse a congregational member to convey thanks at the end of a service.
- Arrange for an appreciation card signed by the congregation to be sent or presented to the pastor.
- Give a book voucher from a local Christian bookshop.
- Arrange with a couple of other families to take the pastor and family out for a meal.
- Subscribe to an encouraging series of tapes.
- Arrange for a family ticket to the zoo.
- Turn up for church with enthusiasm every week.

The apostle Paul said to one group of Christian churches, "One who is taught the word must share all good things with the one who teaches" (Gal 6:6). Two of the most effective "good things" are thankfulness and thoughtfulness, appropriately expressed in words or demonstrated in actions. Everybody wins from this kind of kindness, not least pastors.

Someone told me the story of a pastor who had been taken to a football game. His friend remarked on how well their team was playing. The implication of their conversation was that the church might be doing better if the pastor had as much enthusiasm as one of the key players. The bemused pastor commented, "I would probably play as well as him if I had as many people cheering for me!"

Dr Louis McBurney, who with his wife runs a retreat ministry for pastors and their spouses, comments: "Over twenty years ... we have seen increasing pain and distress among the clergy ... if there is to be healing among the clergy, it must include, in fact begin with, the lay people of the church".

Ian Mears was until recently responsible for in-service training of clergy in Sydney's Anglican Diocese. The ten tips he offers for helping clergy remain fit for ministry provide an ideal catalyst for the supporting of pastors. Church members may find it valuable to work through these tips with one another; certainly, congregational leaders will find them invaluable in their own ministry to their pastor. This will be the topic of the next chapter.

1. Keep your minister focused on gospel work

- The reward of seeing tangible tasks completed, like building and renovation, can be seductive.
- Don't confuse ministry with counselling. A parishioner's problems, whether relational, psychological or physical are easily felt by a compassionate minister.
- Planning and administration are necessary tasks. But meetings can easily chew up time at the expense of front line ministry.
- Encourage your minister in gospel ministry. Remind others to do the same.
- Pray that your minister will be focused on the ministry of the word.
- Offer support when others exert pressure to do 'good' things that aren't central to ministry.

2. Keep your minister devoted

- Your minister needs to maintain a personal faith and devotion to Christ. All Christians need to maintain themselves but the minister is pivotal. If the minister loses faith many become disillusioned.
- Make sure your minister's program allows time for daily Bible study and prayer. From time to time, ask how these are going.
- Share your own experiences to encourage your minister to pray and read God's word.

3. Keep your minister resourced

- Be a generous giver of yourself. Christ has chosen to work through people. He has gifted them for the task. Ministry can suffer from a lack of commitment to fulfil the strategies in hand.
- Encourage others to give not just money, but time, talent and effort.
- Sometimes ministry suffers from unrealistic plans, although often ministers try to do more than they are capable of. Help your minister to be a realistic observer, and to gain confidence to delegate.

4. Help your minister to stay empowered

- Respect your minister's authority. After all, if a doctor says go to hospital, we're inclined to say, 'when?' If an engineer says this bridge is safe, we drive over it in half-tonne cars. But with ministry, everyone feels they know how it should be done.

5. Help your minister to be a visionary

- Let the minister fulfil their primary task: teaching and what Timothy calls 'overseeing'.
- Encourage the congregation and yourself to take on tasks that will free the minister to prepare well and to think ahead. Busyness and pressure undermine many ministers' ability to do these essential tasks.

6. Keep your minister from isolation

- We all need space, but recognize your minister's need for friendship.
- Encourage your minister to maintain friendships 'outside the parish'.

- While the whole church are a family, some will be able to share with each other better than others. Be a good listener but also be trustworthy. You may not be such a confidant (it is not a failing), in which case don't be jealous, and respect the need of your minister to have close friends.

7. Help your minister to be physically fit

- It's important that your minister exercises regularly, eats a balanced diet, and has sufficient sleep.
- Ministers sometimes feel they don't live up to the congregation's expectations. This can drive them away from relaxation and exercise which would have enabled them to be far more efficient.
- Instead of the joke 'ministers only work on Sunday', help your minister to feel that you think they work hard enough.

8. Keep your minister financially secure

- Remember that although the parish provides a home, upon retirement or disablement your minister may have nowhere to live.
- Don't think that it's a good model for your minister to follow unless you're prepared to do the same.
- Financial problems can be a high cause of stress. Be generous to your minister. A minimum stipend is often set by the denomination. Some ministers volunteer to accept less. Many wealthy parishes only offer the minimum stipend.
- If your minister is happy in the job, there will be less temptation to think about previous occupations that paid twice as much.

9. Keep your minister a happy 'family man' (or woman)

- Respect the clergy family's privacy.
- Don't ring on their day off or at unreasonable times.
- Don't use the minister's spouse to lodge your complaints. Spare the children such criticism too.
- Don't burden the minister's spouse with parish gossip.
- Don't put inappropriate expectations on the minister's family. • Encourage and love them.

10. Keep your minister confident

- Australians are great 'knockers'. For the person who lives on the job 24 hours a day, whose parishioners and friends (and enemies) are all in the same circle, being 'brought down to size all the time' undermines ministry.
- Too many clergy have low self-esteem and lack of confidence.
- Help them to see themselves with a sober mind. Offer criticism with respect and humility. A confident person is creative and energetic.

Since it is in everybody's interest to see their pastor affirmed, energetic and balanced in their ministry, these suggestions are well worth pursuing.

13
A word for local church leaders

A congregation cannot be an authentic Christ-centred church when led by persons who have only seniority, talent, money, and social standing. Above all else, the congregational pillar must know Christ.
H. B. LONDON AND NEIL B. WISEMAN

For by the grace given to me I say to everyone among you not to think of himself more highly than he ought to think, but to think with sober judgement, each according to the measure of faith that God has assigned. For as in one body we have many members, and the members do not all have the same function, so we, though many, are one body in Christ, and individually members one of another. Having gifts that differ according to the grace given to us, let us use them.
ROMANS 12:3-6

For the early Christian, 'koinonia' was not the frilly fellowship of church-sponsored bi-weekly outings. It was not tea, biscuits, and sophisticated small talk in the Fellowship Hall after the sermon. It was an unconditional sharing of their lives with the other members of Christ's body.
RONALD SIDER

LOCAL CHURCHES ARE, in reality, outposts of heaven. They are a concrete earthly reminder of the future reality of heaven. On that great Day when the Lord Jesus comes in glory, with all the redeemed who have died to meet those believers who are still alive, church will gather for the first time.

Yet all who will be there will have had some opportunity of gathering in an earthly group, a local church. We catch a glimpse of the wonder of it all, and the resultant responsibility of leaders in these local churches, in the New Testament. Churches have different polities allowed by the New Testament. But that same New Testament sets forth characteristics of church leaders, no matter what style of church government is adopted. The characteristics are essential to what we might call paid and non-paid leaders. Local church leaders can be a source of great encouragement or of despair for pastors. Before suggesting some practical ways church leaders can be a source of encouragement to their pastors (thus contributing greatly to their self-care), we would do well to consider briefly the character traits that Christians in general and leaders in particular ought to be cultivating. By gathering us into local communities, God reminds us that our character growth as disciples of Christ can only be fully developed as we meet and work with each other.

Herein lies the joy and challenge to all Christians. While it may be attractive to be a lone-wolf Christian (one who never meets with others or one who meets without really engaging with others), it is not a real New Testament option for any Christian. As we allow ourselves to be changed through genuine interactions with those who are brothers and sisters, as well as fellow workers, we will be encouraging one another through care and example. When local church leaders and their pastors are clearly striving to allow Christlike character to develop, especially toward one another in their working relationships, work will be a joy rather than a burden.

There are many ways in which Christian character traits could be outlined. What follows is but one suggestion, given in the hope that local church leaders, pastors and church members might use it as a way of testing whether or not their attitudes and actions are a source of encouragement or discouragement to one another. Underpinning them is the conviction that we are all 'works in progress'. None of us has arrived; therefore we need to heed regularly Paul's exhortation to "examine yourselves, to see whether you are in the faith." (2 Cor 13:5); and Peter's gracious promise, "Therefore, brothers, be all the more diligent to make your calling and election sure, for if you practise these qualities you will never fall"(2 Pet 1:10).

Leaders who encourage others

Leaders who encourage their pastors and other believers will be converted people, trusting in Jesus Christ as their saviour and living under his lordship (Rom 10:9-13), who:

Want to see Jesus Christ:

- proclaimed to unbelievers (2 Cor 5:14)
- formed within themselves (Gal 4:19)
- remain the foundation of the church (1 Cor 3:10-11)

Love to:

- pray to the Father (Rom 8:15-17)
- imitate the Son (Phil 2:1-14)
- keep in step with the Spirit (Gal 5:16-26)

See ministry:

- as a gift received from God to be exercised for others without seeking personal kudos or gain (1 Pet 4:10-11)
- to be engaged in joyfully, supported financially and prayed for regularly (Rom 12:3-8)

Are conscious of:

- their accountability to God (Heb 4:13)
- their modelling ministry to others (1 Cor 11:1)
- their part in the team (Eph 4:16)

Are passionate:

- for truth (2 Tim 4:1-5)
- for serving fellow believers (John 13:12-17)
- for winning unbelievers to Christ (2 Cor 5:20-6:2)
- for God's glory (Jude 24-25)

Run the race:

- confidently (Phil 1:3-6)
- seriously (Heb 12:1-3)
- to the end (2 Tim 4:6-8).

Local churches provide us all with room to: observe one another; practice our obedience; find encouragement, rebuke and correction; and receive and offer forgiveness. I can say that I thank God for all the congregational experiences that I have had, both in giving and receiving, which have helped me to find great joy and strength in God. They have come through pastors, members and leaders. Whether they were specific encouragements giving me confidence to try out ministry and endorsing God's call to ordained ministry, or simply the week-by-week experience of caring community and authoritative, relevant teaching, they were all within the context of Christians travelling together.

I saw Christians, young and old, male and female, having different temperaments, seeking to follow Jesus. I knew them well enough to know they weren't perfect, but they were consistent in the way they were humbly seeking to follow Jesus by thoughtfully serving each other. The background noise of these Christian character traits was unmistakably clear, and to my ears, a compelling and attractive tune orchestrated by their common allegiance to Jesus. The heavenly Conductor had well equipped the local leadership to gather the team, discover their gifts and learn to play their part.

Local leaders who are able to lead in ways that enable this complementary partnership to work well offer a great service to pastors. London and Wiseman make this plain with their exhortation addressed to "church pillars":

> Remember as you form your strategy, a minister's greatest satisfaction is to build people up spiritually. Nothing brings a faithful pastor greater fulfilment than knowing lay leaders are growing in their relationship with Jesus Christ and together they are helping to develop the congregation into a genuine New Testament church. Just as marriage partners when they are the best mates possible give incredible gifts to themselves, the commitment to be an authentically Christian change agent becomes a magnificent gift you give yourself and your church. Everyone wins in the process. You delight your pastors heart. You impact others with Christ's love. You

undermine the influence of congregational wounders. And you enrich your walk with God, your attitude, your commitment to Christ; and the joy of your faith helps shape your church, edify it and make your pastor enjoy the excitement of seeing people develop spiritually (London and Wiseman, 1996, p. 141).

Practical matters

There are many practical ways that local church leaders can contribute to their pastor's heart being delighted and excited. These include attending to:

- physical aspects of ministry
- permission given to pursue self-care plans
- planning for mission
- priorities to be pursued
- prayer
- perfectionist expectations
- participation.

Physical

All pastors will need adequate pay, housing, support and study-office facilities. Local church leaders convey real commitment to their pastor if they take the initiative in attending to these essential aspects of ministry. Wisdom would dictate that these matters be dealt with in concert with the pastor. Issues of pay, motor vehicle allowance and housing are very often dealt with by denominational guidelines. Where these are in place, the spirit with which they are followed will speak volumes to the pastor, and especially their spouse. Where the local church is autonomous, not only a willing and generous spirit but a well-articulated and documented schedule should be known by the pastor and leaders.

Sometimes church members and leaders can convey the grudging attitude, "Well, don't forget it's our house. You should be extra grateful for its provision". My wife and I have our house provided for us, and we are grateful, not so much for the house but because we have not been made to feel that we should be grateful! Leaders are able to convey a generous attitude toward their pastor by:

- affirming that "it is your house to live in"
- ensuring that adequate maintenance and repairs are made
- encouraging church members to respect the privacy of the pastor and family
- demonstrating appreciation where improvements or maintenance have been paid for or carried out by the pastor.

Adequate office space should be provided for pastors. Many are finding that it is more helpful to work from the church buildings, rather than from home. Good reasons can be made for this decision, since it allows pastors to have a line of differentiation between work and home. Since many pastors are reticent about asking for anything that is different to their predecessor's way of working, or which will involve the spending of money, it is really the responsibility of local church leadership to take the initiative here. It is best done before a new pastor moves into place, and should also be part of a regular review of the pastor's needs. To have such a review in place speaks volumes about appreciation, and if genuinely done, would lift the heart of every pastor. Good office space will include adequate shelving for books, telephone and other electrical equipment, plus room for counselling and other small meetings. Secretarial support, paid or voluntary, together with adequate equipment and space, are essential if your pastor is to be released to exercise the primary ministries of prayer, pastoring and preparation.

Does your pastor have a budget out of which materials for use in visitation, evangelism, discipling and counselling can be purchased? Ideally every pastor should have a 'minister's discretionary account' from which purchases concerning ministry can be paid. This has the practical effect of saving time from having to go to the treasurer for a cheque, and the associated morale-building consequence of conveying trust and committed partnership by financially resourcing the ministry. Such an amount could be made available by an annual allocation, or monthly top-up to an agreed level. Ministry requires money. Giving your pastor a special ministry account, be it a credit card or cheque account, conveys an important message of partnership that removes one area of potential hurt—that of real or perceived carelessness in the practical resourcing of ministry.

Permission

Local church leaders should talk with their pastor about the importance of regularly:

- taking days off
- working/marking out some evenings to spend at home
- taking annual holidays
- never being expected to return from holidays for a church function or funeral
- attending good in-service training
- spending time every week reading
- having an exercise program
- working to build friendships within and outside the church.

As they do so, church leaders are conveying permission to be intentional about self-care.

Given that there are still unrealistic expectations about how pastors should live, the open discussion initiated by leaders can be wonderfully helpful to pastors. Sometimes pastors won't talk about these matters because church members are quick to point out how a previous pastor never took a day off, or came back from holidays for funerals. To raise the issue can therefore be threatening to the pastor, making him appear lazy. On the other hand, some pastors *are* lazy, and by insisting on rights and not putting themselves out, make it difficult for *conscientious* pastors to articulate their desire to build in self-care strategies. Leaders who take the initiative in addressing these issues will be offering their pastors (and families) a great gift.

When these initiatives are backed by thoughtful expectations and offers they are doubly helpful. If, for example, the suggestion that the local church expected their pastor to engage in appropriate in-service training was backed by the policy that there should be a minimum number of days per year and a specific amount provided from the church budget to cover costs, a strong affirmation is delivered to the pastor. Similarly, if the church gives the pastor a budget for books, clear permission is being given to keep up professional and personal reading. It is not that pastors cannot ask for these things, but when they are given or at least offered, they convey powerfully our appreciation of the nature of pastoral ministry and the pastor's important role. They then become concrete expressions of partnership in the work of ministry.

Planning

Plan your work and work your plan. Local church leaders offer a great gift to their pastors when they:

- make sure that the church has a plan
- convey to the pastor what part in the plan, and the planning process, the pastor has
- encourage the pastor to have their own plan.

It sounds like common sense, yet it doesn't happen often. Why? Churches will only have plans if someone takes the initiative to make it happen. Furthermore, pastors are not always sure whether people want them to lead. So when local leadership takes the initiative in establishing the planning process, pastors at least know that here is a church wanting to be led, and that their contribution in both the process and the delivery is expected and valued. When such a partnership begins through the planning process, hopes are lifted, visions forged, passions fuelled, work shared, goals clarified and strategies put into place.

Since many pastors are discouraged through lack of vision, conflicting expectations, competing agendas and lack of support, this joint planning process offers real hope and contributes to the pastor's effective work and self-care.

Priorities

Once plans are in place, priorities can be established and worked at. Planning that delivers a clear set of priorities takes time. But it is never time wasted, since it frees members and pastors from the tyranny of 'one hundred percentism'. This phrase (coined by Dr D. B. Knox, and seen by him to be Anglicanism's greatest temptation) describes the tendency of churches and pastors to feel they have to have a go at everything.

Clearly articulated priorities enable pastors and churches to concentrate on what can be achieved given the time and people resources and gifts presently available. Pastors whose leaders give clear church priorities, and who themselves have a clear set of their own complementary and mutually agreed priorities, are given a recipe for healthy self-care. Such pastors are in a position to politely but firmly say no to suggestions from local members, or even denominational leaders, and to work without guilt at the agreed priority projects. Furthermore, local church leaders will be in a position, if required, to defend their pastor from criticism for not attending to every possible good work. Every such defence gives an opportunity to articulate the priorities of the church, and demonstrate that the church and pastor are attempting to lead together, and do have agreed priorities.

Prayer

Scripture abounds with examples of people praying, and exhortations to prayer. We are privileged, as John White says, to "eavesdrop on some of the most significant prayers in human history". These people at prayer teach us about God, and encourage us to be people at prayer. The exhortations are similar to the examples, but also teach us that we have the privilege and obligation to pray for one another. The fellowship of believers in Jerusalem who formed the early church following Pentecost, devoted themselves to prayer (Acts 2:42). The apostle Paul was always praying for the churches. He often told them what he was praying, and regularly exhorted believers to be praying for one another. Two typical exhortations are: "Do not be anxious about anything, but in everything by prayer and supplication with thanksgiving let your requests be made known to God" (Phil 4:6), and "Continue steadfastly in prayer, being watchful in it with thanksgiving" (Col 4:2).

Since prayer is a gift from God to his people in which we recognize our weaknesses and his gracious power, we do well to be devoted and systematic in presenting our requests to God. Ephesians 6:10-20 reminds us that Christian faithfulness must take place in the context of supernatural and devilish opposition. All the weapons that God so graciously provides for his children are to be actively and prayerfully taken up. Wesley's hymn emphasizes the fundamental place prayer has in this warfare if we are to stand firm.

> Stand then in his great might
> with all his strength endued;
> and take, to arm you for the fight,
> the panoply of God:
> to keep your armour bright,
> attend with constant care,

still walking in your Captain's sight
and watching unto prayer.

In encouraging us to be "praying at all times in the Spirit, with all prayer and supplication. To that end keep alert with all perseverance, making supplication for all the saints" (Eph. 6:10), Paul alerts us to the ministry of prayer which we can exercise on each other's behalf.

When local church leaders follow this injunction by praying regularly for their pastors, they will be exercising a most valuable ministry. Since God will answer these prayers to stand firm (Eph 6:10-18), to be given the right words and then to fearlessly proclaim them (Eph 6:19-20), the pastor will be uniquely cared for.

There are different ways in which leaders can exercise this ministry of prayer for their pastors:

- private prayers
- praying with the pastor
- encouraging small groups to include prayers for pastors
- encourage those who lead public prayer to pray for their pastor.

When pastors know that their people are praying for them, they are greatly encouraged. Since the apostle told congregations he was praying for them, it is clearly right for Christians to tell each other that they are praying for one another.

Joyce Baldwin puts well the necessity of prayer when she comments: "Divine decree or no, the Scriptures never support the idea that God's purpose will be accomplished irrespective of the prayers of his people".

Leaders who thoughtfully pray for their pastors, and encourage others to do so, are clearly engaged in a great ministry. A ministry that is seeking God's blessing and guidance for their pastor will bring to their pastors great encouragement and thus contribute to their pastoral care in a unique way.

Perfectionist expectations

Both pastors and churches often have expectations of themselves and of each other which can be described as perfectionist. They expect themselves and one another to be perfect. The truth of the matter is that the perfect pastor and the perfect church do not exist. When a pastor believes that it is his or her task to do everything perfectly, everyone is in trouble. It is made doubly difficult when the church expects their pastor to be perfect.

The local leader is in the unique position of knowing the congregation with all its strengths and weaknesses, and is able to observe the pastor's strong and weak points. In this sense, the leader can help both pastors and churches remain realistic by accepting their faults and rejoicing in each other's strengths.

Thoughtful leaders exercise an important ministry every time they encourage their pastor to:

- remember he or she need not attempt everything
- spend adequate time with spouse and family
- say no to unreasonable requests
- focus energies on agreed priorities
- hold members accountable
- see that failure is neither futile nor final
- remember the pressures members face;

and encourage their church to:

- remember that their pastor has limited time
- remember that they have faults
- confront problems and problem people
- question those who want to control the pastor
- work with their pastor
- refuse to use the pastor's spouse as a messenger to their pastor
- have realistic expectations of the pastor's children.

Church leaders are in a position to help interpret and explain the pastor to people, and people to the pastor. When understanding grows, mutual appreciation grows. This in turn can create a situation where unrealistically high expectations are not easily superimposed on one or the other. When expectations are earthed in mutual respect and a genuine understanding of each other's strengths and weaknesses, a more healthy common life will follow. In a sense, church leaders become brokers of mutual understanding when they pursue this kind of leadership. In Jesus' words, they become "peacemakers" who bring blessing to themselves, their pastor and the church. James expresses this ministry in this way: "a harvest of righteousness is sown in peace by those who make peace" (Jas 3:18).

There is one specific area, that of closing a ministry, where local leaders can provide much encouragement to pastors. This is especially so when the expectations of neither church nor pastor have been met. Sometimes flattering words are spoken which neither address reality, nor the hearts of all concerned. Wise local leaders will do well to make sure that an appropriate opportunity is given, first in private with the church leadership, and then in public with the church, for realistic farewells to be exchanged. Realism is required so that disappointments can be spoken about, if either party needs to do so. This will enable gratitude to be expressed for what has been achieved in the same context as the difficulties are acknowledged. Such a farewell, like a funeral, can enable the loss process to proceed, and the raising of difficulties becomes an opportunity for perfectionist tendencies to be addressed. This will be essential for the pastor as he or she goes elsewhere, and for the church, lest the same difficulties emerge to bruise or crush a new pastor. "Speaking the truth in love" is wise advice indeed.

Participation

Recently, I heard that a person is considered a regular churchgoer in the USA if they attend one out of every three weeks. In the UK it was said that church ministry was greatly hampered, especially in spring and summer, by the numbers of church members who regularly go away for weekends. Empty seats are a great discouragement to pastor and people alike. A fellow pastor told me of the man who told him that he wouldn't be in church next Sunday but would be there in spirit. My friend replied, "I'd rather have 10 bodies than 100 spirits any day!"

Leaders provide enormous doses of strength and health-giving vitality to their pastors by:

- being there
- being there awake and alert
- being there awake and alert to ministry opportunities.

Participation is an expression of partnership, enthusiasm and membership. When demonstrated by leaders, it shows the pastor that this church is being led by leaders who want it to go somewhere. It is not about maintenance, but about maturing. The pastor knows that there is a team of leaders who are keen to minister. One of the big factors that leads to discouragement for pastors is the sense of being alone, of everything depending upon the pastor and of having to push to get things done. Participation from leaders is a sure reminder of a team at work, who want to share the load so that the work can be completed. Participation that expresses itself publicly by turning up to church, prayer meetings or working bees, and privately by being available and dependable in following people up or attending to ministry responsibilities, will deliver to pastors the health-giving message: we care, we share, we are a team.

London and Wiseman issue a challenge to local church leadership because they want to affirm the crucial role pastors have in the church, the community and God's purpose:

> Without spiritually committed, courageous pastors, the contemporary church will get steadily worse and society will become more corrupt. Pastors are not the only persons needed for this war, but it cannot be won without them. When pastors are in jeopardy, the church could lose the war ... Try in every feasible way to renew the spirit and stimulate your pastor's courage.

14
A word for denominational leaders

The church Christ is building is his:
It does not belong to the members; they belong to him.
It does not belong to the officers; they belong to him.
It does not belong to the pastor; the pastor belongs to him.
It does not belong to a hierarchy, the hierarchy belongs to him.
... Wherever the church is, it belongs to Jesus Christ alone.
RICHARD HALVERSEN

Jesus cleansed the meaning of greatness when he said,
"The greatest among you shall be the servant of all".
No longer is the man great who has a great number of
servants, but the man is great who serves the greatest number.
STANLEY JONES

THROUGHOUT THE WORLD, we are seeing evidence of clergy in a crisis of stress. Clearly, denominational leaders have an important part to play in the ongoing health of their front line troops—local church pastors and chaplains in specialized ministries.

The comments that follow come from my own observations as one who has worked for twenty-five years in the Anglican church. I am mindful of some differences in the precise nature of problems of pastoral care for pastors across the different denominational and independent church structures. However, as one who has enjoyed close friendships and fellowship with pastors across these different groupings, I know that the issues, and more significantly the means of encouragement for pastors, are substantially the same.[1]

Recognize the primacy of the local church

Local churches are the place where the church is visible and functional. Local assemblies constitute the church. Whatever else denominations or associations of churches are, they are a fellowship where representatives of local churches can meet and offer order for different aspects of their life together. The week-by-week meetings of local Christians are the place where the Great Commandment, of serving love between Christians, can be visible for all to experience and observe. It is also the place from which the Great Commission can be obeyed, supported and its resultant disciples nurtured. The rubber hits the road in local church congregations. Not only is it the place where Christians meet each other, and where Christians are trained to meet the world, but where the world can meet Christ. It is an exciting but difficult place to be. Pastors would want their denominational leaders to understand the difference between 'at the top' and 'down at the grass roots' leadership. Denominational leaders often have paid staff, and may have an authority over pastors akin to employer/employee. Local churches may have some paid staff but membership is voluntary. This is not to say that voluntary members do not display an enormous commitment. Indeed, in my experience, this commitment often shames and outstrips the commitment of us pastors. Local church pastors appreciate it greatly when denominational leaders remember the fundamental difference between leading a local church and a denomination or agency. London and Wiseman make the suggestion:

... have all ecclesiastical leaders spend a minimum of two weeks each year in a local church with an average attendance of fewer than 100. Let them experience first hand the pressures and possibilities pastors continually face. In such a one-on-one relationship, every pastor would get to see the heart of his leaders, and every official would feel the pulse of a local congregation (London and Wiseman, 1996, p. 196).

Wise pastors spend time with their members, learning of the difficulties and joys in their day-to-day lives so as to minister more effectively. In the same way, wise leaders will spend time with their 'pastors on the ground' so that they keep in touch with the real issues of local church ministry. An uninterrupted day once or twice a year is seen by many pastors as being of much greater value than an occasional hurried phone call. When denominational leaders strive to balance the organizational demands of their job with the needs of their pastors for affirmation and encouragement, the whole church is strengthened.

The main thing local church pastors want to know is that their work is valued. Actions speak louder than words. If denominational leaders are always away at denominational conferences, or unavailable because of denominational board meetings, the signal is clear—the denomination takes precedence over the local. Of course denominational planning needs to take place, and denominational leaders themselves need to be envisioned, but it all comes back to the primacy of the local church. The great joys of local church pastoring are watching people come to Christ, and then to share in the process of growing new Christians into disciples. When denominational leaders' time is taken up with committees and conferences, they are robbed of the joys of experiencing the real action of ministry: the new birth and discipling process.

Understanding the middle man

Pastors often feel pressed to meet the demands of both denominational and local church leadership. They are like the meat in the sandwich. This can be a difficult position to be in, especially if the denominational leadership exercises influence in local church appointments. Each party in this equation does well to remember and respect the other. Pastors want their leaders in denominational positions to remember this when planning, implementing and monitoring policies. William Hulme highlights the effect the introduction of new programs can have on pastors:

> Depending on their morale at the moment, clergy may see in these headquarters-initiated programs just one more standard to which they must measure up. Often such new programs are introduced at denominational clergy conferences; one of my clergy friends therefore expressed reluctance to attend such gatherings. "It's all I can do to keep up with what I'm doing", he said. "These new programs are saying that I'm not doing enough, or at least not doing it well enough". He was letting the new ways of doing things exacerbate his already nagging self-judgement (Hulme, p. 9).

Denominational leaders have a responsibility to provide resources and, even more importantly, to offer visionary leadership. If such leadership has the potential to crush the already-discouraged pastor, or imply to the hard working effective pastor that his or her efforts are insufficient or not good enough, how can they lead? When pastors understand that their leaders value them, and by their efforts at meaningful listening know that they are understood, plans will be received without despair. In other words, up-front leadership is never enough; it is only half of the equation. Up-front leadership can distance the leader from local needs and conditions, giving the impression of disinterest. Side-by-side leadership, on the other hand, is one of true partnership. When this is taken seriously, the up-front exhortations and program initiatives will be much more welcome, coming from leaders who are demonstrating partnership in ministry. Side-by-side ministry happens:

- through consultation in the planning process (and even more important consultation as to what programs are needed by the local church)
- regular phone calls just to 'see how you're going'
- friendship visits without any set agenda.

Affirmation

Affirmation tops the list of London and Wiseman's suggestions for how denominations or associations of churches can support local church pastors.

"Affirm a minister's importance as a member of the pastoral team. The attitude should be 'How can our association of churches or our denomination enable the called, anointed servant of the church to do front-line ministry?" (London and Wiseman, 1996, pp. 194-5). Not surprisingly, it dominated the thoughts of my colleagues when we spoke of this issue. All of us need to be wanted and appreciated. Most of us will go the 'extra mile' for the people we know respect and value us and the work we are engaged in. On the other hand, if people don't care about what we do and show no interest in us, it is easy for us to allow the natural tendency to discouragement to grow into the terrible twins of despair and depression. Affirmation must not be confused with insincere flattery.

My own observation is that the affirmation pastors need most is that of being remembered. This is especially powerful when it comes from denominational leaders, from those set in a place of authority over us in the Lord. The impact of a phone call, a note of encouragement or a visit with no axe to grind, no issue to be pursued and no other agenda in mind can be a very powerful and effective means of exercising pastoral care. When done, it proves not only to be a wonderful tonic to the pastor, but also a timely model that will hopefully encourage the pastor in his or her ministry to others.

Local church ministry is surely the most strategic and difficult ministry around. It is a noble task. But given the multiple responsibilities of a typical one-pastor church, the nobility of the task can be lost, clouded over by the multiplicity of tasks and expectations. The denominational leader is uniquely placed to affirm pastors by consistently affirming their work. The apostle did this very clearly by his direct affirmation: "The saying is trustworthy: If anyone aspires to the office of overseer, he desires a noble task" (1 Tim 3:1). Indeed Paul models this affirmation every time he mentions and highlights his large group of fellow workers (e.g. Rom 16). Of course, it is our own responsibility as pastors to make sure that we have in place ways that affirm the uniqueness of our role and ministry. This comes primarily through reading of Scripture, remembering our ordination (in whatever form that took), and the friendship of supportive peers and fellow Christians. However, denominational leaders can play a strategic and powerful role in our care by honest affirmation. This affirmation derives its power from the knowledge that someone has remembered and taken the time to inquire. It is sad when inquiries come only after a problem has been reported. When these checking up inquiries are the only means of contact, resentment is understandable and attempts at pastoral care prove counter-productive.

It has been suggested that listening is the greatest gift we can offer one another. Most of us know that we have problems to face, and usually know what is required to either solve or live with them. What we want is someone to listen to us, someone who will affirm us, redirect us, and offer us wisdom, but mostly just understand us. "A problem shared is a problem halved", may sound simplistic but it is true; and it can become a problem doubled by adding "no-one cares about me" to the original difficulty! No-one expects denominational leaders to anticipate or know about all our specific problems, but what I think is a reasonable expectation is for health-promoting 'listening posts' to be in place. This surely is a responsibility for denominational leaders to exercise. Clearly the denominational leader is not alone in this health strategy. Local church leaders and members all have a significant and primary part to play in this affirmation through listening. A wise denominational leader will know those who have, and those who don't have, support from these means. By their own ministry and by encouraging networking with other groups or pastors, these needs can in time hopefully be met. Of course we pastors must want to be helped and ministered to! Complaint is always unfair where we maintain an arms-length attitude to our leaders. When denominational leaders take the initiative in setting up listening times, such as a known open door policy supplemented by personal visits and lunch dates, a very powerful preventative program that delivers much health to pastors is in place. When listened to, lone church pastors will feel affirmed knowing:

- I have been remembered
- I am more important than paperwork and denominational programs
- Here is someone who understands me, or at least is seeking to.

This ministry of affirmation, like all ministry, is a two-way street. When it is an intentional and regular part of a denominational leader's weekly schedule, we should not be surprised if they too are affirmed. Criticism, so easily levelled toward denominational leaders, is much more difficult, and therefore much less likely, between listening friends who are seeking to understand and support one another, than unknown and distant officials. The question 'who pastors the denominational leaders?' is easily dealt with when they are pastoring the troops in the field. The troops will encourage the leaders best when they are viewed as fellow leaders, and are encouraged by leadership characterized by mutual submission and service. In this way, each has the privilege of affirming the other in the noble tasks to which they have both been called.

Pastor of the pastors

In episcopal systems (such as Anglicanism) with a well-developed leadership structure, the long held view is that the bishop is the pastors' pastor. Just how effective this system can be will probably be determined by the influence the denominational leader has, or is perceived to have, in future appointments. London and Wiseman are clear in expressing this potential difficulty when they say:

> Develop a pastor for pastors. This person should have no administrative or credentialling authority over ministers. However caring ecclesiastical leaders may be, it is difficult for a pastor to discuss personal issues with one who has authority over future placement (London and Wiseman, 1996, p. 195).

The Churches of Christ in Perth have a pastor of the pastors who has no administrative influence in their denomination. Some Anglican Dioceses have experienced clergy in similar positions, available for pastoral care but removed from the normal 'hierarchy'. Does this mean that those who are the official leaders can exercise no real pastoral care of pastors? In my judgement, officials can exercise a very powerful ministry of affirmation precisely because they are the denominational leaders. There is need for the realism expressed by London & Wiseman; the difficulty, however, can be minimized where the placement system is not dominated by the denominational leaders or officials. Where the local church has either equal representation, or the principal power of calling pastors, or if there is a clear conviction amongst pastors that personal issues will remain confidential and not used as barriers to future placements, the difficulty decreases.

Denominational leaders prove themselves to be pastors to the pastors when they set up opportunities (as outlined previously) to convey affirmation and then work at encouragement. Two very practical matters make for encouragement and are therefore highly valued by pastors. The first is prayer. Prayer offered with us is a timely reminder that we are both involved in God's work. Apart from the efficacy of joint prayer, a modelling of humility and a reminder of God's rich resources and promises are conveyed through prayer. Prayer takes time, and where it is not hurried or 'tacked on', tells us that we are important to the leader and reminds us that we are important to God. When prayer is offered together, the promise "I'll pray for you" is more likely to be believed and therefore appreciated.

Appreciation is always a tonic for pastors. In marriage, it has been suggested that where there is a proportion of five parts appreciation to one part criticism the relationship will last, indeed grow. Applying this to pastors and their leaders, we are reminded that both appreciation and criticism are important. We have seen the value of rebuke in the chapter on friends. One of the reasons for having a denominational or associational leadership is to provide accountability. But when will criticism be best received? Surely in the context of a valued relationship where affirmation and appreciation are already firmly in place. Larry Crabb makes this point very clearly in his book *Encouragement: The Key to Caring*. I am much more likely to receive, and then respond, to godly admonition when it comes to me from someone who has clearly demonstrated that they are for me as a person.

This is where the hours invested by denominational leaders in the ministry of affirmation and appreciation, through the listening times during visits, over meals, and phone calls, will bear fruit. When and if correction needs to be made, it is likely to be heard.

All of this is asking much of denominational leaders, who are often pushed for time. Although most leaders want to pastor their pastors, it is often easier to be involved in national and international meetings and local committees rather than in ministry to those working at the coalface. Visibility is higher, and it looks more important, but it is rarely as valuable or important to the real church. The local church must, however, accept some responsibility for allowing it all to happen. We create boards, and we feel that it is important to be represented on national and international bodies. The whole thing grows and develops a life of its own which can, unchecked, survive without any real reference to local churches.

Somewhere, sometime, the vicious cycle of exhausted and absent denominational officials, wanting to, but unable to, invest the time or spiritual energy in ministry to local church pastors must be broken. My suggestion for my own denomination is that a two-year test be conducted along the following lines. All meetings involving nation-wide ministry would be held during a single two-week jamboree in one city. At a Diocesan level, no leader would be allowed to spend more than one evening and one two-hour daytime period each fortnight with meetings that are not connected to local church ministry.

The time, energy and more importantly the goodwill released by such a commitment to pastoring local church minsters would be enormous and possibly revolutionary. Without having done any research into it, my feeling is that the fastest growing parts of the Anglican Communion, namely Africa and Asia, do not put as much time into centralized meetings. The energies of all leaders are focussed where the churches are growing at the local level.

Pastors want the support and encouragement that their denominational leaders can give. To do so, denominational leaders need to spend time focussed on the local church task. Rested, rather than rushed, leadership is in a position to effectively lead. Tired leadership tends to become faddish, picking up ideas and programs from elsewhere with the assumption that they will be a cure-all solution for us. Local church pastors want their denominational leaders to do less and to do it better. To consult from the ground up. To sit beside and to listen. To pray with and to encourage. To rejoice in triumphs and to walk us through our failures. Yes, we want and certainly need our denominational leaders to place the big picture before us and to admonish us for small dreams, to rebuke us when lazy and to help us grow. The exhortations to grow and to lift our game will be appreciated and welcomed, in direct proportion to the amount of time thoughtfully invested in listening, understanding and affirming us in personal and quietly caring ministry. This is the way of the pastor. Leading, but leading gently; leading by walking beside; as much involved in the process as the plan.

Resourced

Denominational leaders will do a great work for their pastors if they are able to make sure they know what resources are needed for their work. No one person can know or provide all the resources that are available today. The problem is not a shortage, but an overload of resources. Imposed resources are not what is required, any more than suggestions that a particular resource will solve all one's problems. Gatherings with displays, review sheets setting out different materials, or reviews from pastors who have tried different resources will all prove helpful. The denominational leader who acts as a catalyst for such gatherings is a great encourager, especially where a wide variety of resources is reviewed. Here is a way for the average local pastor, who will probably never be asked to speak at the conference or preach at the ordination, to be affirmed. Each person has ideas, and more importantly experience, to contribute to the whole.

Encouragement of pastors of small congregations

Christian culture is almost the same as secular culture in the way we promote the pastors of large churches as the successful pastors. Clearly, gifted pastors who have demonstrated faithfulness and have been able under God to lead churches to real growth need to be heard. Wisdom dictates that we can learn from those who have succeeded in planting new churches that continue to grow. However, many pastors, equally faithful in their work, do not see the church they pastor grow in a spectacular way, nor become as large. Yet they have many insights to share. Denominational leaders need to remember to encourage these faithful ministers of the gospel. We do well to remember that even in the USA where there are a number of very large churches, 75% of churches have fewer than 80 members. What is more, 80% of missionary and ministry candidates come from these small churches.

Church growth writers or speakers who fail to recognize these facts only discourage many local church pastors. This of course is very unfortunate because there are many helpful insights to be found in church growth principles.

Denominational leadership will bring encouragement if all faithful pastors are given opportunities to share their insights. This is part of building a team, and will mean that the busy are not overburdened, the successful not tempted to pride, and the faithful plodder encouraged. Such encouragement will make it possible for gifts to be discovered and partnerships developed. Certainly it takes wisdom, a wisdom that will follow intentional listening and pastoral care. However, I suggest that it will result in invigorated pastors who know they are appreciated.

Provide opportunities for development

One place where visiting speakers and local pastors alike can minister to pastors is in ministry development opportunities. When these are initiated or developed by pastors themselves, they will be particularly effective. Most denominations have their own annual conferences, in-service training and retreat opportunities, which seek to provide times for refreshment, training and encouragement through fellowship. Denominational leaders can help pastors by encouraging church boards to set aside funds to make it possible for their ministers to attend. Where local churches cannot afford this, London and Wiseman suggest that denominational leaders "encourage larger churches to give scholarships to minsters serving churches with limited financial resources" (London and Wiseman, 1996, p. 195).

Needless to say, if denominational leaders want these conferences and training days to be taken seriously, they also need to attend and be seen to be giving their enthusiastic support.

My own observation of clergy conferences and small groups has been that they are less effective in providing encouragement when they become issue based, involving the sharing of personal experiences or the "way I grew my church" type presentations. On the other hand, where the focus has been on either exposition of Scripture or the application of Scripture to the big pastoral issues, more encouragement and support has accrued. I think this is because the latter approaches tend to help us firstly lift our vision away from our own immediate concerns, and secondly model to us the principal means of grace by which God chooses to nourish and give health to his people. The personal issues and experiences, triumphs and hardships can then be discussed, shared, prayed over and worked through with those from the larger group whom we know well and trust. Denominational leaders often need to take the initiative at this point after consulting widely, since it is easy for calls for 'relevance' to dominate, and the consequent tendency for issues relevant only to a few to set the agenda.

The permission given to take 'time out' for personal growth together by attending such conferences will encourage clergy growth and well-being. Denominational leaders who work at providing this ministry will be making a great contribution to pastors, if for no other reason than reminding us that we are disciples who need to remain fresh if we are to grow.

Remuneration

Our Lord's word "the worker deserves his wages" is affirmed by the apostle regularly. Denominational leaders and leaders of independent churches do well to remember these exhortations.

London and Wiseman put this obligation clearly when they say to leaders:

> Establish a plan of minimum compensation and insurance benefits for pastoral families. Such benefits could be classified as full support or bi-vocational. No church should expect to have a full-time pastor when it does not pay a minimum full-time salary. Neither should a pastor with small pastoral responsibilities serving in a bi-vocational role expect full-time support (London and Wiseman, 1996, p. 195).

Remuneration should be adequate and provide sufficiently for the pastor to house, clothe, feed, educate and care for his or her family and provide transport for work. I understand that in many independent churches this can be a real difficulty. The withholding of money should never be a method of removing a pastor. This should be handled in other ways which have been agreed to prior to appointment.

The reason for adequate compensation, apart from obedience to the New Testament injunctions, is to enable the pastor to minister without anxiety. Where anxiety is allowed to develop through carelessness over finances, the pastor and their family can easily be overcome by worry and a sense of being unappreciated. Appreciation shown by adequate compensation will demonstrate itself in a returned joyful sacrifice. Denominational leaders who attend to this basic compensation, and make provision for financial help in emergency situations, refresh the hearts of their pastors and their families.

Fair hearing

Closely related to the question of adequate remuneration is the issue of disagreements and disputes. Once again, London and Wiseman make the point clearly:

> Provide a system of due process and interim compensation for pastors whom churches abuse. Pastors are too often cast aside at the will of a few malcontents and then viewed as suspect for the

remainder of their ministry. Congregations who mistreat a pastor should be censured by the larger church body and held financially liable until the wronged pastor can be reassigned. On the other hand, a plan is also needed to be sure a pastor is faithful in doing ministry—no slothful servants should be tolerated in the saviour's service (London and Wiseman, 1996, p. 195).

Denominational leaders have a responsible part to play when disputes arise concerning the pastor's competency. As suggested by London and Wiseman, decisions made affect pastors for a long time. For pastors who live in church-provided homes, and who do not own a home, the stakes are high. Add to this the disruption to children's education if moving is required, and denominational and local leaders have an important responsibility to discharge.

Where denominational leaders have failed to spend time with pastors in general care, the local church situation is unlikely to be understood. Sometimes local churches need a real shake up. Outward respectability can conceal very real problems. Genuine gospel ministry is sometimes offensive to those who do not want their comfortable complacency challenged. Denominational leaders do everyone a service when they listen well and listen long before taking the side of either pastor or the congregation. Pastors who have become indolent, abusive, unfaithful to our received traditions and the Christian creeds, or immoral, need censure, discipline and sometimes even dismissal. Of that there is no dispute. But this must be handled fairly. One important scriptural guideline is: "Do not admit a charge against an elder except on the evidence of two or three witnesses" (1 Tim 5:19). When this principle is followed, misunderstanding has a good chance of being minimized, and genuine care for pastor and people maximized.

A worthy model

The concept of leading by example is strong in Christian teaching. It is indeed implied in the word 'disciple', and nowhere is it as plain and challenging as in Philippians 4:9 when the apostle says, "What you have learned and received and heard and seen in me—practise these things, and the God of peace will be with you". These words, sometimes used to label Paul an egotist, are in fact the words of a realist. Paul knew that those in leadership in the church would be observed. The real question is, will my example be seen to be worthy or unworthy of emulation? That Paul was not an egotist but a humble Christian who wanted his words and way of life to count, can be seen from Philippians 3:17 where he makes it plain that there were others whose lives should be noted as well. "Brothers, join in imitating me, and keep your eyes on those who walk according to the example you have in us."

Amongst these were surely Timothy, of whom Paul says, "For I have no-one like him, who will be genuinely concerned for your welfare" (Phil 2:20), and Epaphroditus, whom he commends with the words "So receive him in the Lord with all joy, and honour such men, for he nearly died for the work of Christ" (Phil 2:29-30). For Paul, modelling was simply an expression of obedience to Christ. He says, "Be imitators of me, as I am of Christ" (1 Cor 11:1). The godly leader whose life is an example of consistent and open discipleship will bring health to pastors and church members alike.

When pastors see a congruence between what is asked of them and what is practised by their leaders, they rejoice. Integrity in leadership is far more important than ideas. Prayerfulness is much more powerful than a proliferation of programs. Honest sincerity is preferable to style. As John Stacey has said, "The essence of the minister lies in what God has created him to be rather than in what the church has authorised him to do" (John Stacey quoted in Robbins (ed.), p. 60). This of course is what each pastor must seek with all his or her heart, soul, mind and strength. We must ask nothing of our leaders that we would not want others to ask of us.

After affirming our salvation through faith in Christ, rather than our own works, the apostle charts our course, and at the same time assures us that it is one for which we have been well equipped. He says: "For we are his workmanship, created in Christ Jesus for good works, which God prepared beforehand, that we should walk in them" (Eph 2:10).

One such good work of the denominational leader is the modelling ministry of affirmation, encouragement and example that shines through clear biblical teaching and godly example. God's grace can be counted upon for such work, and such work will prove to be a means of grace for all of God's people, not least those who pastor local churches.

ENDNOTE

1. I am indebted to the 1997 Pastors Pit Stop group that met the fourth Tuesday of every month and the Joondalup Area Deanery group of Anglican clergy for helping me formulate and clarify these suggestions.

15
Finishing the race

In Acts 20:24, Paul stated, "I consider my life worth nothing to me, if only I may finish the race and complete the task the Lord Jesus has given to me". Herein lies the model I choose to follow. I want neither to burn out nor rust out. I want to finish the race.
JAMES D. BERKLEY

The test of a vocation is the love of the drudgery it involves.
LOGAN PEARSALL SMITH

... let us run with endurance the race that is set before us, looking to Jesus, the founder and perfecter of our faith, who for the joy that was set before him endured the cross, despising the shame, and is seated at the right hand of the throne of God.
HEBREWS 12:1-2

PASTORING, LIKE PARENTING, seems to be a never-ending task. Is the task completed only when our life is about to be taken from us? Our Lord's confident cry, "It is finished" (John 19:30), and his apostle's assertion, "I have finished the race" (2 Tim 4:7) were spoken at the end of their earthly lives. Is it possible to enjoy rest from the seemingly never-ending work of pastoring each day? Can we enjoy regular satisfaction from 'a job well done'?

These are important issues to resolve, lest what we love becomes a drudgery, a chore rather than a joy. When joyless drudgery becomes the commonplace experience of pastors, nobody wins. Congregations, pastors, their spouses and families all become discouraged and despairing. Self-care can provide the key to joyful ministry that can be sustained for a lifetime. Sustained ministry will be enjoyed by pastors who are able to rest regularly because they have learnt to see each of the tasks that make up their work as completed.

Running the final lap of a distance race can be the most difficult of all. Reserves of energy need to be tapped as the temptations to slow down or give up grow stronger. Pit stops in Grand Prix races are designed to attend to necessary maintenance and refuelling requirements, so that the racing car will be able to finish the race. To finish the race, the car needs to be performing up to its full capacity. So too in ministry. We want to be able confidently to assert, "I have finished the race". Thankfully, unlike the racing car drivers, we are not competing against each other. There is more than one winner. Faithfulness flowing out of faith in Christ is the requirement for victory in the Christian life. The apostle makes this plain when he confidently reflects upon his life of Christian ministry, "Henceforth there is laid up for me the crown of righteousness, which the Lord, the righteous judge, will award to me on that Day, and not only to me but also to all who have loved his appearing" (2 Tim 4:8).

We shall return to the stimulus this great assurance brings to all faithful Christians, but there are some other issues that we do well to address if we are to finish joyfully the tasks assigned to us.

We are wise to rest

It was sad to learn from some lay leaders' responses to my survey that their desire to listen to and support their pastor was not fulfilled because their pastor was too busy to stop. Christian ministry can take as much time as we are prepared to put into it. For a number of years (which will vary according to our physical constitution), it is possible for a pastor to simply keep on working. However, this is an open invitation to the ravaging effects of burnout, breakdown, illness and the law of diminishing returns. The damage is not limited to the pastor's own physical tiredness and spiritual dryness, but also contributes to family tension, ineffective leadership and a poor witness to the church.

Imitation of Christ's example, who took time to rest, pray and spend time with friends, and obedience to the fourth commandment, are good reasons for pastors to rest. It is often difficult for us to rest, because we are involved in too many ministries. This can arise from others' expectations, having a Messiah complex, a desire to be noticed and appreciated, or any combination of the three.

The ability to rest can help us to keep on course both by refreshing us, and by giving time for reflection that will enable us to check, and when required, rechart our course. It is inevitable in the complex world of competing expectations and demands, together with varied ministry contexts, that adjustments to the course of our ministry will need to be made. Such adjustments can only be made wisely when there are regular times for rest and reflection.

We do well to distinguish between two kinds of rest. The first is that enjoined upon us by the fourth commandment. My understanding of this is that we ought to cease our normal labours for one day in seven. This kind of rest is usually supplemented by annual holidays, which I think also have God as their source. Holy days, in the life of God's people, Israel, gave time to rest from work with a view to gathering, celebrating with family or community, and thanking and worshipping their God. Pastors do well to make sure that these set days—one in every seven and annual leave each year—are taken, used thoughtfully, and seen as a good gift from God.

The second kind of rest is what we could describe as times of refreshment through reflection. This can be done on the job, during each day and each week. Whether it be the early part of the day spent in prayer, Bible reading and meditation, the relaxed lunch spent with a fellow pastor or friend, the uninterrupted time given to preparation and planning, or the reading of some helpful book. These all contribute to the pastor's own health and the good of the church.

Yet often these reflective times are approached with a feeling of guilt, and given a very low priority or ignored completely. These times of reflection will only be entered into with a full and joyful expectation of receiving God's refreshment if we are assured of our value and worth, and know that it is God to whom we are to be faithful. If we locate our worth in our own efforts, and are more concerned with being seen by others to be busy, we will not set aside the time necessary for refreshment through reflection. We will always be worried by remarks such as "incomprehensible on Sundays and invisible during the week", and threatened by the insinuations of Satan that actions are always more important than words, and much more so than prayer and reflection.

It is important to note in passing that if a pastor's self-esteem is founded upon faith in Christ and faithfulness to God, she or he will be kept from an imbalance in the other direction, of too much reflection, refreshment and rest.

When we take time for rest and reflection, we are in fact recognizing our dependence upon God. Just as trades or business people who close their doors on a Sunday are demonstrating their faith that God will provide for their material needs in six days' labour, so the pastor is demonstrating faith that God will do his work through them when they work diligently for six days. If this is good theology, then we should not be at all surprised that it works well pastorally. With pastors being refreshed daily, the congregation will find that there is more real time for them to spend together. Why? Because rest and reflection will mean that the pastor is more refreshed and will have more to give.

At the same time the reflection will inevitably mean a more thoughtful use of time by the pastor. Failure to take time for reflection may result in our doing things which might well be seen as unnecessary, since they were at best the product of a confused mind, and at worst were done in order to be seen and appreciated. Furthermore, the gifts of lay people will be better encouraged and facilitated by a reflective pastor than a busy one. When the whole body is functioning as it should, the pastor will not labour under the false notion that they are the only one competent or expected to do the work.

One fruit of rest and refreshment is the ability to be unhurried. This wonderful characteristic communicates a welcome to church members that hurried pastors easily forfeit. Thus more will be achieved, since people will feel comfortable about coming to see the pastor. Dr Eugene Peterson has a brilliant short essay called 'The unbusy pastor', in which he outlines his own personal journey from being hurried to unhurried, with the ensuing benefits for him, his staff and his parishioners. He comments:

> ... if I vainly crowd my day with conspicuous activity, or let others fill my day with imperious demands, I don't have time to do my proper work, the work to which I have been called, the work of pastor. How can I lead people into the quiet place beside the still waters if I am in perpetual motion? How can I convincingly persuade a person to live by faith and not by works if I have to constantly juggle my schedule to make everything fit into place? (Peterson, p. 141).

Completed tasks—unfinished work

I would imagine that when a builder hands over the keys of a completed building, he would experience a considerable amount of personal satisfaction. The last three, six, twelve month's work has been worth it. The hold-ups of materials, the disputes with contractors and the inclement weather are all things of the past. They do not just fade into the background; they are quite overshadowed by the sense of accomplishment. The job has been completed, the client happy and the contract settled; there is now freedom to move onto the next venture. But every pastor knows that the building he or she is involved in is much more than concrete, bricks and mortar. It is as the apostle Peter writes a "spiritual house" made up of "living stones", people who have put their trust in Jesus the "living cornerstone".

Christians in general, and pastors in particular, are involved in building this spiritual house, and at the same time are seeking to grow and mature themselves. Without a shadow of doubt, this is a great privilege for any person. However, the 'unfinishedness' of the task can easily swamp the pastor with feelings of anxiety, despair and failure. I am aware that many Christians, not only pastors, feel the immensity of the task, and struggle with the unfinished nature of Christian ministry. They are burdened with the twin tasks of reaching and winning those who are not Christians, and of building up the church, so that is an attractive servant to outsiders and working properly in building up its members. Even when these things are happening there is always more to be done.

For pastors, it should be remembered, this is our vocation. There is no distinction between work and ministry. Our fellow Christians, who share the burden of evangelism and edification, may have through their work, past or present, a sense of completed fulfillment to encourage and build them up. Pastors are only too aware that whilst their work is being seen and recognized by God (and indeed will be vindicated along with Jesus upon his return), at the moment it appears to be very fragile, insignificant and incomplete. I feel this very much, and often long to be in a job about which I can say at the end of each day or period of time, "It is finished". For this reason, I find that on my day off I derive great satisfaction from doing some woodwork, or simply mowing the lawn. The woodwork I see completed every time I use it, and I can sit back and enjoy the transformation of the lawn at least for a couple of days.

How can a pastor resolve this problem?

By learning to see each task as a completed whole

This involves the prior discipline of setting both long-term and short-term goals. These goals should be broken down into manageable tasks. Once this has been done (especially when the goals have been developed by and shared with the leadership of the church and then understood, owned and shared by the congregation), we can confidently work away at each task. I find it interesting to reflect on how God has divided our time into days and nights, weeks and seasons. Perhaps the reason is the same as for breaking down our tasks into manageable portions. We can handle most days, one day at a time. Since the building up of God's people is such an important ministry goal, it is essential for its implementation that it be broken down into interrelated, consecutive and appropriate parts.

I am often overwhelmed by the number of people I should follow up, or the preparation that needs to be completed each week. When I itemize these into my diary, I do not have less work, but am less confused and can see and plan a way to accomplish what is required. As I complete a pastoral visit, make a phone call or do the initial preparation on the text for Sunday morning's sermon, I mark it off in my diary. Sometimes I do this in red to highlight for myself the completion of a task. This is therapeutic, in that the generalized feelings of frustration and panic are dissipated, and replaced with a quiet sense of accomplishment. One real side benefit of spending the few minutes at the beginning of each week and each day in this exercise, is that we are better equipped to assess a request made of us to do something else during the week. We can say 'yes' or 'no' with a clearer conscience and proper motivation. This is important because if, as we check our diary, we are conscious of achieving our goals, we are far less likely to say yes to somebody just because we know they will thank and appreciate us for doing so. On the other hand, if we are organized and not confused or frustrated by lack of planning, we may well be able to say yes and gladly fulfil the request.

The apostle Paul was able to say that he had "finished the race" when he was nearing the end of his earthly life. Judging from his desire to proclaim the gospel, it is hard to imagine that he meant that he had had enough of ministry. I think he meant that under God's good providence, he had been faithful in each mission field, church and task assigned to him. He knew he could not do it all, and he recognized the work of many others involved in gospel ministry. But he did do well what he was able to do. He could then conclude with a humble confidence that he had "finished the race" that was his to run.

By remembering that it is God's work we are engaged in

It is surely right for pastors to dream dreams and to "expect great things of God". This is where vision, motivation and leadership come from. At the same time, pastors do well to remember that the ground is often unfruitful and always uneven, as the parable of the sower makes plain. Ultimately God is the one who must convict people of sin, draw them to Christ, enable new birth to take place and bring growth to the church. These truths (which can never be used to excuse thoughtless, prayerless or careless ministry) serve as reminders to us that pastors are God's servants. The pastor's task may well be unfinished, in that both individual Christians and congregations alike need to be fed and nurtured by others, but it is nevertheless completed every time it is exercised faithfully. Whether fruit is borne or not is up to God, and the response of the people or congregations. This truth is vital to all pastors. Those whose churches are large and whose ministries are 'successful' must recognize that success is measured by God, and is due to his sovereign will. On the other hand, pastors of small churches who are not necessarily recognized as successful by the wider Christian community or even their own church or denomination, will be sustained by the knowledge that it is God's work they are engaged in, and it is God's assessment of their ministry that matters.

I have been challenged and helped by a distinction Dr Larry Crabb makes between desires and goals (Crabb and Allender). A desire, he says, is something that I pray for, since it depends for its fulfilment upon the co-operation of others, whereas a goal is what I work for since its accomplishment depends on me alone and cannot be blocked by anybody else. For example, my desire is that our church grows both in quality of life together and in numbers. So I pray for this to happen. My goals are to consult with the congregation, lead and teach faithfully. I work for these goals. Crabb makes the point that we often do the reverse; we work for our desires and pray for our goals. In working for our desires we not only forget to seek God's strength and guidance, but are bound to become frustrated, since the growth of the church depends upon the willingness of each member to grow and be actively engaged in welcome and witness. When I pray but not work for my goals, I am failing to work at the one thing people cannot block me from doing: faithfulness in each task that is mine to do. Put another way, the work may remain unfinished, but faithfulness in my tasks and God's faithfulness in his work are accomplished every day.

By remembering that the work of ministry is like a relay

In a relay we find both teamwork and the baton change. We are engaged in team work, and a vital part of our work is to hand the baton on to others. What we may not finish, through lack of time or ability, others will be able to complete in the present as they run with us, or in the future as we pass the baton to them. From the pattern of his ministry and his teaching, it seems that this was the nature of Paul's work. His words "and what you have heard from me in the presence of many witnesses entrust to faithful men who will be able to teach others also" (2 Tim 2:2) encapsulate the relay model and ideal.

The time between the commencement of disciplemaking, and the time a disciple is ready to pass on what he has learnt, is long. The outward growth in numerical terms may be slow, and a charge of favouritism can be levelled by church members who are not seeing quick results. Therefore, it is not surprising that many of us never build a relay team and therefore have no-one to whom we can pass the baton. However, if it is true that the finished work is God's, and each part of the discipleship process is to be seen as a completed whole, then the nurture of teachable disciples is surely worthy of our energies. This is the only way to ensure completion of the task in the long-term and the maintenance of our health in the short- and mid-term.[1]

The final product

Ultimately the work of ministry will be completed when the church is all gathered around Christ in the new heaven and the new earth. Just as Christ's work of redemption was finished upon the cross, so too there will be a Day when all the redeemed will be gathered into his completed kingdom. Our work, along with God's work within us, will remain incomplete until that Day.

We work in expectation. If the task is important and there is joy in being part of God's people now, then the prospect of sharing in the completed plan and purpose can work to encourage and stimulate us greatly. We need not panic that the work is incomplete, nor should we be thrown by the disappointments, hardships and hard work on the way. The prospect of a future holiday or visit from loved ones can stimulate and focus our efforts. In the same way the prospect of the coming of Christ, when he will vindicate his own name and that of his people, thus bringing to fruition and making public all that he has been accomplishing through his people, will stimulate faithful work. All Christian people have the promise and guarantee of Christ's resurrection and the gift of his Spirit as 'down payments' of the completed and glorious future.

Dr Peter Jensen, in his book *At the Heart of the Universe,* takes as his starting point for Christian doctrine and conduct the future completed work of Christ. With our final destiny secure and sure, he then shows how this acts as a great source of confidence and motivation for Christian ministry and conduct. The fact that the end result will be both completed and splendid can help us come to grips with the unfinished and even disappointing aspects of our work as pastors. Just as the pastor's work ensures the completion of God's great work, so does the prospect of Christ's coming to complete his work ensure that the unfinished and often heartbreaking work of pastoring will itself be completed. All this will contribute to the joy of ministry for the pastor. The pastor will derive great joy from being called to be one of God's children, and from the opportunity of contributing to God's purposes. To stand on that great Day and observe the fruits of their labours which have stood the test of time, and to know that in one way or another their work has made it possible for others to be there, will produce joy unspeakable. Not only will pastors share in the joy of being with Christ and of seeing Christ glorified, but will see their work, much of which appeared to be unfinished, unsuccessful or misunderstood, fully mature and complete.

When watching the film of Betty Cuthbert winning the inaugural 400 metres race for women at the 1964 Tokyo Olympics, I can remember being overwhelmed with joy, and tears came to my eyes. Nationalism and pride in the sporting achievements of national heroes, especially someone like Betty Cuthbert who was making a comeback after her 1956 Melbourne successes, often overwhelm me. However, that is nothing when compared to the splendour and unimaginable joy of standing with countless others on that great victory Day. This is certainly worth looking forward to and worth all the effort required in fighting the good fight, finishing the race and keeping the faith.

Nothing is as significant in God's purpose as the church. Few of us would have sought to be the pastor of the Corinthian church with its many problems and its unwillingness to welcome even Paul the apostle as its pastor! Yet the apostle knew that they were the church of God (1 Cor 1:2), whom he thanked God for (1 Cor 1:4) and clearly loved (1 Cor 16:24).

Always having before us the glorious final product, and our unique privilege of contributing to that final gathering, will keep us from downgrading our work and criticizing the church. Nothing can be more debilitating to the work of pastoring and to the health of pastors than a critical spirit toward those to whom we are called to minister. As Bonhoeffer says:

> A pastor should not complain about his congregation, certainly never to other people, but also not to God. A congregation has not been entrusted to him in order that he should become its accuser before God and men (Dietrich Bonhoeffer in Robbins, p. 57).

This, of course, does not rule out correction through admonition, but it does remind us that the church, with all its blemishes, belongs to God. As pastors, our great work as his servants is to help bring to maturity the church in which we have been placed. This can be a difficult task, but there is no doubt that it is God's purpose. To be a part of that purpose as a local church pastor is the greatest privilege available to men and women. One day, as the apostle reminds us, the church will be presented to Christ "in splendour, without spot or wrinkle or any such thing, that she might be holy and without blemish" (Eph 5:27). The local churches, which we pastor and with whom we fellowship, contain people who will be part of that triumphant and universal church presented to Christ as his radiant bride. Just as criticism in a marriage is debilitating and contributes to a dysfunctional relationship, so it does in the church. Since (as the author of Hebrews reminds us) a critical and bitter spirit breeds and spreads seeds of destruction, both pastor and congregational members do well to cultivate attitudes that make for the building up of the body. The contrast between these two passages from Hebrews is striking.

> See to it that no-one fails to obtain the grace of God; that no 'root of bitterness' springs up and causes trouble, and by it many become defiled (Heb 12:15).

> Let us hold fast the confession of our hope without wavering, for he who promised is faithful. And let us consider how to stir up one another to love and good works, not neglecting to meet together, as is the habit of some, but encouraging one another, and all the more as you see the Day drawing near (Heb 10:23-25).

We are not members of some worldly club or special interest group. We are God's people, drawn by the grace of God to Christ, and sustained by the grace of God until that great Day when Christ and his people will be glorified. This hope will sustain us, and give us the nerve to stand firm. The hope of a transformed and radiant people will keep us from destructive criticism and the like. The knowledge that we and all of God's children are engaged in building up a people whose destiny is gloriously eternal, and whose works play an integral and essential part in the fulfilment of God's purpose, will sustain us.

No other earthly group has such a destiny. Even local churches have their day. Sometimes through time or schism, what was good withers away. The only way for the ensuing discouragement to be handled is to remember that men and women, boys and girls, who have come to know Christ, will be standing with Christ on that great Day. Ultimately it is God's work. Pastors are under-shepherds who are exhorted to work hard and to build well.

Nowhere is this so plainly spelt out as by the apostle in his first letter to Corinth.

> For we are God's fellow workers. You are God's field, God's building.
>
> According to the grace of God given to me, like a skilled master builder I laid a foundation, and someone else is building upon it. Let each one take care how he builds upon it. For no-one can lay a foundation other than that which is laid, which is Jesus Christ. Now if anyone builds on the foundation with gold, silver, precious stones, wood, hay, straw—each one's work will become manifest, for the Day will disclose it, because it will be revealed by fire, and the fire will test what sort of work each one has done. If the work that anyone has built on the foundation survives, he will receive a reward. If anyone's work is burned up, he will suffer loss, though he himself will be saved, but only as through fire.
>
> Do you not know that you are God's temple and that God's Spirit dwells in you? If anyone destroys God's temple, God will destroy him. For God's temple is holy, and you are that temple.
>
> This is how one should regard us, as servants of Christ and stewards of the mysteries of God. Moreover, it is required of stewards that they be found trustworthy. But with me it is a very small thing that I should be judged by you or by any human court. In fact, I do not even judge myself. I am not aware of anything against myself, but I am not thereby acquitted. It is the Lord who judges me. Therefore do not pronounce judgement before the time, before the Lord comes, who will bring to light the things now hidden in darkness and will disclose the purposes of the heart. Then each one will receive his commendation from God (1 Cor 3:9-17; 4:1-5).

Here, then is a work that is worth doing.

- God works through pastors.
- We are God's fellow workers.
- It is God's building.
- God's grace is given.
- God's Son, Jesus Christ, is the only but sure foundation.
- God watches over our building methods.
- God's Spirit dwells within us.
- God has entrusted us with his truth.
- God judges his people.
- God's Son will return.
- God's praise will be our reward.

A work like this is worth doing well. The disappointments that the apostle must have felt keenly in Corinth (division, immorality, lawsuits, the questioning of his authority and integrity, the odious comparisons with super-apostles and the like) could only be dealt with by a firm grasp of the glorious finale. This final manifestation of God's purposes was guaranteed by:

- God's calling of ordinary people through the preaching of Christ crucified (1 Cor 1:18-31);
- God's creation of a new people of God, the church of God (1 Cor 1:2);
- God's raising of Jesus from the grave, with a transformed physical body, on the third day (1 Cor 15:1-11); and
- God's gracious gift of the anointing of the Holy Spirit as the guarantee of the glorious future (2 Cor 1:21-22).

The race is worth running. The obstacles under God:

- will be but stepping stones to maturity (2 Cor 6:3-10);
- will make us more able to comfort others (2 Cor 1:3-7);
- will increase our reliance upon God's all sufficient grace (2 Cor 1:8-11; 12:7-10);
- will prepare us for glory (2 Cor 4:16-18).

Hard work will be required. Self-care knows nothing of slackness or laziness, but will prove to be a means by which we can rest long enough to be able to reflect upon the great purposes of God revealed to us in the Bible. This time for reflection, and purposeful drinking from the deep wells of living water, will enable pastors to remain fresh for the work of ministry. Out of these wells we will be able to refresh others. Refreshed people are able to encourage one another and reach out to others. Refreshed people will want to feed more and more upon Christ, by allowing God's gracious Spirit time to change them. Paul speaks of this transformation in Second Corinthians and links it to perseverance in ministry.

> And we all, with unveiled face, beholding the glory of the Lord, are being transformed into the same image from one degree of glory to another. For this comes from the Lord who is the Spirit. Therefore, having this ministry by the mercy of God, we do not lose heart (2 Cor 3:18-4:1).

Self-care is like the regular intentional training of the middle distance athlete. The stamina so painstakingly built up in the everyday training sessions is called upon in the race, especially in the last lap. To use another analogy, self-care is like the balanced diet consumed day by day, week by week and month by month. If I were to ask you, "Which meal made you healthy?" you would say, "None in particular, but the ongoing cumulative effect of many meals over many years". Junk food will keep us going for a while. An occasional missed meal can be compensated for. Food can be grabbed on the run. However, these are no substitute for the balanced diet. Self-care is a mechanism which ensures that we benefit from God's gracious resources. It becomes the means through which his grace is mediated and appropriated by pastors. It keeps us from shallowness and emptiness. It enables us to feast now upon all the resources God has in his storehouse for us. As we do so, it whets our appetite and gives us a taste for eternal realities, so that if we do lose heart we will be quickly revived and given strength to keep running to the end. The big picture, the final product, the prospect of sharing in and contributing to the glory of God when Christ is revealed, will keep us in the race.

Paul the apostle bases two of his exhortations on the certainty of believers sharing in the fruits of Christ's bodily resurrection. They form an abiding exhortation and assurance to all Christians engaged in obedient discipleship.

> Therefore, my beloved brothers, be steadfast, immovable, always abounding in the work of the Lord, knowing that in the Lord your labour is not in vain (1 Cor 15:58).

> So we do not lose heart. Though our outer nature is wasting away, our inner nature is being renewed day by day. For this slight momentary affliction is preparing for us an eternal weight of glory beyond all comparison, as we look not to the things that are seen but to the things that are unseen. For the things that are seen are transient, but the things that are unseen are eternal (2 Cor 4:16-18).

ENDNOTE

1. The enemies of effective ministry are the principles of expediency and urgency. Charles E. Hummel in the *The Tyranny of the Urgent* outlines how easily the urgent can crowd out the important things in our lives; Bill Hull in *The Disciplemaking Pastor* applies this principle to the pastor's difficult role as disciplemaker.

16

Justification by faith—a truth that works!

We walk by faith, not by sight.
2 CORINTHIANS 5:7

We are human beings, not human doings.
ANONYMOUS

Therefore, since we have been justified by faith, we have peace with God through our Lord Jesus Christ.
ROMANS 5:1

AT THE TIME OF WRITING it is the 'annual report season' of many of Australia's large companies. Questions are being asked about the salary packages of CEOs and Directors. Experts are divided as to whether this transparency of reporting will bring excessive packages down, or cause a round of discontent and covetousness when others salaries are revealed. It is only natural, one commentator observed, "to measure our value by the salaries of others". The propensity for pastors to be self-driven and to measure their worth by the performance of others, when added to the dominant community tendency to endorse this works-based philosophy of life, can become an unbearable burden.

Is there a better way for Christians in general and pastors in particular? There is—one which takes faithfulness in duties seriously, yet locates our value in something far more secure and sure. It is the doctrine of justification by faith.

Ever since I became a Christian at age 17, I have always regarded doctrine as both fundamentally and eminently practical. When tested in the crucible of experience, this great Christian doctrine is verifiably real.

If I had to rank any one teaching of Scripture as of primary significance for my own nourishment as a person and as a pastor, I would choose 'justification by faith alone'. It was Martin Luther who suggested that justification by faith was the article of a standing or falling church. My own view is that it is also the article of a standing or falling pastor. This is not the place—nor am I the person—to discuss this great doctrine in detail, but I do want to attempt to show how it can keep us standing firm as we give our life to ministry.

This great truth, I know, presupposes a guilt and condemnation that stood against me. In this light, the doctrine's power, in terms of its irresistible comfort, becomes dominant in understanding myself and others. Despite my sinfulness, I am now pardoned through a simple, yet wholehearted acceptance of what Christ Jesus has done for me through his sinless life and sacrificial death. The realization that behind my move toward God and my acceptance of Christ was the grace of God working in me, gives me a further powerful and compelling understanding of how valued I am. Justification will mean not only that I am forgiven, but that I am welcomed into his presence now and for all time. This is possible since the penalty of my sin has been dealt with. No longer am I under his condemnation, but have free access and welcome into his presence in prayer. There will be a day when I will enter finally and fully into his presence, but in the meantime he is present within me by his Holy Spirit.

What has all this got to do with the care and support of the pastor in ministry? At one level, it assures me that God cares for the pastor, and at another it becomes the model upon which Christians see themselves and each other. Writers such as Larry Crabb, David Seamands, William Hume and Louis McBurney have taken up this theme and have shown very effectively, I believe, the important link between justification by faith and a person's sense of self worth, value and significance.

Self-esteem

Just as every building needs to be constructed on a solid foundation, so a pastor's life needs to be built on a solid foundation, if growth, perseverance and an ongoing effectiveness is to be maintained. Clearly the foundation for Christian ministry is Christ. The difficulty in working this out in practice is obvious. There are so many factors that can combine to blind pastors to the reality and the joy of Christ. Since this rarely happens in one memorable moment of rejection, or even disillusionment, but rather as the culmination of a dulling process, it is important for us to acknowledge the process and build in healthy correctives.

I have observed that when I am most discouraged and am finding my pastoral work more dreary than joyful, a gradual and dangerous shift has taken place in my thinking about myself. I forget that I am a Christian who has found in Christ a resting-place. The truth that I am a person who, despite my sinfulness, has been accepted and acquitted through faith in the Lord Jesus Christ, is neglected. I seem to become strangely unaware that I have been made, by sheer grace on God's part, a child of God; that he has granted me the gift of his Spirit and that I have experienced the reality of both his presence and power in my life and work. Instead, I focus upon my work as pastor. Then, in a twisted kind of way, undoubtedly fuelled by Satan himself, my attention goes straight to the failures, fears and frustrations of the work. I say 'twisted' because at other times, thankfully, with the refocussing work of the Scriptures and good Christian friends and my loving spouse, it is possible to allow the successes to fill my mind. I suspect this struggle is unavoidable and is the lot of every pastor. It arises from the nature of the role.

For most pastors this is a point of real vulnerability. Every person has a desire to be accepted and needed. It is at this point of need that the gospel is such good news. Through our acceptance of Christ we find that God accepts us. As we reflect upon and interpret our experience of conversion, we discover that it was God who drew us irresistibly to the point where we abandoned any pretence of self-righteousness and self-salvation through our own works or goodness, to joyfully embrace the Lord Jesus Christ. We discovered that he alone is righteous, and through his death deals with our unrighteousness. The realization that our value and worth, at least to God, is not tied to our performance, is liberating and of great profit in the way we view ourselves and our achievements. At one level, I do not need to pretend that I am anything other than who I am. At another level, faithfulness in my responsibilities will be acceptable to me, whether it is to others or not.

My self-esteem or self-worth is found in Christ, and not in my own efforts, or in acceptance by others. This truth, so clearly apprehended and embraced at the outset of discipleship, needs to be built into our thinking and outlook, so that it can be constantly reaffirmed. This foundation, expressed as 'justification through faith alone, in Christ alone, by grace alone' is clearly to be preferred to the shifting sands of acceptance through our own efforts or our approval rating among others. This latter is of special relevance to pastors, since there are so many eyes upon us, observing and assessing our worth by our performance. Many of us try to operate by the unrealistic notion that we can, even must, please 'all the people all the time'. It is sobering but vital to be reminded that not even our chief pastor, our Saviour and Lord, was able to please all the people all of the time. Nor did he seem to be troubled by the fact that he did not. And why? Was it not because he was secure in the knowledge that he was the Father's Son, and content to be faithful to his purposes rather than successful in the eyes of people? Surely our security comes from this. We are not the unique Son of God, but we do become God's children when, through the gracious action of the Holy Spirit, we are drawn to Christ.

Failures

"My own worth and value does not depend upon my performance." This truth has been fundamental to my thinking, and a tonic to cheer me, on many occasions. There have been many failures in performance—failure brought about by laziness, sinfulness, lack of time, or my inability to understand or cope with a person or an issue. Whilst justification by faith does not excuse laziness any more than sinfulness, it is good to know that I do not need to be perfect in my performance to be accepted by God. Sometimes others might expect me to be perfect, but God does not accept or reject me on that basis.

Perhaps the person who is hardest to convince on this issue is myself. Pastors tend to be people who want to work hard, and who want to perform well for many good reasons. Like other people, they are encouraged by success. It is very easy for a pastor to become a person who is driven by the expectations of others and themselves. Justification by faith becomes important, not just to boost us when we fail, but as the motivation that keeps us functioning. We work not in order to gain salvation or acceptance from God, but because we are already accepted in Christ. There is a world of difference between being driven by uncertainty, or confidently responding to God's love. This is especially helpful in times of low performance or failure, and especially necessary in keeping pride and self-sufficiency at bay when successful.

Dr Pat Cleary's practical comments, which clearly have their foundation in justification by faith, help us to recover from stressful experiences.

- Learn from the past but avoid living too much in the past. It may take conscious, prayerful perseverance to break the habit of brooding over failure, our own and other people's.
- Separate what we *did* wrong from what went wrong.
- Take hold of God's forgiveness on his terms not ours. We are justified by faith (Rom 5:1), not by feeling sorry. This process of feeling sorry may subconsciously be an effort to earn (or deserve) our forgiveness.
- Separate fair from unfair criticism (in our humble opinion), processing what seems fair and forgiving the rest.
- Distinguish between rebuking ourselves and punishing ourselves. Sandpapering our gut may be a familiar habit, but it does not right wrongs, nor does it stop the same mistake happening again. It is often a sign of shame resulting from fallen pride.
- Just have another go after failure, rather than feeling we have to have a better go! If we didn't clear the hurdle last time, it seems rather pointless to aim twice as high next time: yet it seems strangely meritorious (Cleary, p. 15).

A healthy theology of failure, which every pastor needs, can only be built upon justification by faith. The failure brought about by willful sin must be repented of, but our assurance of acceptance is grounded in God's grace through Christ, not further frantic effort on our part.

Failure brought about by giving it a go, inadequate support, mistaken reading of circumstances, inability or the stubborn sinfulness of others need not be brooded over or become reason for despair. Justification by faith reminds me that my status with God has not been altered one bit by failure. After all, I gave it a go. It has been suggested that failure is forced growth, God's nudge to redirect us towards another route. Seen in this light, our anger toward ourselves for ever attempting the task, toward others who may have blocked or failed to support us, or even toward God for not stopping us, will not last long enough to sour or cripple us.

Relationships

Justification by faith will also serve as the basis and pattern for my relationships. This will be vital, since pastors are always working with people, people whose support will be a vital ingredient to their own care.

If I see myself as important or valuable because of what I do and achieve, I am very likely going to be hard in my assessment of those who do not appear successful. I will also be less willing to receive encouragement or ministry from others. Instead of accepting people on the basis of who they are, I could very easily adopt a performance-based criteria for accepting fellow Christians. On the other hand, if I am among people to whom justification by faith is foundational in relationships, expressions of weakness, fear and even failure can be expressed without fear of rejection and criticism. Mutual encouragement can flow since God's grace will be mediated by example and word alike.

It is through the ministry of God's word that I become convinced of my need of justification by faith alone, in Christ alone, through grace alone. This is maintained by reading Scripture, and by reminders from fellow Christians. In all of this our minds are of first importance. At the same time, it is through the ministry of fellow Christians, especially those who are fellow members of the congregation, that God applies these truths at our heart level. David Seamands insists that all of this needs to be internalized if it is to have a practical effect in our lives. "It is rather the visceral knowledge of God's unconditional grace and love for us ... it takes an inside job". This, of course, is the work of the Holy Spirit and what Seamands calls "a human paraclete—someone called alongside to be a temporary assistant to the Holy Spirit" (D. A. Seamands, *Healing Grace*, pp. 161, 173, 179). When this kind of caring ministry is experienced (and how we need to welcome and encourage those who seek to draw alongside us), we become greatly affirmed. We are being treated by our fellow human beings as God treats us. Nobody can ever do it as well as God does, who ministers to us primarily through our reading of Scripture and the work of his Spirit. However this experience will be made all the more real, especially at crisis points, when others come alongside and minister lovingly to us.

It has been remarked that "God loves us by accepting us where he finds us, but loves us so much that he will never leave us where he finds us". Unconditional love, both on God's part and our own, will never be an excuse for flattery of others or neglect in our lives. The Reformers' catch cry, "always justified, and always sinning" whilst being remarkably realistic, needs to be balanced by Calvin's dictum, "we are justified by faith alone, but the faith that justifies is never alone". Works must follow justification, and one of the great works Christians can do for each other, and especially for their pastors, is to take the time to show that they accept and love them as they are; to accept them in the same way that God, in Christ, has accepted them. Out of this both encouragement and correction can flow.

Correction is a vital ministry we must give to each other in the church: Christian to Christian, pastor to members and church members to pastors. The fact that it must be exercised with great care (Matt 7:1-5; Eph 4:15; Jude 22-23) does not mean that correction should not be part of a healthy and caring congregation, but it does mean that it must be done humbly. Justification by faith provides the basis upon which correction takes place, and by which it can be received. We are more likely to receive admonition from people who have demonstrated their love and commitment to us. I will be much more likely to accept admonition as a gracious gift from God, from those who have welcomed and accepted me on the basis of grace not performance. So when corrected, whilst I may be put out, I can view the correction through the lenses of justification by faith. My standing with God is not affected. I am still loved. If the correction is warranted, I will see you as a messenger, an expression of our heavenly Father's love in calling me back into line. If, on reflection, it is not warranted, I will not be defeated and put down, since my standing with God through faith in Christ will sustain me.

We see this at work in the apostle Paul, enabling him to handle unjust criticism in Corinth (2 Cor 3:2-6; 10:17-18), and to rejoice when Christ is preached by those who are hurting him by their selfish ambitions (Phil 1:15-18).

Justification by faith keeps us from the need for self-justification, or the need always to be noticed or praised by others. As such, it is a powerful remedy to self-delusion and despair.

Leads to real work

If I am always dependent upon the assessment of others for approval (be they the congregation, local or denominational leaders), chances are I will put my energies into work that will win the most approval and applause. In so doing, I will be failing to do the real work of pastoring, and even what real work of pastoring I do will be done from improper motives. Justification by faith will provide me with the glue that will enable me to stick to my real tasks, seeking the approval of the One who really counts.

Whilst our work as pastors does not form the foundation of our self-esteem, which is found in Christ, it can certainly contribute greatly to it. Here I need to be well focussed. For if I do not measure up to standards that either I or others have set for me, standards that are not in accord with God's, then I will live in despair. God's standards for ministry are better described in terms of excellence and faithfulness, rather than success. Faithfulness to God's standards can be achieved by all pastors. It may bring us into conflict with denominational or local leadership expectations, but when pursued faithfully will contribute to our sense of worth.

When this foundation is in place, and is constantly being reinforced by a healthy mindset fed by Scripture and caring fellow Christians, pastors are freed from the tyranny of always feeling a failure. An honest appraisal of Scripture and our own performance should, I believe, cause us to expect a performance gap. It is healthier to acknowledge this gap in ourselves, and not be surprised at its existence, than to expect ourselves to be perfect. Far from being an excuse for tardiness or unfaithfulness to either our Lord or our pastoral task, this realization will keep us humble, with our eyes fixed very firmly upon our sure foundation. Seen in this light, justification by faith in Christ will serve as an incentive and motivation for faithful

JUSTIFICATION BY FAITH—A TRUTH THAT WORKS! 251

ministry. Ephesians 2:8-10 makes this connection crystal clear:

> For by grace you have been saved through faith. And this is not your own doing; it is the gift of God, not a result of works, so that no-one may boast. For we are his workmanship, created in Christ Jesus for good works, which God prepared beforehand, that we should walk in them.

Faith in Christ, itself a gift from God, is the great incentive to faithful work for God. We work as pastors not to earn or prove our worth to God, ourselves or anyone else, but because we have been graciously received by the heavenly Father at the expense of his beloved Son. Hulme, in showing how different this is to our prevailing culture's understanding of our worth, also explains how practical and liberating this can be.

> Dealing religiously with stress thus means breaking the chains that bind us to stress-producing values. It means affirming a radically different understanding of human worth, in which the distinctions of *winner* and *loser* have no meaning.
>
> The liberating influence of this Good News has something to do with why we get up in the morning. Rather than awakening to the pressure to get moving before someone gets ahead of us, we can greet the new day with the joy of being, because nothing has to be proved. Arise then, for 'this is the day which the Lord has made: let us rejoice and be glad in it' (Ps 118:24) (Hulme, p. 33).

This in turn leads to a way of viewing ourselves and our work, that can sustain us. It can sustain us because it is based upon the reality of the gospel, not the false and perverted views that follow our self-centred way of constructing reality.

It can be expressed diagrammatically:

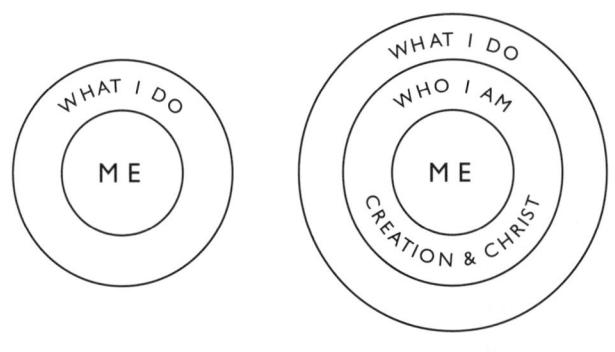

Figure 1

Figure 2

Justification by faith offers me a realistic view of life. If my life is circumscribed by what I do (Figure 1), I will be driven by fear. Even if I love my work and do it well, what happens if I am laid off (through no fault of my own) or need to retire? All is lost. I will have missed out on the richness I could have experienced from relationships with others.

When I understand and can live by justification by faith, I derive my value from my relationship with God, both as a human being and as a Christian. In Figure 2, my work as a pastor will be secondary, valuable to my worth but not essential or primary.

This way of viewing life and ministry, far from making me lazy or careless about work, will enable me to work well because I will be living well. My life will be bound up in Christ; I will be content to derive my praise and my power from him. This will keep me from seeking it in the shifting and uncertain place of human applause. Paradoxically, it will also enable me to draw upon the God-given resources all around me, be they the beauty of creation, the support of friendships or the refreshment of the creation ordinances of Sabbath and nightly rest. Far from suffering, work will be rejuvenated because it is in its rightful place.

Helps me to think straight

I find that when I begin to think of myself as a 'human doing', whose worth is bound up with my performance, or when despair sets in as I contemplate my failures, I need to 'change tapes' in my mind. The self-defeating tapes need to be replaced with the realism afforded by justification by faith. For through faith in Christ I am:

- loved
- pardoned
- accepted
- a child of God
- indwelt by the Holy Spirit
- bound for glory.

My thoughts need sorting out. Dr Hart speaks of 'reality thinking'; that is, thinking that is grounded in the twin realities of our frail and sinful humanity, and in God's grace to us through Christ. He contrasts irrational and rational thoughts.

Irrational thought	**Rational thought**
I am only a worthy person if I do what others expect of me.	My self-worth is not dependent on the acceptance of others. I am therefore free to choose my own actions.
Things should always turn out the way I expect them to.	There is no law that says my expectations should always be fulfilled. I must, at all times, only expect what realistically can be achieved.
My happiness is dependent on others doing what pleases me, or giving me the respect I crave.	My happiness is determined by my own actions and attitudes and not by others.
Because others expect me to be perfect, I must continue and strive at all costs to live up to their expectations.	I am only human and therefore I am imperfect. It is unreasonable for others to expect me to so distort my life as to live up to their expectations.
No-one must dislike me. I must dislike no one.	I cannot expect everyone to like me. I am called to love others, not necessarily like them. Christ loved the unlikeable.
I can be extremely happy without doing anything to achieve it.	Happiness is not automatic. It is achieved by hard work, dedication to God's purposes and the grace to accept failure as the means of growth.

Justification by faith will help us to think straight, because it takes us to the heart of our relationship with God and our consequent value to him. It also helps us to see the congregation we serve in its true light.

The precious flock

When I see myself as a child of God, valued and loved, I am in a position to think rightly about the church. If this is important for all Christians, it is essential for pastors. The people whom I am called to pastor, like me, are 'forgiven sinners', work in progress, with warts and all. Justification by faith will keep me from either idealizing or, more likely, criticizing or resenting the congregation for its imperfections.

Far from finding it surprising that churches will have problems, we should expect it as the norm. God loves sinners. Christians are forgiven sinners, but sinners nevertheless. Groups of sinners are the only people to pastor! Churches can only be pastored by sinners!

The range of exhortation addressed to Christians in the New Testament constantly amazes me:

- be patient with one another
- forgive one another
- speak the truth to one another
- flee immorality
- do not lie to one another
- do not gossip.

Yet the apostles always address these people as Christians, as saints, as brothers and sisters. Why? Because they are justified by faith.

Justification by faith keeps me from feeling that I will only be able to pastor you joyfully if you are perfect. This in turn will help me to value and see the local church I'm part of as:

- Christ's bride
- a precious flock
- a royal priesthood
- God's own people.

This will give me the incentive to pray, to work, to love, to rebuke and to labour hard. It will keep me from either being cynical or careless. It will remind me that the work that is to follow justification, that of sanctification, is one that God has graciously called me to. Just as he has brought justification, so he can surely be relied upon to strengthen me to be faithful in the ongoing pastoral work that contributes to the sanctification of his people.

17
Summing up

The main thing is to make the main thing always remain the main thing.
GERMAN PROVERB

I praise you, for I am fearfully and wonderfully made. Wonderful are your works; my soul knows it very well.
PSALM 139:14

For we hear that some among you walk in idleness, not busy at work, but busybodies. Now such persons we command and encourage in the Lord Jesus Christ to do their work quietly and to earn their own living. As for you, brothers, do not grow weary in doing good.
2 THESSALONIANS 3:11-13

I HAVE ENDEAVOURED TO SHOW that there is no real conflict between caring for ourselves as a pastor and the gospel obligation to "deny oneself". The responsibility of the pastor is to minister this gospel to men and women, both by word and example. When we take thoughtful steps to ensure that we are receiving good pastoral care, we are in fact acting responsibly in making sure that our life is an example to others, and that our ministry can be sustained and effective for as long as possible.

Since the ministry of pastors in local church congregations is so important in the building up of God's people and the fulfilment of his purposes, it should not surprise us that in the doing of ministry God will supply the means of care required to sustain us. The foundations of ministry, justification by faith and the word of God, will combine with the fruits of ministry, the Christians amongst whom we work, to provide the framework for our self-care.

Pastors, and their fellow Christians, do well to be intentional in pursuing what makes for their care and support. Given the numerous pressures we face, it cannot be left to chance. These pressures can be self-induced in the form of high or unrealistic expectations, or external in the form of resistance to gospel truth or the competing expectations of church members. Pastors, local church members and leadership, together with denominational leadership, can combine to set in motion, maintain and encourage strategies that will promote care and support for those involved in pastoring. When this takes place everybody gains. Pastors will be able to do more effective pastoral ministry at a pace that will invite support, and encourage thoughtful dialogue. Churches will benefit, because the pastor will be more able to spend time with God, and unhurried time with people. Pastor's spouses and families will benefit, since cared-for pastors are likely to be less preoccupied with themselves, and therefore more able to care for their families.

When we are ready to receive support and care from others, we are demonstrating our humanity. We have a God-given task, and we are endowed with God's Spirit, but are nevertheless very human. It has been said that "most ministers don't burn out because they forget they are ministers. They burn out because they forget they are people". Church members can offer a great gift to their pastors by treating us as people. It is not good for us if we are idolized, or placed upon a pedestal. Respect is one thing, but reverence is entirely inappropriate.

We pastors need all the help we can get in being reminded that we are people. This will keep us from pride, from isolation, from a Messianic "I can do it all" complex, and from burnout through overwork and anxiety.

The way the apostle Paul faced the unwarranted criticisms of the so-called "super apostles" from Corinth was to point to his faithful and ordinary work for the gospel. Paul's strength, which he was sure the faithful Christians of Corinth would recognize, was his weakness, which caused him to depend upon God for reward, recognition, results and power.

> And, apart from other things, there is the daily pressure on me of my anxiety for all the churches. Who is weak, and I am not weak? Who is made to fall, and I am not indignant? If I must boast, I will boast of the things that show my weakness. The God and Father of the Lord Jesus, he who is blessed forever, knows that I am not lying (2 Cor 11:28-31).

> But we have this treasure in jars of clay, to show that the surpassing power belongs to God and not to us (2 Cor 4:7).

Many of us may not be expected to be "super apostles" by others, but still have this unhealthy expectation of ourselves. Its effect is debilitating. Joy is quickly drained and reliance upon God is easily neglected.

The gospel message is a treasure of great value. So too are Christian pastors, not only because we are pastors whose mandate is to carry that message, but primarily because we are Christians, people who have responded to the gospel. The God who called us knows how frail we are. When we exercise our ministry faithfully, and express our weakness in humble prayer for wisdom and strength, we can count on God's surpassing power. Prayer is one expression of our weakness and reliance upon God; the other is our intentional enjoyment of the resources available to us. These resources can be expressed like this:

- Because we are people: friendship, family, rest and the beauty of creation.
- Because we are Christians: fellowship, prayer, God's word and sacraments.
- Because we are pastors: peer support, leaders, time for preparation and fellowship in the congregation we serve.

Every Christian, pastors included, is in a 'no lose' situation. This is expressed by the apostle Paul in his moving words, "for me to live is Christ and to die is gain" (Phil 1:21). However, this is no excuse for a lifestyle that disregards the provisions God has made to meet the needs of our frail humanity or the pressures of ministry.

Self-care is not an excuse for laziness in ministry. Rather, it is a way of making sure that we "live for Christ" for as long as he has work for us to do. There is no virtue (indeed one could say it would be an expression of disobedience) in burning out before our time, because we failed to take appropriate care of ourselves. Reality demands that we face up to our frailty and mortality. The saying "Every day I die a little. The big question is: Am I dying too fast?" helps us address this stark reality with confidence and hope.

The German proverb "the main thing is to make the main thing always remain the main thing" can be applied to the care of pastors. Intentional self-care which is worked at individually, and received from fellow Christians, keeps the pastor on track doing the main thing. 'Time out', paradoxically, means more real time available for the work of pastoring. The chief pastor, of course, is God himself. All pastoral care finds its beginning and end in him. To be doing his work and to be living his way, is the main thing in life.

When a pastor cares enough to take 'time out' in order to find refreshment from God and others, thoughtful pastoring of people will not only take place but will be sustainable over a lifetime. Ultimately our lives are in God's hands. However, we will have been able to complete the task assigned to us, rather than burn out by a careless approach to ministry, if we have taken steps to take and receive care throughout our life.

In taking positive steps in self-care and in being gracious enough to receive care from fellow Christians we are:

- being wise and humble in cooperating with and depending upon God
- expressing real gratitude for the gift of eternal life
- living as a responsible steward before God and as a faithful servant of his people
- demonstrating to God that we want to do it as well as we can, for as long as he chooses to work through us.

Appendix I: Bible study and discussion guide

Written by Denis Kirkaldy

Introduction

The study guide is set out in three sections:

(i) Bible study

Bible passages which are mentioned in the chapter, or which relate to the content of the chapter, are set out with questions to consider. The exploration of the deeper meaning of these passages will lead to a greater understanding of the principles in the chapter.

(ii) For discussion

This is designed for you to use with other pastors or with friends. It is meant to allow a sharing of ideas and experiences. As the book suggests, we ought to be very responsive to the help and insights we can receive from others. This section would be best used with others who are reading the book, but it is designed to work without that.

(iii) Activities

This is time for your personal response to issues in the chapter. A book such as this is easy to read and then put aside, having mentally noted what it teaches and planned to do something about it 'some day'. This section is designed to help you react in a practical way as you read each chapter. Often it is suggested that you write down your thoughts and plans. You may find it helpful to use an exercise book to write your responses in this section so that you can go back over them throughout your ministry. Many of the questions ask you to consider things which may take on a greater relevance at other stages of your ministry. Plan to keep this book private—and be brutally frank and totally honest in your responses.

Finally, include regular prayer in your time for reading this book and doing the study guide exercises. Many of the issues are complex and many of the suggestions are not easy for Christians to put into practice. You will need God's help, so make prayer about what you are reading a *planned priority*.

I: The importance of self-care

Bible study

1. Is Berkeley's interpretation of Acts 20:24 correct (p. 10)? Read the verses in Acts surrounding verse 24. What do they teach us about Paul's view of his ministry?
2. What is the basis for the exhortation in Hebrews 10:24? Read verses 19ff.
3. What is the basis for Paul's assessment of his own ministry gifts in 2 Corinthians 11:21-31?
4. How does Paul exhort us not to lose heart in 2 Corinthians 4:7-18?
5. What is the 'cross' Jesus calls us to take up in Luke 9:23? How does this fit with the need for self-care?

For discussion

1. Is self-care selfish or is it the primary responsibility of a pastor?
2. "[P]astors are busy because they are lazy!" (p. 21). What does this quote mean? How should pastors set priorities in their ministry?
3. How do you deal with the 'numbers matter' mentality?
4. For today's pastor, what could you substitute for the horse in the McCheyne quote (p. 20)?

Activities

1. Make a list of things where proper self-care will help you as a pastor. (Begin with 'being aware of false teaching'.)
2. What, in your ministry, could you hand over to others in order to take the pressure off yourself?
3. Keep a diary of time spent in prayer and preparation. How can you change your timetable to give them the priority that they deserve?
4. Analyze your activities and consider whether you have a 'Messiah complex'. How can you change that?

2: Burnout—friend or foe?

Bible study

1. Read Hebrews 11 and ask how many of these 'heroes of faith' experienced failures and doubts. What does this tell us about God's attitude to our desire to 'succeed' in the eyes of others?

For discussion

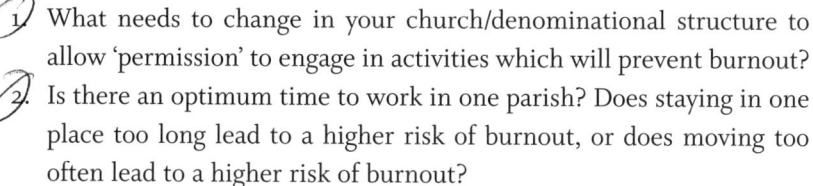

1. What needs to change in your church/denominational structure to allow 'permission' to engage in activities which will prevent burnout?
2. Is there an optimum time to work in one parish? Does staying in one place too long lead to a higher risk of burnout, or does moving too often lead to a higher risk of burnout?
3. How can we go about setting goals for our church that will help us to re-organize our ministry priorities?

Activities

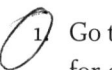

1. Go through the symptoms of burnout on pages 28-31 and rate yourself for each one on a scale of 1-10. Then prayerfully consider:
   a) how close you are to burnout;
   b) what you can do to change so that you reduce each symptom.
2. Make a list (no matter how impractical) of things you could do to take periods of 'time out'. Once you have made the list, go through and place a tick beside the ones that are more practical. Set a time to sit down and actually plan these in your diary (right now would be good!).
3. Make a list of the things you should have said 'no' to in the past month. Consider each one and devise a strategy to help you say 'no' next time. (This exercise may be done best in conjunction with a fellow pastor or your spouse.)

3: Stress and the demands of ministry

Bible study
1. In 2 Corinthians 11:28 Paul speaks of his anxiety. What is it for? How did Paul deal with it in his ministry?
2. Philippians 2:1-12 is about servanthood. It seems to run counter to some of the advice in this chapter. Study it carefully and ask how it relates to the concepts in the chapter. Can you find evidence in the ministry of Jesus where he applied the principles set out in this chapter? For example, what is the meaning of Matthew 15:21-28? Why did Jesus leave Palestine and go to the coast? What was his attitude to the woman who interrupted his time with his disciples?

For discussion
1. Commit time over an extended period to work through the chart on page 41 with a few other pastors. Analyze each factor in the first two columns. Discuss their meaning, acknowledge the part they play in ministry, and discuss practical ways of dealing with them.
2. Make a list of the variety of activities in your weekly programme. Rank them in order of importance. Explain to another pastor(s) your reasons for this ranking and then discuss whether changes need to be made.

Activities
1. Take the chart on page 41 to your doctor and ask him/her to give you a complete medical check-up. Ask especially about the issues set out in that chart.
2. Since words of affirmation and encouragement are important, offer these to some people who are important to you. You may do this face to face or by telephone. You will find it a rewarding exercise to write short letters of encouragement to people who have had a significant influence on your life.
3. Make a list of a few things you should have said 'no' to over the past few months.
4. Work through each of the 'Ten Preventative Measures' (pp. 48-49) and write down practical things for you to do for each one.

4: Stress and adrenalin

Bible study

1. In John 10:10, what does Jesus mean by abundant life?
2. How does Romans 8:28-39 help us to deal with the stress we can face in ministry?
3. Paul's exhortation in Philippians 4:4-7 is very helpful. But what can we do to make this a part of our experience?

For discussion

1. What causes stress in ministry? Discuss this question, identify areas of agreement, and then discuss how these can best be dealt with.
2. How do you find a balance between work and rest?
3. How do you deal with the "4 A's" (pp. 58-59)?
4. Share with others how you spend your day off and how they spend theirs. Are there better ways that you can relax more?
5. Discuss the issue of choosing friends with whom to share your pressures. What are the limitations of family and parishioners as people with whom to share?

Activities

1. Make a list of regular weekly activities and then consider which ones you would withdraw from in a time of great stress (such as the lecturing mentioned in the book).
2. Think through part of your ministry. Write down times when you were depressed and then see if you can find reasons from this chapter which may have led to this distress.
3. Look at your diary for *last week*. Pencil in what you could have done to provide a more balanced programme with 'hills and valleys'.
4. Make a list of things that you can do which will reduce stress. Add them to your diary.
5. The chapter contains an example of how to prepare a sermon (p. 63). Consider how you prepare for your preaching and think of ways you could utilize the lessons of this chapter to prepare 'better' sermons.

5: Depression doesn't have to be depressing

Bible study
1. Go to a concordance and look up all of the New Testament passages that use the words "one another". How should these affect our relationships with others?
2. Hebrews 10:24-25 is important but difficult. How can we "stir up one another"? What are the difficulties with this? How can they be overcome?

For discussion
1. How do you deal with common causes of depression in ministry? For example:
   - a key congregation member moving elsewhere;
   - you receiving criticism which you don't feel you deserve;
   - you receiving discipline from a superior;
   - you moving from a parish to a new ministry.
2. How much should you share your weaknesses and problems with your congregation? Why is it better to let them see your flaws than to try to hide them?

Activities
1. Analyze where you are at in your attitude to depression (on a scale of naivety to understanding).
2. Make a list of the passages of Scripture that you find most helpful in times of depression. Consider putting them together in some form and having them in a prominent place in your office or study.
3. Analyze your ministry and ask yourself if there is some unresolved loss/failure that needs to be dealt with. Deal with it first with God and then, if necessary, with others.
4. Analyze each of the 11 suggestions on page 80 and consider what changes you need to make to the way that you minister to others.

6: Anger—using it constructively

Bible study

1. What does James 1:19-20 say about anger?
2. Does Ephesians 4:26 help us to understand when anger becomes sin? What is the context for this verse (4:11-5:21)?
3. What was Jesus' attitude to being treated unfairly, according to 1 Peter 2:23?
4. Go to a concordance and look for 'anger' and 'self-control'. Look up each reference and analyze what it says. What practical help do you get from these verses?
5. What practical things should you do to make the ideas expressed in Romans 12:17-21 real in your experience?

For discussion

1. What situations in your ministry lead to you becoming angry? How can these be dealt with positively?
2. How can we deal with 'failures' in ministry?
3. Why does the Bible contain so many passages about anger and self-control? What are the implications of this for our Christian walk and ministry?

Activities

1. Think through two or three situations where you not only felt angry but also expressed your anger in an unhelpful way. What were the consequences? How could you have handled the situations better?
2. Write down your goals. Organize them in a general order of importance and, for each one, ask yourself if it is realistic. Think about what people can do to block each of those goals and work out ways of coping positively if that happens.
3. Are there one or more people in your past who have wronged you and whom you have not forgiven? Seek God's help in genuinely forgiving them.

7: The pastor's family

Bible study

1. 1 Timothy 3:1-13 sets out the requirements for church leaders. Go through each requirement, determine what it means, and then consider why it is so important.
2. How does Hebrews 4:14-16 help us in our family relationships?

For discussion

1. How can you balance your responsibilities to both family and ministry? What practical things can be put in place to help ensure you get this balance right?
2. How important is it to plan 'ordinary' activities in the parish rather than just 'spiritual' activities? Share ideas that have worked.
3. How can we teach our congregations to have more realistic expectations of the families of their leaders?
4. "Would you come back from holidays to take a parishioner's funeral?" Discuss your response with reference to the comments made in this chapter (p. 113).

Activities

1. Look at your diary for *last week*. Add to the appointments a list of times you spent with your family. Mark the occasions when this was quality time rather than just being there. What proportion of the week did this fill?
2. Set aside a special time in a quiet place to ask your spouse to share their frustrations. Commit yourself to not justifying anything but to going away and prayerfully considering what changes you might need to make. Then report back to them what you plan to do and ask them to help you keep your plans. Do the same with your children.
3. Work through the table on working or living the role (p. 108). You will probably find that you do not entirely fit into one or the other. Where are there problems in your attitude? What can you do about them?
4. Plan some 'time out' periods for the next few weeks.

8: Sexual temptation in ministry

Bible study
1. What does Paul mean in 1 Timothy 5:1-2? What is purity?
2. Hebrews 13:4-7 warns us about two temptations. What are they? Why is faithfulness in marriage so important?
3. If 1 Corinthians 10:13 is true (and it is!), why do so many Christians fall into temptation? What do I need to do to ensure I find the "way of escape"?
4. What reasons are given in 1 Thessalonians 4:1-8 for the need for sexual purity?

For discussion
1. Discuss the "framework for the proper expression of sexuality" on page 127. Clarify each point and expand on it. Find Bible references to support each point.
2. How do we respond to modern teaching on sexuality, both secular and from within the church, that differs from 'orthodox' or 'conservative' teaching? How does the Bible help us determine what is right and wrong when many current issues are not specifically dealt with?
3. How can we encourage each other to remain sexually pure?
4. How do we deal with transference and counter-transference in counselling situations?

Activities
1. Read Matthew 5:8. What did Jesus mean in this beatitude? What pressures are there on you to not be pure in heart? How can these be dealt with?
2. Can you identify needs within yourself which could make you vulnerable? What can you do to provide a proper fulfilment for these needs?
3. "There are bound to be a number of people to whom we are attracted" (p. 132). Is this true for you? How have you dealt with it in the past? How should you deal with it in the future?
4. What practical steps can you take to accept your vulnerability in this area, and to guard against temptation becoming sin?

9: Friendship

Bible study

1. What do Proverbs 27:17 and Ecclesiastes 4:12 tell us about friendship?
2. What does John 15:9-17 teach about our friendship with Jesus? What are our responsibilities and what are his promises to us?
3. Is the exhortation in 2 Timothy 4:2 to "reprove, rebuke and exhort" confined just to preaching? How can we make each of these a regular part of our pastoral ministry?
4. In Titus 2:15, how does the exhortation to encourage and rebuke with *authority* apply to friendship?
5. What are the features of Paul's prayer in Philippians 1:9-11? How can you encourage others to pray for you in this way?

For discussion

1. How did Jesus model friendship in his ministry?
2. How can a pastor develop appropriate friendships? What are the difficulties involved in doing so?
3. What are the dangers of being friends with people in your congregation? How can these dangers be minimized?
4. What needs to be done to your church structures to enable pastors to be pastored more effectively?

Activities

1. Make a list of your close friends. Spend a few moments in prayer for each one. Resolve to contact them within a few days simply to say how much you value their friendship.
2. Take this list of friends and note beside each one the role that they fulfil in your relationship—encourager, rebuker, etc.
3. What role(s) do you play in your friendship with others? Which role do you need to work harder at doing successfully?
4. Using Mallison's characteristics of "a good Christian mentor" (p. 154), make a note of areas you need to work on to become a better mentor. What will you need to do to strengthen those areas?
5. Make a covenant, as suggested on pages 155-156, with at least one close friend. Then work through the 12 questions mentioned on page 157 with that friend.

10: Principles and strategics of self-care

Bible study
1. In 1 Corinthians 6:19-20 what does Paul mean by "glorify God in your body"?
2. As you read this chapter, have your Bible open at Luke 10 and read each of the verses referred to in the chapter. It would also be helpful to have a good commentary to help you to gain an even deeper understanding of these important principles.

For discussion
1. What is the Sabbath rest? What does it mean, practically, in the life of a pastor?
2. How can pastors ensure that they continue to learn? Share what you do with others and listen to them.

Activities
1. Look at each of the eight principles from the example of Jesus set out in this chapter (pp. 160-166). Work through what each principle means and then make a list of things you need to do to put that principle into practice in your Christian life. Put together a strategy that will enable you to implement these effectively.
2. Put together a 'study programme' to help you to continue your learning. As part of this, go to a friend or a colleague and get a list of books they consider important to read. Alternatively, you can ask the manager of a good Christian bookshop what new books should be looked at. You could also check sources for book reviews and determine to read one new Christian book regularly.
3. Seek out possible courses you could attend.
4. Consider what you need to do to make your 'Quiet Time' (Bible reading, meditation and prayer) more regular and more effective.
5. Organize a regular routine to keep yourself physically fit (if you do not already have one).

11: Where the rubber hits the road

Bible study
Look up the word 'humility' in a concordance. Read each verse and note how it might be applied in your life.

For discussion
1. Analyze the quote from Eugene Peterson on page 172 and discuss the truth of each part. What could be done so as to be 'less busy'?
2. Find a recording of *Cat's in the Cradle* to listen to and then discuss Chapin's insights.

Activities
Create your maintenance plan, basing it on the principles in this chapter. Make it as detailed as you can. Then set aside a time to share it with others—your spouse and family, other church leaders, members of your congregation, friends who you have chosen to mentor you, etc. *Make sure your plan is workable and your goals are achievable, not impractical.*

12: A word for local church members

Bible study
1. Read Hebrews 13:17. Why should you obey your leaders?
2. Read 1 Timothy 5:17. What is meant by "double honour"? How do you apply this verse?
3. Read Ephesians 4:11, 1 Timothy 3:1-13, Titus 1:5-7, 1 Peter 5:1-4, Acts 20:17-28, 1 Timothy 5:17, and 1 Thessalonians 5:12. How do each of these passages help us to better understand the relationship between the pastor and his people? What special responsibilities does each have?

For discussion
How can we help our congregations gain a better understanding of the relationship between pastor and people?

Activities

1. Work through this chapter carefully, looking at the way you react to your 'elders' or those who are in authority over you. Until you have done this in a detailed way, you cannot expect to profitably share it with those over whom you have authority.
2. Given that most of your congregation will not read this book (though they should be encouraged to do so, because most of it applies to them as well as to their pastor), you need to organize some way to make the contents of this chapter available to them for discussion. You can:
   - summarize it and add questions for discussion;
   - photocopy sections such as Ian Mear's ten tips (pp. 197-200).

   Get them to discuss the issues and suggestions in small groups, led by the elders in your congregation and *without you present*. Providing questions for discussion may be helpful.

13: A word for local church leaders

Bible study

1. How does Romans 12:3-6 help to put your leadership role in perspective?
2. Carefully read each passage referred to in the section 'Leaders who encourage others' (pp. 203-205) and seek to apply it.

For discussion

1. How can the 'body' image used in Romans 12, Ephesians 4:11-16 and 1 Corinthians 12 be implemented in our congregations? What needs to change for this to happen?
2. What makes the local congregation so important in our Christian growth? How can we convey this to others—especially those who claim that they can be Christians without going to church?
3. Rather than 'have a go at everything', what are principles you can use to determine what you attempt and what you decide is to be left undone?

Activities

1. If you are a local church leader, look at the list under practical matters (pp. 205-213). Go through each of the seven sections and note the expectations of your church in each area. Make a list of the things which need to change and plan how you will discuss this with other decision-makers in your congregation.
2. If you are a pastor, encourage your leaders to read the chapter and do the activity above.
3. Here is a list of 11 suggestions as to how you might encourage your pastor:

   - Love your pastor into greatness.
   - Believe in him as a holy person.
   - Apply his preaching to your life.
   - Release him from repetitive routines.
   - Make the logistics of his living as easy as possible.
   - Don't waste his sacrifice.
   - Encourage him to dream big dreams.
   - Treat him as generously as you treat your boss.
   - Start an affirmation campaign about your pastor today.
   - Try to see your church through the eyes of the Saviour.
   - Commit to be a holy person who pleases God in all things.

Aim to implement each of these points. When you have done so, jot down the noticeable effect it had on your pastor.

14: A word for denominational leaders

(The exercises for this chapter are designed for denominational leaders—suggest that they read the book.)

Bible study

1. Read 1 Timothy 3:1. Why does Paul see the role of overseer as a noble task? How does this relate to his own experience of ministry?
2. Read the beginning and end of each of Paul's epistles. What sort of model does he provide for a church leader?

For discussion

1. How relevant is this quote for your denomination: "A congregation can not be an authentic Christ-centred church when led by persons who have only seniority, talent, money, and social standing. Above all else, the congregational pillar must know Christ". How should the denominational structures relate to the local congregation? Are they there to serve? Do they hinder the work in the local congregation?
2. How can denominational leaders gain a better understanding of what local pastors are experiencing?
3. How can denominational leaders be pastors to the pastors when they are involved in the furthering of careers?
4. Does your denomination need a pastor for pastors who does not have administrative or credentialing authority? What can be done to put such a position in place if it is needed?
5. What does your denomination do to ensure that remuneration for pastors is adequate? What changes need to be made?
6. What structure does your denomination have for dispute resolution? Is it fair on all involved? How could it be improved?

Activities

1. Work through the list of pastors you are responsible for and ring each one with a word of encouragement. If this is difficult because you don't know what they are doing, put in place plans to find out more about them.
2. Plan a programme of either inviting the pastors for whom you are responsible to visit you at home or visit them. Make this a purely social getting-to-know-you occasion.
3. Look at your diary for the *past two weeks*. How much pastoring of pastors have you done? (This does not include responding to crises that have been brought to your attention.) How can you re-order your priorities to ensure that you do more to encourage and affirm those for whom you are responsible?
4. Make a list of the committees you are on where your input is not really needed. What should you do about this?

15: Finishing the race

Bible study

1. What do you understand to be the implications of the 'race' image in Acts 20:24, 2 Timothy 4:7 and Hebrews 12:1-2?
2. What are the implications for us of Paul's attitude to the Corinthian church (1 Cor 1:2, 1:4, 16:24)?
3. Work through the other references in the Corinthian letters (as set out on pages 241-242) and relate them to your ministry.

For discussion

1. What would be the advantages of making times for leisure, prayer and reflection in your diary?
2. How do you deal with the 'tyranny of the urgent' (endnote, p. 242)?

Activities

1. How much rest of both types do you get each week? What can you do to change that?
2. Are you willing to try use your diary to plan leisure, prayer and reflection? If so, block out times for a period of about a month. Give the answer, "My diary won't permit it" when asked to do things at times you have blocked out. Keep a record of how you feel when you do so. After at least a month, reassess whether this is a technique that will work for you.
3. If you do not have clearly set out short and long-term goals for your ministry, then you should begin to set them. If you are not sure how to do this, ask someone; almost every business sets goals and many people can help you to do it effectively.

16: Justification by faith—a truth that works!

Bible study

1. What is the doctrine set out in 2 Corinthians 5:7 and Romans 5:1? Go to a book on theology and refresh your understanding of this central doctrine.
2. How does Paul's experience in 2 Corinthians 3:2-6, 10:17-18 and Philippians 1:15-18 help us to face criticism and hurt?
3. How does Ephesians 2:8-10 put you and your ministry in proper context?

For discussion

1. What examples are there in Jesus' ministry to show that he did not try to please everyone or do everything?
2. How can we help pastors cope with failure?

Activities

1. Write down some evidence from your life that shows: a) God cares for you; b) you know that God accepts you. How does this affect your self-image?
2. Write down some examples of your failures. Analyze them. Confess those that were due to your own sinfulness before God, and seek forgiveness. How many others are there? Are they really failures? How would God treat them?
3. Work through some examples of irrational thought (p. 253) which you have experienced. Note what the rational response would be.

17: Summing up

1. Spend some time going over the notes that you have taken. How successful have you been in following through plans you made to change?
2. Make a list of resolutions on a single page that you plan to implement permanently and then commit them to God.
3. If this book has been helpful, as a part of your ministry of encouragement, send a brief note to the author, Peter Brain.

Appendix II: Our life and doctrine

When St Paul advised Timothy to "keep a close watch on yourself and on the teaching" (1 Tim 4:16), he was reminding pastors that our doctrine is not only relevant and applicable to our life, it is the wellspring of our life and our calling.

It got me thinking about which doctrines are particularly worth watching in regard to our unique calling to be pastors. I will limit myself to commenting on how these great truths are applicable and fundamental to our life as pastors. My purpose is to encourage pastors to persevere. My hope is our perseverance will save both ourselves and our hearers (1 Tim 4:15-16).

Creation

The doctrine of creation is vital to the pastoral life. We are accountable to God and we would be wise to recognize that our humanity comes with the need to rest (Exod 20:8). We should grasp the opportunity to enjoy the good gifts of family, marriage, worship, friendship and food (1 Tim 4:1-5, 5:1-2). Thanksgiving which leads to contentment is an attitude we should nurture in ourselves and model to others (1 Tim 4:1-5, 6:6).

Sin and grace

The doctrines of sin and grace are vital because they will keep us from disillusionment, surprise, bitterness and harshness. That we are all sinners is self-evident, yet we still trip up when we see its ugly head rise up in our churches and in ourselves. We will be kept from disillusionment when we remember that there is only one type of person at church—a sinner. We will be kept from bitterness and harshness when we remember that we pastors are sinners as well.

This healthy diagnosis (made so clearly by our Lord in Mark 7:20-23) keeps us humble but it also magnifies the great doctrines of grace which dominate God's dealings with people from Genesis to Revelation.

1 Timothy 1:15 captures this remarkable grace so clearly. As recipients of God's grace, we must not only preach grace (2 Tim 1:8-12) but be driven by it (1 Cor 15:10; Eph 2:9-10), and become models of grace in our pastoral and personal lives (Rom 15:7; Eph 4:32-5:2).

At a practical level, these doctrines will keep us happy and humble (as sinners who did not deserve but have been shown God's grace) and so like Paul, we will want to magnify the Lord (1 Tim 1:15-17). These doctrines will also keep us reliant and prayerful, knowing that the work of grace in regeneration is God's work. We will then be faithful in the work (of preaching, pastoring, praying, equipping) and will rely upon God to continue to do his work (of regeneration, quickening, humbling, enriching) through the Holy Spirit, just as Jesus did his work upon the cross for us.

God's providence and sovereignty

These are precious doctrines for pastors. To know that God has called us to Christ and to ordained ministry, and that he has led us to our current place of ministry, is vital. This is especially so when the going is hard, we are tired, or family and life difficulties are engaging our minds and hearts. We do not minister in a vacuum; we are subject to all the normal pressures of life from an unbelieving, unresponsive and careless world, as well as extra assaults from Satan who would, by every means, seek to deflect, discourage or deceive the servants of God. Yet we are not on our own. God is with us and for us, and, providentially yet mysteriously (in that we cannot always see or know how or why), he is at work for us and his people. God, not Satan, is in control. Our work is God's work. And God always has his hand upon his servants. We see this in Paul when he remains confident despite the prospect of impending death and disappointment about the desertion of believers (2 Tim 4:16-18, 4:6-8, 4:9-10).

To know that our Lord is in control and is lovingly ordering all things for our good (and our good is that we and others grow to be like Christ— Romans 8:29, following the grand promise of 8:28) is the remedy against despair (where growth is slow), pride (where growth is fast), the temptation to be covetous of someone else's church or gifts, the unsettling tendency to want to be somewhere else, or the sin of feeling sorry for ourselves. Here is a doctrine that, rightly applied, is full of health for pastors.

Justification by faith

The doctrine of justification by faith will keep us from beating ourselves up when something we have done fails; it will keep us from living in fear of what others (especially our peers in ministry) think of us; and it will keep us from slipping back into an unhealthy works-based assessment of ourselves (or others).

Thinking about 'who is in my grandstand' will remind us that it is the same God who forgave us all our sins when we accepted Christ on the basis of his life, death and resurrection who will continue to watch over and hold us in his hand. Our works and faithfulness in ministry may well increase our experience of fellowship with God (they will certainly increase the joy of our fellow Christians) but they will never change our status with God. That has been settled. We are saved through Christ (1 Tim 1:15).

So when we fail, we learn and, if necessary, we confess, and we press on confidently as God's sons and daughters. We need not fear comparisons, for that is not how God deals with us in Christ. When tempted by Satan (and fuelled by the unrealistic expectations of parishioners or, alas, ourselves) to make our works the grounds of our acceptance by God, we go straight to this fundamental doctrine of justification by faith alone in Christ alone through grace alone for strength.

The authority of Scripture

The doctrine of the authority of Scripture is precious to the pastor because in the Bible we have the complete quarry from which to build up God's people, the complete granary to nourish them and ourselves, the complete canon (or measuring stick) by which we can discern error, and the complete well from which the thirsty find refreshment (2 Tim 3:16-17). Put simply, we don't have to spend our time worrying about whether we are right, where we will go for Sunday's sermon, or what we will say to the suffering, broken-hearted, careless, dying or bereaved. Rather, we humbly devote ourselves to Scripture in private (1 Tim 4:6-8) and in public (1 Tim 4:13) and to its prayerful public and private application (2 Tim 4:1-5, 2:2). We don't know everything and we must remain humble, but we do know what we need to know (2 Tim 3:17), and we are responsible to faithfully discharge this duty under God.

Christ's return

The doctrine of Christ's return to judge, reward and rule is fundamental to the pastor's work. There is a goal for which we work: there will be a day when Jesus will be vindicated along with his people and their pastors. All around us, others might scoff and mock us, the church, our Lord and the message we preach, but when Jesus returns, all will be revealed. Far from giving us joy in wanting judgement to come on our detractors, it drives us on to be lovingly faithful and urgent in our appeal, filling us with the joy of knowing our labour will not have been in vain (1 Cor 15:58). All of these aspects of Christ's return can be seen in Paul's exhortations and advice to Timothy and us in the pastoral epistles. 1 Timothy 6:11-16, 2 Timothy 1:12, 2:12, 4:1-2 and 4:6-8 and 18 are deserving of our meditation since those parts of God's word can always be relied upon to help us keep our head, avoid despair, maintain our allegiance, and help us remember that we are God's co-labourers who will share in the great harvest and final manifestation of his glorious kingdom.

HERE ARE JUST SIX DOCTRINES that are worth watching closely. The words behind "Keep a close watch on yourself and on the teaching" encourage an ongoing fixing of our attention to these matters. They are flanked in 4:15-16 with words like "Practise these things, devote yourself to them …" and "persist in this". The benefit and blessing of this exhortation ("for by so doing you will save both yourself and your hearers") will not come to the careless, distracted or half-hearted pastor. Instead, they will come to all who are conscious of their Creator, to all who are humbled by their ongoing struggle with sin, to all who are experienced in and overwhelmed by the magnitude of God's grace, to all who are joyful and prayerful under God's providence, to all who are secure and responsive to God's verdict of 'justified', to all who are obedient and submissive to his word, and to all who are eagerly waiting for the return of Jesus Christ. We do well to actively encourage each other in these truths.

Appendix III: Staying happy in ministry

Some have said that "in choosing ministry, one chooses to command an outpost of unequalled danger which threatens from within and without", and "to keep happy in ministry requires much effort".

John Piper tells of an older Christian leader who said that "it is the first responsibility of a pastor each morning to pray himself into happiness". How is this happiness achieved and sustained?

A strong basis for personal happiness in ministry can be woven together from the following strands, all drawn from Ephesians:

1. Remember that **it is God who called us to become Christians** (Eph 2:8-9). This was entirely his work—an expression of his deep love for us, not based upon our life's performance or ministerial efforts but on his grace. Our new status is not improved upon by our ministerial performance.
2. We are called to be pastors into his church and amongst his people. **It is one of the good works he has prepared for us** (Eph 2:10). We are part of his means for growing his church (Eph 4:12-16) and this should always be a cause for gratitude and honour to God.
3. If we begin to doubt God's purposes or plans, we would do well to remember that the work we engage in is both **very special to God and essential to his purpose** (Eph 4:1-14).
4. We focus upon the gospel of a crucified and risen Saviour and we look forward to his return, when he will consummate and complete all the gospel work of the ages—**including what we've been privileged to be engaged in.** This means that our involvement is of eternal and glorious consequence (Eph 5:24-32).
5. **God's word is the basis** for not only our knowledge of God and his purposes, but also for joyful faithfulness in ministry. As the Bible is carefully read, prayed over and preached, it will yield its rich treasures to the pastor and be a constant source of happiness, especially as the pastor prayerfully prepares. (See Paul's words to the Ephesian elders at Miletus: Acts 20:20, 27, 32; Eph 6:17; cf. Eph 5:18; Col 3:16.)

6. **God's people are the fruits of gospel ministry.** They will provide rich fellowship for the pastor when they are loved and gladly accepted as gifts and from God. Spending time with, praying with, meeting with, submitting to, and fellowshipping with God's people will result in joy (Eph 5:18-21).
7. **God's Spirit can be relied upon** since he is given to all believers at conversion (Eph 1:13-14), and because he is the giver of pastoral gifts and the source of joy and happiness in pastoral work (Eph 4:4, 5:18, 6:17-18).
8. The way our church members respond to one another will be a vital variable, contributing either to our happiness or unhappiness. Either we or they will be grieving (Eph 4:30) or welcoming (Eph 5:18) the Holy Spirit. Though we receive God's Spirit as individuals, our congregational life is a place where God's Spirit is also active (Eph 2:22). The context of Ephesians 4:30 and 5:18 is clearly congregational. Though we cannot take responsibility for how our church members respond to God's word, his Spirit or one another (a truth worth remembering if we are to maintain happiness in ministry), we must take responsibility for **how we respond** to both the ungodly or godly responses of our brothers and sisters. The exhortations of Ephesians 4:25, 29, 32 and 5:5, when heeded, may well be the most effective ministry we exercise, contributing greatly to the happiness of ourselves and possibly the happiness of our churches.

At the end of the day, the pastor, like any Christian, must choose to be happy in life and ministry. There will always be reasons for personal and congregational disappointments. These can so easily conspire to rob us of happiness, and deliver anger and its destructive second cousins, bitterness, malice and slander. All these are clearly works of the evil one (Eph 4:27) who longs to deflect, discourage, disappoint, disable and destroy those called to pastor God's people.

Being able to focus clearly on the glorious big picture will be a matter of choosing to live one's life upon the gospel of the Lord Jesus Christ. To be happy in ministry, a pastor will need to draw upon the traditional means of grace: Bible reading, personal prayer and Christian fellowship. Each of these will serve to remind ministers of the gospel realities which combine to drive away the unhappy guests of self-interest, self-pity and self-effort. Through these means, the happy guest, God the Holy Spirit, will be daily entertained. With his presence to nurture us daily, happiness will be our inevitable and growing experience.

BIBLIOGRAPHY

An Australian Prayer Book (AAPB), 1978, Anglican Information Office, Sydney.
Cleary, Pat, 1997, 'Coping With Stress', *Southern Cross*, February, p. 15.
Crabb, Larry & Allendar, Dan, 1984, *Encouragement: The Key to Caring,* Zondervan, Grand Rapids MI.
Donovan, Kath, 1991, *Growing Through Stress,* Anzea, Homebush West, Australia.
Ducklow, Paddy, 1995, 'Dear church! We quit!', *CRUX,* originally in *GRID,* June.
Friedman, Edwin H., 1988, *Generation to Generation,* The Guildford Press, New York.
Grenz, Stanley, 1995, 'When the pastor fails', *CRUX,* vol 31.
Hansen, David, 1994, *The Art of Pastoring: Ministry Without All the Answers,* IVP, Downers Grove IL.
Hart, A. D., 1984, *Coping with Depression in the Ministry and Other Helping Professions,* Word, Dallas.
— 1988, *Adrenalin and Stress,* Word, Dallas.
— 1987, *Counselling the Depressed,* Word Books, Waco TX.
— 1990, *Unlocking the Mystery of Your Emotions,* Word, Dallas.
Hull, Bill, 1988, *The Disciple-Making Pastor,* Fleming Revel, New Jersey.
Hulme, William E., 1985, *Managing Stress in Ministry,* Harper & Row, San Francisco.
Hummel, Charles E., 1971, *Tyranny of the Urgent,* IVP, Downers Grove.
Jensen, Peter, 1991, *At the Heart of the Universe,* Lancer, Sydney.
Knox, D. Broughton, 2003, *Selected Works, Vol II: Church and Ministry,* Matthias Media, Sydney.
Lee, Cameron & Balswick, Jack, 1989, *Life in a Glass House,* Zondervan, Grand Rapids MI.
London, H. B. & Wiseman, Neil B., 1993, *Pastors At Risk,* Victor, Wheaton IL.
— 1996, *Your Pastor is an Endangered Species,* Victor, Wheaton IL.
London, H. B., 1996, *Refresh, Renew, Revive,* Focus on the Family, Colorado.
Mace, David & Vera, 1987, *How to Have a Happy Marriage,* Abingdon Press, Nashville TN.
MacDonald, G., 1996, *Restoring Joy,* Inspirational Press, New York.
Mallinson, John, 1998, *GRID,* World Vision Australia, Winter.
McBurney, Louis, 1986, *Counselling Christian Workers,* Resources for Christian Counselling, vol 2, Word Books, Waco TX.
Mears, Ian, 1998, 'Ten tips for ministry', *Southern Cross,* June, p. 17.
Merrill, D., 1985, *Clergy Couples in Crisis,* The Leadership Library, vol 3, Word, Dallas.
Minirth, F., Hawkins, D., Meier, P., & Thurman, C., 1990, *Before Burnout: Balanced Living for Busy People,* Moody Press, Chicago.
Minirth, F., Hawkins, D., Meier, P., & Flournoy, R., 1986, *How To Beat Burnout: Help for Men and Women,* Moody Press, Chicago.
Muck, Terry C. (ed.), 1989, *Sins of the Body,* The Leadership Library, vol 19, Word, Dallas.

Packer, J. I., 1961, *Evangelism and The Sovereignty of God,* IVP, Chicago.
— 1995, *A Passion for Faithfulness,* Good News Publishers, Wheaton IL.
Peterson, Eugene, 1980-85, 'The unbusy pastor' in Robbins (ed.).
Robbins, Paul D. (ed.), 1980-1985, *When It's Time to Move,* The Leadership Library, Word Books, Waco TX.
Stott, J. R. W., 1992, *The Contemporary Christian,* IVP, Leicester.
Warren, N. C., 1990, *Make Anger Your Ally,* Wolgemuth & Hyatt, Brentwood.
White, John, 1982, *The Masks of Melancholy,* IVP, Downers Grove IL.

Feedback on this resource

We really appreciate getting feedback about our resources—not just suggestions for how to improve them, but also positive feedback and ways they can be used. We especially love to hear that the resources may have helped someone in their Christian growth.

You can send feedback to us via the 'Feedback' menu in our online store, or write to us at PO Box 225, Kingsford NSW 2032, Australia.

matthiasmedia

Matthias Media is an evangelical publishing ministry that seeks to persuade all Christians of the truth of God's purposes in Jesus Christ as revealed in the Bible, and equip them with high-quality resources, so that by the work of the Holy Spirit they will:
- abandon their lives to the honour and service of Christ in daily holiness and decision-making
- pray constantly in Christ's name for the fruitfulness and growth of his gospel
- speak the Bible's life-changing word whenever and however they can—in the home, in the world and in the fellowship of his people.

It was in 1988 that we first started pursuing this mission, and in God's kindness we now have more than 300 different ministry resources being used all over the world. These resources range from Bible studies and books through to training courses and audio sermons.

To find out more about our large range of very useful resources, and to access samples and free downloads, visit our website:

www.matthiasmedia.com.au

How to purchase our resources

1. Direct from us over the internet:
   - in the US: www.matthiasmedia.com
   - in Australia and the rest of the world: www.matthiasmedia.com.au
2. Direct from us by phone:
   - in the US: 1 866 407 4530
   - in Australia: 1800 814 360 (Sydney: 9663 1478)
   - international: +61-2-9663-1478
3. Through a range of outlets in various parts of the world. Visit **www.matthiasmedia.com.au/information/contact-us** for details about recommended retailers in your part of the world, including www.thegoodbook.co.uk in the United Kingdom.
4. Trade enquiries can be addressed to:
   - in the US and Canada: sales@matthiasmedia.com
   - in Australia and the rest of the world: sales@matthiasmedia.com.au

> Register at our website for our **free** regular email update to receive information about the latest new resources, **exclusive special offers**, and free articles to help you grow in your Christian life and ministry.

Mission Minded

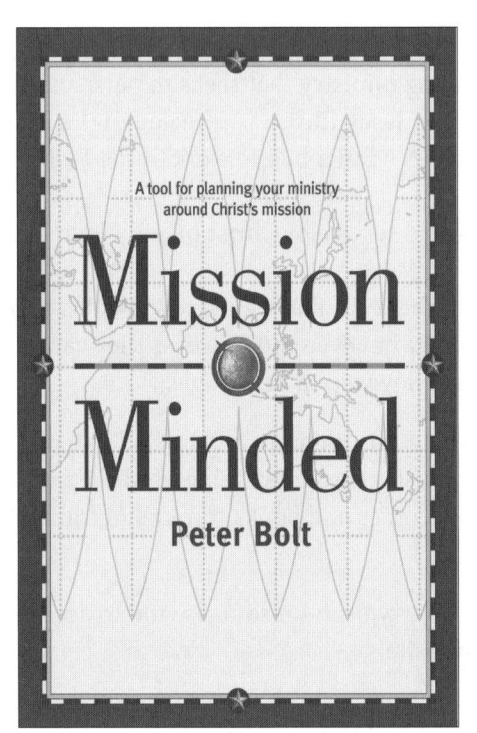

Mission Minded assumes we would all like to be more evangelistically orientated, and keen to see our churches enthusiastic for the task. But how do you turn good intentions and enthusiasm into a well-directed, mission-minded enterprise? This clever little book by Peter Bolt, shows you how to plan a purposeful, gospel-centred ministry and how to get evangelism going in your congregation or small group.

FOR MORE INFORMATION OR TO ORDER CONTACT:

Matthias Media
Ph: +61-2-9663-1478
Fax: +61-2-9663-3265
Email: sales@matthiasmedia.com.au
www.matthiasmedia.com.au

Matthias Media (USA)
Ph: 1-866-407-4530
Fax: 724-964-8166
Email: sales@matthiasmedia.com
www.matthiasmedia.com

D. Broughton Knox Selected Works

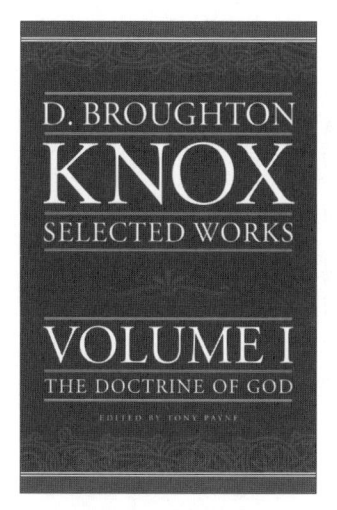

Volume 1: The Doctrine of God

This excellent reference volume contains a selection of Broughton Knox's varied writings on the doctrine of God. The centrepiece of the volume is 'The Everlasting God', Dr Knox's most well-known work. It is reprinted here with the addition of extensive Scriptural footnoting. Part 2 contains a selection of theological works, ranging from sermons to scholarly articles and radio talks, all related in some way to the Christian worldview as it is shaped by the doctrine of God, Father, Son and Holy Spirit. This is an ideal book for Bible Study leaders, theological students and pastors.

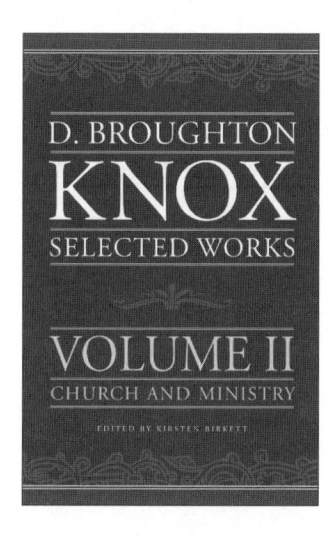

Volume 2: Church and Ministry

The second volume in the series of D. Broughton Knox's works brings together a selection of his writings on church and ministry, many of them previously unpublished. It includes:

- material relating to Dr Knox's influential doctrine of church, known as the 'Knox-Robinson' thesis.
- a fascinating study on New Testament Baptism, previously unpublished.
- statements on the Lord's Supper, and a refutation of Roman Catholic views.
- as with the first volume, there are general and biblical indices.

FOR MORE INFORMATION OR TO ORDER CONTACT:

Matthias Media
Ph: +61-2-9663-1478
Fax: +61-2-9663-3265
Email: sales@matthiasmedia.com.au
www.matthiasmedia.com.au

Matthias Media (USA)
Ph: 1-866-407-4530
Fax: 724-964-8166
Email: sales@matthiasmedia.com
www.matthiasmedia.com

Stay up-to-date

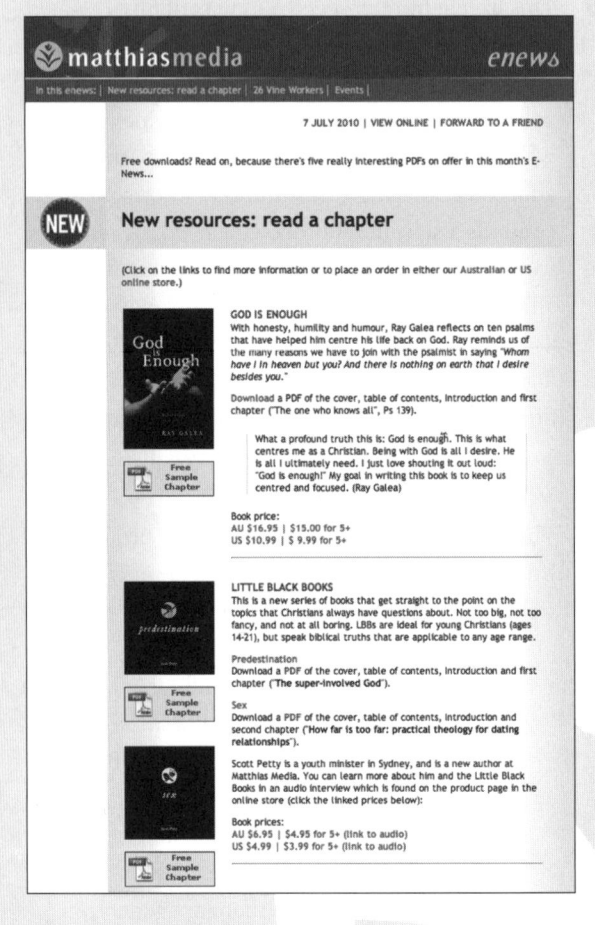

Subscribe to Matthias Media's e-news. It's free.

Each month, we send out a free email newsletter containing special offers and news about our latest resources. It's a great way to stay informed. To get your copy, just go to our website and click the 'Sign up here for our newsletter' button.

www.matthiasmedia.com

matthiasmedia